WHAT'S IT LIKE TO BE CHASED
TO BE CHASED
BY A CASSOWARY?

Felicity Lewis is a Walkley Award winner with more than twenty years' experience in journalism. She is the national explainer editor at *The Age* and *The Sydney Morning Herald*.

WHAT'S IT LIKE TO BE CHASED BY A CASSOWARY?

Fascinating answers to perplexing questions

Edited by Felicity Lewis

PENGUIN BOOKS

UK | USA | Canada | Ireland | Australia
India | New Zealand | South Africa | China

Penguin Books is part of the Penguin Random House group of companies whose
addresses can be found at global.penguinrandomhouse.com.

Penguin
Random House
Australia

First published by Penguin Books, 2020
Text copyright © Fairfax Media Publications Pty Ltd, 2020
All internal illustrations by Dionne Gain except for image on page 112, by Dylan Mooney; jellyfish on page 196 (courtesy Dr Robert Hartwick); stingray on page 198 (courtesy Sarah Speight/Flickr); and snake on page 200 (Shutterstock/Ken Griffiths), which are drawn by James Rendall.

Map on page 284, by James Mills-Hicks, Ice Cold Publishing

Every effort has been made to contact the rights holders of images in this book. If you have a query about the rights or credits for any image, please contact Penguin Random House.

Cover illustrations by Dionne Gain; background texture courtesy Here/Shutterstock.com
Cover design by Alex Ross © Penguin Random House Australia
Text design by James Rendall © Penguin Random House Australia
Typeset in 12/16 pt Times New Roman by Post Pre-press Group, Australia

Printed and bound in Australia by Griffin Press, part of Ovato, an accredited
ISO ANZ/NZS 14001 Environmental Management Systems printer

A catalogue record for this
book is available from the
National Library of Australia

ISBN 978 1 76104 082 5

penguin.com.au

MIX
Paper from
responsible sources
FSC® C009448

Contents

INTRODUCTION

Felicity Lewis

What's it like to be chased by a cassowary is a question that was possibly not top of your mind before you saw this book. Sometimes, though, an offbeat question can lead to an intriguing answer. Some birds squawk or screech when they're cross, but the cassowary emits an alarming boom – and that's just the warm-up act. It propels its bulky body with lightning speed and wields its middle toe like a ninja.

The cassowary question is among the most popular, if unlikely, to emerge from the explainer desk of *The Age* and *The Sydney Morning Herald*. A dedicated editor and reporter as well as journalists across the newsrooms regularly step back from the hurly-burly of breaking events to decipher the latest buzzwords, to decode geopolitical hotspots and, generally, to set out the how and why of events – in explainer form.

But why 'explainers'? Isn't that what journalism is for in the first place?

Well, yes, but amid an ever-faster news cycle, it's easy to miss the start of a story, or key developments, and to lose track of where it fits into the bigger picture – let alone its relevance to you. Our readers are inquisitive and savvy and want to think through issues for themselves. They value lucid journalism that cuts through claims and counter-claims, and equips them with the knowledge to form their own opinions. Good news reports do that, but explainers are *designed* to catch you up, fill any gaps and offer rich context – to place events within the flow of history, and to show how they matter now.

Of course, 'explainer' has become a bit of a buzzword itself, with media outlets worldwide recognising the value of the concept. More than mere recaps, ours involve extensive reporting and research, reframing issues and revealing fresh insights. They should also give you some nifty fast facts to deploy down the pub.

As well as examining matters arising in the news, explainers look at who we are and how we got here: what does 'mate' actually mean? How has slavery been part of Australia's history?

They can touch on the human condition and the concerns we all share. Our explainer about exactly what happens to the human body as we die resonated powerfully with readers when it was first published.

We also examine some of the critical questions of our time, such as how the Esky became a cultural icon. And our innocent inquiry into why cicadas sing at dusk ends up grappling with the big stuff (spoiler alert!), namely sex and death.

There's no glossing over complicated bits, either. Take cricket's reverse swing, a peculiar phenomenon that has confounded the world's finest batsmen for years. Asked how it works, many cricket buffs will assure you that *of course* they know – it's just that they, er, don't have time to explain it right now. In our quest for a definitive account, we consulted elite cricketers, fluid mechanics experts and scientific texts. 'It's really very complex,' I confided to our executive editor, in quiet desperation. 'So is nuclear fusion,' he said, 'but it can be explained. Keep going.'

On 26 November 2011, a spacecraft blasted off from Cape Canaveral bound for Mars. It was carrying a robotic laboratory, or rover, its mission to find out whether the red planet could have ever supported life. At the time of writing, the rover was still performing experiments beamed back to Earth – and, all the while, it has borne the signature of a schoolgirl called Clara Ma.

Back in 2009, when she was a 12-year-old student at Sunflower Elementary School in Kansas, Ma won a competition run by NASA to name its new Mars rover. She chose Curiosity. 'Curiosity … makes me get out of bed in the morning and wonder what surprises life will throw at me that day,' she wrote. 'Curiosity is the passion that drives us through our everyday lives. We have become explorers and scientists with our need to ask questions and to wonder.'

Curiosity sometimes gets a bad rap – it can be seen as distracting, troublesome, dangerous even. On the other hand, curiosity is a great navigational aid. Following it can lead to exciting discoveries, and hopefully you have fun along the way. So enjoy these explainers – and keep wondering.

1

WHY DO CICADAS SING AT DUSK?

They make a din in our backyards in summer but how do these ancient insects produce their high-decibel song? And who is their true audience?

Liam Mannix

It is the background sound to sausages being turned on the barbecue, to kids splashing in the pool, to the crack and fizz of opening that first beer – the dull, droning song of the cicada.

Some love the song, others hate it, but for many people, especially those with large backyards, it is ever present during the warmer months, a sound that seems to come from an insect you can never find, no matter how much hunting you do … And then, towards the end of summer, the sound ends abruptly and the only evidence of it you can ever find is strange, brown shells that crumple to the touch.

> *'It is ever present during the warmer months, a sound that seems to come from an insect you can never find, no matter how much hunting you do.'*

'It is just a normal part of the summer celebration, the soundtrack of summer,' says one of Australia's few cicada experts, Professor David Emery. 'And there used to be loads of them around. I used to catch them and bring the shells home and put them on the Christmas tree.'

While they may evoke sweet associations for us, a cicada's life is, in fact, one of solitary, years-long darkness punctuated by a sudden festival of sex. Then death. The song we hear at the height of summer is the cacophony of carnal festivities as the creatures go out with a bang.

What are cicadas and why do they make such a racket? Why does it happen at dusk? Why only in summer? And how are cicadas faring in the modern world?

What is a cicada?

Cicadas are a wonderfully diverse and ancient insect. Fossilised versions date to more than 200 million years. There are about 3000 described species and perhaps 1000, named and unnamed, roosting across Australia – no one really knows the true number. Australia has by far the highest diversity of cicadas of anywhere in the world (South-East Asia and the Americas are next), probably because the creatures have been here for so long – at least since the last Ice Age, says Emery, a professor of veterinary parasitology at the University of Sydney.

'We don't know a hell of a lot about them – there are only a limited number of cicada scientists about. We don't really know what the triggers are for them to emerge, except for rain. But what causes the major plagues we see some years, and virtually none next year?'

Today's cicadas come in all shapes, colours and sizes, ranging in length from about 10 millimetres to 12 centimetres – and each has its own distinct song.

Scientists who study them clearly care deeply about these creatures because they give them some truly fantastic names: Blue Moon, Black Prince, Yellow Monday. The Floury Baker looks as if it is covered in white dust. As the name suggests, the Cherrynose – also known as the Whisky Drinker – has a red 'nose'.

The Greengrocer (*Cyclochila australasiae*) is the most common cicada in Sydney and Melbourne. Its luscious, leafy-green shade is just part of the colour spectrum of the *australasiae* species, which ranges from yellow (thus the Yellow Monday) to turquoise (the Blue Moon).

A cicada's life begins as an egg tucked in the cracks of tree bark. 'And they take a long time to hatch, usually over one hundred days,' says Dr Max Moulds, an entomologist and senior fellow at the Australian Museum, although some can hatch in as little as ten days. After hatching, the tiny cicada (known as a nymph) falls from the tree and tumbles to the ground. It weighs so little the fall does not injure it. But rather than flutter away to begin a perilous journey to adulthood, the nymph digs a hole for itself – down towards one of the tree's roots, which it latches on to. A Greengrocer will spend six years down here in the depths – although no one is sure exactly how long – feeding on the tree's sap, becoming fat, brown and misshapen with huge front legs and tiny hind legs, a subterranean creature.

'Most of their life is spent underground,' says Emery. 'Depending on size, they only get a week to six weeks above ground. And during that time, your whole energy is spent on finding a mate – a very justifiable pursuit.'

Eventually, when a cicada is mature, it will emerge from the ground, crawl up the trunk of the tree and hold on for dear life. This happens between September and November, usually after a big rain. The cicada then begins to moult. A crack appears along its back and, over about two hours, the creature pushes out through it, emerging as a fully grown, winged and colourful adult.

'They usually emerge at night. They climb to a safer position and dry their wings,' says Moulds. 'Usually, by the next day, the males are ready to sing.'

To the human eye, all that remains are brown shells attached to the tree or strewn around its base, the husks of cicadas' former selves, discarded as they crawl, finally, towards the main event of their lives.

How (and why) do they sing? And why won't they shut up?

After its years underground, the newly hatched Greengrocer cicada is frantic. It has just weeks to find a mate before it dies. To do that, it uses song. Think of the cicada's song as a homing beacon. In the larger cicada species, the female cicadas will fly towards the sound, zeroing in on their mate's location. The sound also lets a female cicada distinguish between different species. Cicada songs are sufficiently distinctive that scientists use them as the basis for designating between closely related species.

'Every species has a slightly different song, either in frequency or the pattern of the pulses. Some have a continuous sound; others produce little pulses of sound in various combinations. That's what the females recognise,' says Moulds.

That's the simple story. But a cicada's call is also as diverse as a book of songs. Many, including Greengrocers, have a warm-up sound. 'It sounds like a rev-up at the start, like a *brum brum brum*,' says Emery, imitating a car engine.

They move into the calling song, as it is known, which for the Greengrocer is a long, monotonous burr. Then, as a female draws closer, the cicada will generally shift to a quieter courting song, calling her to his exact location. 'That tends to be more muted, as you might expect – you cannot go shouting in your partner's ear,' says Emery.

Many cicadas will also make a distress call, which sounds like a sharp squawk, if they are picked up by a bird or a human. Most mate in silence but some excitable species make a lot of noise during sex, the sound 'a bit like a distress call, particularly Greengrocers,' says Emery.

The Hairy Cicada, which lives only in Australia's alpine regions, is one of the world's oldest cicadas – probably one of those left over from an Ice Age – and is a bit on the quiet side. They don't make a sound we can hear at all; instead they vibrate branches to send messages to potential mates.

It's a shame that the type of cicada we're most used to hearing, the Greengrocer, also happens to have one of the less flamboyant calls. Compare more rowdy types, such as Queensland's Bagpipe Cicada, which can inflate its abdomen to a huge size and use that air to power its song. The Golden Emperor can sound like he's yodelling. The Double Drummer produces a deafening ruckus if you're standing too close. Others emit more offbeat sounds akin to fishing-rod flywheels or lawn sprinklers. Still others have structures on the wing and the back of the head they can rub together, akin to playing a fiddle, which sounds a bit like rubbing a pencil across a mesh-wire door. Then there are the 'tickers': they communicate using wing flicks, which sound a little like finger snaps. The males fly around, ticking their songs and listening out for a female wingsnap in response. But the way most cicadas make sound is by using a pair of ribbed membranes on their abdomen called timbal (sometimes spelt tymbal). The insect rapidly lengthens and contracts the membrane using muscles. Differences in the shape and ribbing on the timbal give the species their unique songs.

To get an idea of how this works, think of holding a piece of cardboard between your hands and wobbling it to make a *wup wup* sound. Now imagine doing this with a tiny piece of cardboard up to 10,000 times a second. The *wup wup* turns into a deafening drone. A hollow abdomen acts like a drum, amplifying the sound. The larger the insect the larger the drum and the louder the call, which helps females pick out bigger mates.

It's long been said the cicada's call is the loudest of any insect, but *Guinness World Records* does not keep this data. In 2014, University of Florida entomologist John Petti decided to find out. After consulting his colleagues and reviewing the scientific literature, he came upon the Shrill Thorntree of Africa, which can make sounds of up to 106.7 decibels from 50 metres away. Yet Moulds has measured Australian cicadas, including the Greengrocer, at over 120 decibels at close range – that's the amount of sound a jet makes taking off. Why don't cicadas go deaf? To protect themselves, their ears tighten up when singing.

Why do they sing at night? And in summer?

It's as the sun sinks that many cicadas really find their voice. Not only do they tend to sing at night but also during hot weather, and as a pack. Why? To escape predators. A single, singing cicada is extremely vulnerable. Programmed to go all out on displaying its ardour, it makes itself an easy target, signalling 'come and get me' to suitors and predators alike. Birds, ants, spiders and bats all love a crunchy cicada – and they can follow the sound right to the source.

'If you've ever watched currawongs in the evening, when an isolated Greengrocer starts singing, they will find him, they will pick him off,' says Emery.

But if cicadas sing together, odds are only a few will get taken – not ideal, but better than the alternative. As an extra line of defence, the nature of the sounds that resonate from their hollow abdomens makes it hard for humans (but not female cicadas) to tell exactly where the song is coming from. If you get close enough to a cicada, it sounds as if the song is coming from everywhere. Bladder Cicadas, which have enormous abdomens, have extremely dull and resonant songs, making them impossible for birds to find. Instead, cunning currawongs will wait nearby and pick off the females when they start to fly towards the males.

If you really want to find a cicada, try looking on tree trunks in the early morning, particularly sites where you've already found shells, suggests Emery. Others sit in a tree's canopy while still others set up in hedges, shrubs and grass. 'They all have their niche,' he says.

Early in the season, when there are fewer cicadas and individuals are more vulnerable to predation, they will wait for the cover of darkness to sing, but as Christmas nears and their numbers swell, they will boldly belt out their song in broad daylight.

Why do they start to sing in the heat? Scientists aren't sure. Perhaps because in extremely hot weather most predators are likely to be sheltering in the shade and not hunting for a meal; or, suggests Moulds, cicadas' muscles work better at higher temperatures.

Most females mate once before finding a slit in a tree's bark to lay their eggs. Males, on the other hand, seem able to mate several times before dying. 'My daughter found a Yellow Monday we called Stud because he sang very loudly in our azalea,' says Emery. 'He mated three times – that we saw – before he died.'

If they are vulnerable, are they also endangered?
Fewer and fewer Australians get to experience the cicadas' distinctive summer din every year, says Moulds. 'In the cities, they are certainly under threat.'

The traditional nature strip, especially ones with trees running between footpath and road, is an increasingly rare sight in many inner-city suburbs. 'Now it's all paved. There is nowhere for the little babies to get under the ground or get up from the ground,' says Moulds. 'In metropolitan areas, they are pretty well gone.' And female cicadas prefer to lay eggs in young trees. Many of the trees that remain in the inner city are old – for a cicada.

The insects are also under threat at beaches where spinifex once thrived, providing a home for small cicadas known as sand fairies, which would reliably harass beachgoers sweltering in the sun. Storm surges and the erosion of sand dunes have reduced their numbers, leaving many beaches silent now but for the crash of the waves.

'If you really want to find a cicada, try looking on tree trunks early in the morning.'

2

WHY DO WE HAVE LEAP YEARS?

Every four years, more or less,
the world is gifted an extra day. Why?
What would happen without it?

Sherryn Groch

Sydney salesman David Cameron celebrated his ninth birthday in 2020 but he turned thirty-six. The chances of being born on 29 February are estimated at 1461 to one. Yet, at odds of 2 million to one, Cameron also shares his leap year birthday with his young son, Jaxon, who was born the last time the world enjoyed an extra day, in 2016.

Without this particular quirk of the Gregorian calendar, scientists estimate our clocks would already be eighteen months into the future – Australia would be in the grip of its blistering summer peak in the middle of the year, instead of at the start, ahead of a cold, wintery Christmas. Of course, depending on the historian you ask, society could also be falling apart.

Who came up with leap years? What did Cleopatra have to do with them? And how does the maths work?

Why do we have leap years?

The Earth takes twenty-four hours to complete each rotation on its axis, turning day to night and forming the building block of our calendar. Each year is 365 of those days, roughly charting the Earth's orbit around the sun. The problem is that it actually takes the planet six hours longer than that – or approximately 365.2422 days – to complete the journey. So each solar year is about a quarter of a day too long for our calendar. Over time, that drags our calendar out of sync with the seasons we use to guide everything from crop-planting to religious holidays. So an extra day, 29 February, is slipped back in every four years to balance the books. But even that is an overcorrection in the astronomical maths. In the very fine print, we also skip adding in a leap year every one hundred years – except when the year is divisible by 400. (For example, the years 1700 and 1800 were not leap years but 1600 and 2000 were.) 'Leap seconds' are also sprinkled in from time to time by scientists as the Earth's orbit slows down minutely and unpredictably with the pull of the tides.

Conveniently, leap years seem to arrive whenever we need more time, coinciding with the Summer Olympic Games and US presidential races. But the Earth's solar year will never fall neatly within the boundaries of a calendar made of whole days, and history is littered with humanity's failed attempts at timekeeping – including the strange ten-month-long tangle of early Rome, where extra days were often tacked on here and there, mostly at the whim of politicians, until the seasons seemed back in their proper place.

What do leap years have to do with a steamy ancient Roman affair?

By the reign of Julius Caesar, from 49–44 BC, Rome's calendar was off track by three months. In the depths of his famous affair with Cleopatra, Caesar was inspired to adopt Egypt's 365-day system instead, with a leap year thrown in once every four years. Egyptians, the same as most of the ancient world, largely set their clocks by the stars, though some historians suggest they might have guessed the year was about 365 days long thanks to nilometers, which measured how high the Nile flooded at different points of the year. Because of Rome's keen admiration of Egypt's calendar, historians can pin nearly any event that occurred after 1 January, 45 BC to an exact date. (One of the first traceable events in the record books is Caesar's own assassination on 15 March 44 BC.)

Unfortunately, the priests left in charge mistakenly added a leap year every three years instead of four. This was later corrected but the underlying maths was still not quite right and, by the 1570s, the calendar was out again, this time by ten days. With Easter askew, Pope Gregory XIII organised an overhaul, bringing in the rules we observe today. (Some countries held out until the 1700s over fears of a Catholic plot but eventually, albeit with a riot or two over those lost ten days, the world synced up.)

Still, even the careful choreography of the Gregorian calendar isn't perfect – it's off by about twenty-six seconds. By 4909, that will add up to a full day, meaning we may decide to scrap it altogether, opting for something based on weekdays or moving to the atomic clocks used by astronauts (and your GPS), which measure time more precisely by tracking the natural rhythms of atoms. NASA's Deep Space Atomic Clock, launched into the stars in 2019, loses only one second every 10 million years, while the most accurate clock built so far, by scientists in Colorado, is said to be off by just one second every 15 billion years – or roughly the age of the universe.

What's it like being born on 29 February?

Cameron shrugs. '[Birthdays] don't tend to be a big thing,' he says. 'But for my son they will be great. This year [2020] is his "first", he's turning four. And next [leap year] is my fortieth so it'll be a big one.'

While Cameron has not ventured into the 'leaper clubs' and parties that spring up around the world on 29 February, he admits he's always been curious. 'I haven't really met many others, well, [apart from] Jaxon.'

The Honor Society of Leap Year Day Babies was established in 1997 and boasts more than 10,000 members. 'Leapers', as they are sometimes known, have banded together to launch awareness campaigns and fight back against so-called deniers who always leave out the twenty-ninth. They've asked more than one US president to make 29 February a national holiday, and convinced stores such as Toys R Us to include the twenty-ninth on birthday cards and gifts every year. And, of course, when the day does come around, they throw wild parties.

Outside a leap year, leapers tend to pick either 28 February or 1 March to celebrate their birthday. ('I tried the twenty-eighth when I was about to turn eighteen and wanted to get to the pub a day early,' Cameron says.) But in some countries there are legal rules

The chances of being born on 29 February are estimated at 1461 to one.

already in force to ensure leapers such as Cameron aren't served beer or issued a driver's licence early. In China, the civil code has been interpreted to mean a leaper must observe their birthday before February ends but in Hong Kong as well as countries such as New Zealand, the law explicitly names 1 March as the date. Most countries from the United States to Australia don't have a hard rule and age is instead counted in days from birth.

In one strange Canberra case, a leaper was charged with a crime on 28 February – the day before her eighteenth birthday in the leap year 2000. That left lawyers confused over whether she should be tried as an adult – had she turned eighteen the day of the crime or the day after? Initially, the ACT Children's Court ruled she should be tried as an adult but this was later thrown out on appeal by the Supreme Court (though not before it heard some memorably tedious definitions of a calendar month).

In a US court, one man (unsuccessfully) challenged the length of his state prison sentence because leap years were omitted when it was calculated. Leap years can also cause headaches with pay slips and bills, although sometimes, as it did in 2020, the extra day of trading can actually boost economic growth.

Do women really propose on 29 February?

The leap-year tradition of women popping the question dates back centuries in Irish and British lore – possibly starting with an Irish nun known as St Brigid, who insisted women needed at least one day every four years to propose. There's also a tale that in 1288, Margaret, the Maid of Norway, passed a law to improve women's odds after she inherited the throne of Scotland – any man who turned down a proposal had to pay a fine or present the spurned woman with a silk gown to make up for his bad attitude. (Inexplicably, Margaret was just five at the time and still living in Norway.)

Historian Katherine Parkin has tracked leap-year traditions and instead points to parties that sprang up in the 1780s – on the one night when girls were allowed to ask boys for a dance. An elite New York City party ran every four years from 1924 to 1968, except during World War II, sometimes at the Ritz-Carlton. At this event, women were even permitted to cut in on dances.

Today, while some surveys show that women consider the tradition that only men propose marriage to be outdated, they also show they're not rushing to get down on one knee either – although experts say leap years can offer a kind of 'cultural cover' from the enduring perception that a woman asking is somehow 'pushy'.

Do leap years cause bugs in computers?

There's usually a nervous gulp in IT departments as the clock ticks over to a new year but computers now have leap-year counters built in. Of course, every now and then they make errors in their calculations – known as 'leap-year bugs'. In 2016, a glitch in algorithms saw 1200 pieces of luggage miss their flight at a German airport. Over the years, phones have frozen, programs crashed and even smelting plants shut down.

Leap seconds tend to pose bigger problems for timekeeping computers – the very concept of an extra sixty-first second is almost circuit-frying. Companies such as Google run Network Time Protocol servers – the clocks your computer sets its watch to – and so have invented neat hacks to trick computers into taking the leap. Both Google and Amazon opt for time 'smearing' instead of straight-up insertion. Clocks are slowed down by a fraction over the ten hours before the second and the ten hours after, thereby splicing in the extra moment without confusing servers.

At least someone knows what's going on.

3

WHY DO PEOPLE POST LIZARDS IN THE MAIL?

The black market in wildlife is booming – and Australian creatures are in demand. What drives the trade and how are detectives fighting it?

Sherryn Groch

There was a dead lizard in the mail. But that wasn't the strange part.

Australia's wildlife 'coroner' Dr Lydia Tong performs hundreds of autopsies on native and exotic animals each year, many of them from zoos, others, such as this shingleback lizard, the victims of a multibillion-dollar trafficking racket gone wrong. This time, the reptile carried its own unusual traveller – a parasite never before seen in a shingleback. 'Straight away that was a clue that it might have been handled with another species; maybe there had been a jump,' says Tong, a forensic veterinary pathologist. 'The wildlife trade is a melting pot for these kinds of diseases.'

From live reptiles smuggled through customs to tigers shot or farmed for their bones, wildlife, dead or alive, is in soaring demand, spawning the world's fourth-largest contraband market – right behind drugs, humans and guns. Gram for gram, rhino horn and endangered turtles are worth more than cocaine. But while business is booming, enforcement is thin on the ground – international trade is regulated by a slow-moving and largely toothless United Nations treaty and park rangers often stand as the only line of defence for rare species sought by poachers in remote corners of the world.

In late 2019, a deadly virus emerged in a Chinese wildlife market. Within months, it had morphed into the worst pandemic in a century, and suddenly a trade that had long hidden in the shadows, lining the pockets of criminals, terrorists, even governments, was thrust into the global spotlight.

Calls are now growing for a ban on all wildlife trade to protect people as well as animals. But is COVID-19 really a watershed moment in the fight against wildlife trafficking? Are roadside zoos such as the bizarre world glimpsed in Netflix documentary *Tiger King* part of the problem? And how are new technologies and *CSI*-style wildlife forensic labs helping investigators close in on smugglers?

What does the wildlife trade have to do with coronavirus?

You probably hadn't heard of the world's most trafficked animal until the COVID-19 crisis hit. It's called a pangolin and it looks like a scaly anteater, but it's more closely related to dogs. Small, shy and now highly endangered, the pangolin is prized for both its meat and the unproven medicinal value of its scales – in the past decade millions have been snatched from the wild for use in traditional Chinese remedies. Despite the efforts of conservation groups on the ground, the pangolin might have stayed endangered, or even become extinct, in relative obscurity. The United Nation's Convention on International Trade in Endangered Species of Wild Fauna and Flora (CITES) didn't even outlaw its sale until 2017. But in 2020 pangolins became big news when early research on the pandemic suggested they may have been the very species that first passed COVID-19 to humans.

As people push further and further into the world's last wild places, more diseases previously unknown to humanity are making the leap across species (70 per cent of new outbreaks originate in animals). Vet and epidemiologist Dr Jon Epstein says habitat loss, global travel and a persistent appetite for wildlife have created a 'perfect storm' for human pandemics; and Asia's infamous wet markets – where both the deadly 2002 SARS outbreak and now the latest coronavirus are thought to have started – remain ground zero.

'As people push further and further into the world's last wild places, more diseases previously unknown to humanity are making the leap across species.'

Every day, scores of live animals are trucked into these markets across Asia and beyond as part of an enduring cultural preference for fresh meat over frozen. Some of them have been caught from the wild, sold on from remote or poorer communities to vendors or smugglers, both legally and as part of a thriving underground trade in 'wild tastes' and exotic products. As local animal populations dwindle, endangered species are taken from more faraway locales in Africa, South America and even Scandinavia and then thrust close together in cages – putting unfamiliar species and their microbes on a collision course.

'These markets are often really dirty and cramped, you might have bats on top of rabbits on top of rodents … dogs or hedgehogs,' Epstein says. 'They're stressed out, trading body fluids, there's faecal matter, blood [when] they are butchered. That's the perfect opportunity for a virus to jump.'

So why do people trade wildlife?

Beyond the dinner plate, demand for exotic pets and attractions has surged as the internet makes stars of creatures such as the slow loris. The body parts of other species, including the endangered tiger and rhino, are believed to offer healing and even sexual powers in traditional Chinese medicine, though science is yet to find any evidence for this. An estimated 20,000 elephants still die each year so their ivory tusks can be turned into furniture, jewellery and trophies.

> 'One in six of all known vertebrates on Earth are traded, putting about 9000 species at risk of extinction.'

Bears are caged and 'milked' for the bile of their gall bladder; smaller mammals, including foxes and civet cats, are bred for their fur; the skins of predators such as lions and polar bears are used as trophies, and their young are smuggled overseas to live in petting zoos. Monkeys are even caught in the wilds of South-East Asia for sale to Western research labs. In one extraordinary case in 1997, a long-tailed macaque bound for the United States escaped from its crate on a flight stopover in Paris and caused chaos on the tarmac. And far more tigers now live in basements, backyards and roadside zoos across the United States than in the wild.

The fate that awaits animals caught up in the trade is invariably cruel – many die on the journey or at the end of a butcher's knife. Birds and monkeys are sewn into jacket pockets or stuffed down underwear, and stingrays are shoved into special bags, called reverse osmosis bags, so that they can be smuggled; fins are sliced off sharks for soup and tusks hacked out of the faces of elephants while they are still breathing.

One in six of all known vertebrates on Earth are traded, putting about 9000 species at risk of extinction. The main corridor of trafficking runs through China, Indonesia, Vietnam, Laos and Myanmar. At TRAFFIC, an international group that monitors the illegal trade, Dr Richard Thomas says China is still the world's largest market, although the United States and Europe are also big consumers.

Not all poaching is coordinated and clandestine, sometimes it's merely opportunistic. For crime bosses, gaining a slice of a black market worth at least US$20 billion each year is enticing. (Legal wildlife trade, meanwhile, is estimated to pull in US$300 billion). And demand is growing fast alongside increasing middle-class wealth in developing Asian countries, and the rise of online shopping.

'Now even internet fads can affect trade,' Tong says. 'Lately we've been seeing those albino hedgehogs turn up everywhere, even here in Australia.'

Recent police investigations have revealed deep links between Australia and overseas trafficking syndicates. Data since 2017 shows Border Force has made about 500 seizures of illegal wildlife products a year, including turtle shells, ivory and animal skins, most of them imports. There's even a macabre collection beneath government offices in Canberra, a 'dead shed' of polar bear rugs, lion's paw 'gloves' and orangutan skulls, all seized on Australian soil.

Is Australian wildlife caught up in the trade?

The Department of Agriculture, Water and Environment says Australia's unique wildlife is highly sought after abroad as pets and has been reported in Asia, Europe and North America. 'They're cute,' Tong explains. 'And they're really rare.' While she says koalas and echidnas are not routinely snatched from the bush, reptiles, in particular, are targeted by smugglers as they are easier to move long distances.

At the Australian Museum, wildlife forensic scientist Dr Greta Frankham helps identify animal victims and gather evidence for police taking cases to court. That means DNA tests – under CITES' complex regulations, even a difference in subspecies can warrant a starkly different penalty. 'CITES is important but it has the same problem as the UN – it's slow,' Frankham says. 'It's not agile enough to respond to what's happening on the ground, what new species need protection. Countries all have to agree.'

Still, that convention, which Thomas describes as 'intensely complicated to understand let alone implement', is what allows prosecutors to build their case.

How do detectives solve wildlife crimes?

Compared to human forensics, the science of wildlife crime has a great deal of uncharted ground – and species – to cover, with a lot less resources. But, thanks to collaboration between labs scattered across the world, new technologies are already emerging: high-powered fingerprinting kits for ivory; rapid genetic tests for rhino horn developed by Frankham's team; and, hopefully soon, a wildlife 'smell detector' for airport and postal screenings, although Thomas notes that 'man's best friend, sniffer dogs, are still one of the most effective solutions'.

'A whole new arsenal' of gadgets is also helping rangers catch poachers in the act, he says – think eye-in-the-sky drones, heat cameras and computer programs that can predict poaching patterns across vast swathes of forest. Still, Thomas says innovation is a 'double-edged sword' – smuggling rings are themselves becoming more sophisticated, coordinating through encrypted messaging, cultivating their own intelligence networks and using night vision and even helicopters to make fast getaways in remote jungles and savanna. They are also getting bolder. A group walked into a French zoo in 2017, shot dead a beloved four-year-old rhino named Vince and walked out with his horn. No one has been arrested over the crime.

Interpol says police are stepping up their work with border officials. A series of carefully choreographed raids around the world in June 2019 seized live animals and illegal timber worth millions, including twenty-three primates, thirty big cats and nearly 10,000 turtles.

Frankham, who describes live Australian parrots packed into suitcases and reptiles 'secreted in electronics and Milo tins', says prosecution rates globally are still low, and penalties often 'just a slap on the wrist'. But the high-profile bust of an international smuggling ring led in Australia by former rugby star Martin Kennedy has set the tone for tougher prosecutions locally. After the government challenged his earlier good-behaviour bond, Kennedy was jailed for four years in October 2019, convicted of smuggling stingrays and snapping turtles from Thailand and exporting native Australian lizards to Sweden. Even sugar gliders were caught up in the plot, until it was thwarted by an undercover police sting.

A government spokesperson stressed that stopping wildlife crime was a priority, and Australia now has some of the toughest penalties in the world – up to ten years jail and $210,000 in fines.

What is 'wildlife laundering'?

Many animals have only partial protection under CITES – while they can't be taken from the wild, they can be bred for sale. (In China, even tigers are farmed for their parts.) This has allowed organised crime to expand the trade in plain sight through 'wildlife laundering': passing off animals caught in the wild as captive-bred.

'It's cheaper to take from the wild,' Tong says. '[Authorities] often tell us their hands are tied because they have no real way of proving the paperwork is a fraud in court. The whole thing almost relies on an honour system.' The pathologist has now joined forces with a 'ragtag' group of Australian researchers – from nuclear technologists to animal nutritionists and experts in machine learning – to devise faster, 'Border Force–ready' modes of detecting when wild-caught animals are imported. 'We're sort of like the wildlife Avengers,' Tong laughs. 'The crime's out of control because we don't have the tools yet to fight it.'

Take the case of echidnas. Experts suspect they are being laundered out of the island of New Guinea, the only place to which they are native outside Australia. The clue? The spiny creatures are notoriously difficult to rear in captivity. Fewer than fifty have been born in zoos in the past century, Tong says. So when TRAFFIC found an Indonesian facility selling 'captive-bred' echidnas, often by the dozen, it tripped alarms. Rapid tests developed by Tong and Frankham's respective labs can now spot the difference between echidnas reared in a zoo and those taken from the wild (checking either their spines for dietary markers or their DNA for genetic lineages). Tong's team is now working on a similar test for pangolins, which are almost as difficult to breed in captivity.

Why is there still demand for wildlife?

Market forces largely shape the fate of the world's wildlife. Often the rarer the species, the bigger demand, and profit margins. Despite some new protections introduced in China in recent years, restaurants continue to broker secret deals with poachers and middlemen. In markets, sometimes it's simply a case of keeping wildlife hidden out back or selling after dark.

Most of Asia's pangolins are already gone, so poachers have turned to the African continent to hunt the scaly mammal. In April 2019, officials seized 25 tonnes of pangolin scales in one haul, representing 50,000 animals with a street value of US$7 million. Likewise, when a fish prized in traditional medicine for its swim bladder – the organ that helps it float – became extinct in China, traders zeroed in on a comparable species in Mexico. That fish, the totoaba, is now protected but demand has pushed the price per swim bladder to almost irresistible heights for fishermen – US$5000 a fish, which in turn can be sold for as high as $100,000 in China, according to Ivonne Higuero, the secretary-general of CITES.

Unfortunately, the world's rarest marine mammal, a tiny porpoise known as the vaquita, is also paying the price – getting caught and killed in totoaba fishing nets as bycatch. At last count, there were less than thirty vaquita left in existence, Higuero says. But while people still rely on wet markets and the wildlife trade for income and protein, she argues that regulation rather than outright bans is key.

Other experts such as biologist Professor Diana Bell stress the trade is no longer about poverty in many parts of the world. In Africa, wild animals are hunted in lieu of other available livestock, but China's wild meat is now typically more expensive and consumers of the trade largely wealthy. Products such as rhino horn, sold as everything from an aphrodisiac to a hangover cure, have become about status as well as tradition.

So how likely is an end to the trade?

At the turn of the twentieth century, some North American wildlife was in trouble. Populations of elk, wolves and other animals had been decimated by rampant hunting and trade on the frontier. Suddenly, even the iconic bison was on the brink of extinction. It was enough to push conservation into the mainstream, says zoologist Dr Roland Kays. By the 1930s, every US state had a wildlife agency to regulate hunting and species recovery.

Advocates now hope the tragedy of COVID-19 will be enough to shock Asia into a similar response. By July 2020 Vietnam had banned all wildlife imports and domestic wildlife markets. But in China, the heart of the trade, more than fifty wild species can still be legally sold for their meat and parts, including badgers, Arctic foxes, crocodiles and even bats and civet cats, which have both been linked to past disease outbreaks. During the panic of SARS twenty years ago, a temporary ban on the wildlife trade came into force across China, as it has again during COVID-19. But this time, a campaign for something permanent is gaining traction as younger generations turn away from purchasing wildlife products and eating animals such as bats becomes increasingly taboo. A pandemic could be the ideal moment for a crackdown on the trade – the same lockdowns that have grounded global travel have also slowed down traffickers, according to an undercover investigation by environmental group Wildlife Justice (although poaching has increased in some reserves now empty of tourists).

Yet breaking the trade's hold on Asia will not be easy. As well as deep cultural roots, there is still a staggering amount of money and a huge number of jobs tied up in the market. China, under fire for its decision to reopen the trade after SARS, announced in February 2020 that it would at last outlaw the wild meat trade for good. Experts are cautiously optimistic but warn that loopholes, including allowing trade for medicine, pets and fur, remain wide open for traffickers. By April 2020, Beijing was already offering tax breaks on wildlife products shipped overseas, a perk not even extended to medical supplies, and reopening wet markets. While there was buzz in June that pangolin scales had finally been removed from China's official list of ingredients approved for traditional medicine, on closer inspection of the new law's appendices, the Environmental Investigation Agency found pangolin products were still legal. At the same time, bear bile has been touted by the Chinese Government as a cure for COVID-19, without any scientific evidence.

Some experts point to the strides made in reducing ivory hauls since China finally banned the product in 2017 as a sign that outlawing all trade could work, especially under China's authoritarian government. But Thomas says it will be difficult, even for Beijing, to enforce an outright ban. Epstein adds, 'It will just drive it more underground. The people running the [illegal side of] the trade globally are the same people running drugs and [human trafficking]. The demand's got to stop too. It's a market. And people have to stop buying.'

Fortunately, wildlife is also worth something alive. In some trafficking hotspots, whole generations of poachers are switching sides and finding work as rangers to rebuild their communities around wildlife tourism. 'The trade can hurt [Indigenous] and local people,' Tong says. 'If all the animals are gone, they won't have a [sustainable] income. If all the animals are gone, what happens then?'

4

WHAT IS CULTURAL BURNING?

Catastrophic bushfires have led to a heightened interest in Indigenous burning practices. How do Aboriginal experts use fire to care for the land?

Miki Perkins

Aboriginal and Torres Strait Islander people should be aware that the following chapter contains the names of people who have passed away.

A cool, gentle, creeping fire came to the bushland that surrounds the Tang Tang and Thunder swamps in Central Victoria, north of Bendigo, in 2019. It burnt gently through grasslands and connected up with other fires lit on the forest floor to create a mosaic effect. This fire was lit by Dja Dja Wurrung people, including employees of Forest Fire Management Victoria, and their non-Aboriginal colleagues. It was the first cultural burn in the area in 170 years.

It was a momentous day, says Trent Nelson, the chairperson of the Dja Dja Wurrung Clans Aboriginal Corporation. In the years since cultural burning had been used, the landscape had become degraded and 'sick'. The region, which includes the towns of Daylesford, Bendigo and Boort, used to be cloaked in box-ironbark forests and woodlands but is now one of the most profoundly altered landscapes in Victoria, where agriculture, urban settlement and mining have left ecosystems fragmented. Nelson learnt cultural burning – known as *djandak wii* or 'country fire' – from his father, who learnt from his father before him and other elders. 'We don't make it really, really hot, we burn cool. It's a lot slower than planned burns.'

In the wake of recent catastrophic summer bushfires, there is heightened national interest in the role of Aboriginal cultural burning, sometimes called traditional burning. What is it, and how does it work? And can it reduce the threat of out-of-control fires in an era of climate change?

What is cultural burning?

For at least 65,000 years, Aboriginal people have used cultural land management practices – including fire – to care for country (the term used by Aboriginal and Torres Strait Islander people to describe family origins, ownership and associations with particular areas of Australia).

Cultural burns are done by Indigenous custodians, or people given permission and guidance from those custodians. The use of fire is specific to each location, its animals and flora and their totemic and cultural value. There are many interconnected objectives, which include protecting cultural or natural assets by maintaining the health of surrounding country, ceremony, habitat protection and fuel reduction. But fuel reduction – targeted burning to reduce the amount or density of foliage – is often not the primary objective.

'For at least 65,000 years, Aboriginal people have used cultural land management practices – including fire – to care for country.'

Indigenous land management was critical to preventing catastrophic bushfires, the Royal Commission into National Natural Disaster Arrangements was told in 2020, but Aboriginal voices had been ignored. 'Cultural land management is not an add-on or an enhancement, it's not a practice that can simply be grafted onto the regime of non-Indigenous land managers,' Euahlayi man and Australian National University researcher Bhiamie Eckford-Williamson told the commission. He also said that short-term funding was a barrier to Aboriginal land management. 'It is not possible for groups to develop, to recruit, train and retain staff to maintain that corporate memory, to build relationships with non-Indigenous land management agencies over time, if their funding is not secure,' he explained.

Most Australian wildfires occur in the northern tropical savanna, and most cultural burning also happens in Northern

Australia – about 70 per cent of projects are in the Northern Territory, Queensland or Western Australia, according to the Commonwealth Scientific and Industrial Research Organisation (CSIRO). In Western Australia, for example, the Great Western Woodlands, 16 million hectares of temperate woodland, heathland and mallee, are cared for, in part, by the Ngajdu Nation and the Ngajdu Rangers Group. The Ngadju undertake cultural burns at particular times: when the grass is green, or a few days after rain, or when rain is coming. In the warmer seasons, the fire must be started in the morning before the sea breezes rise.

In early colonial artwork, letters and journals, there is considerable evidence of Aboriginal use of fire. In 1836, naturalist Charles Darwin visited Sydney and commented on the sparsity of trees and the prevalence of grasslands, much of which is now thick scrub. 'The extreme uniformity in the character of the Vegetation, is the most remarkable feature in the landscape of the greater part of New S. Wales. Everywhere we have open woodland, the ground being partially covered with a most thin pasture,' he wrote.

The use of 'prescribed' or 'hazard-reduction burning' is the process of applying fire to a predetermined area to achieve a desired outcome – usually to mitigate the presence or severity of bushfires. While there are some crossovers between the two practices, cultural burning may also be used to clear important pathways or manage vegetation around significant sites. But where fire is a concern, it may be possible to use cultural burning where prescribed burning is unsafe – because of the warming climate, it is becoming more challenging for land management agencies to find periods of time when prescribed burns can be safely lit.

How does cultural burning work?

Most cultural burns use 'cool' fires – smaller, low-intensity fires – which reduce the risk of extreme, high flames that can burn whole trees and forest canopies. Protecting the canopy is considered paramount in cultural burning because it holds many precious resources – insects, bird nests, bats and shade. And canopy removal fundamentally alters the surrounding ecosystem – sunlight breaks through and dries out the soil. Unlike hazard-reduction burns, where lines of fire can create walls of flame, cultural burning tends to use spot ignitions, creating a mosaic of fires. This leaves space for wildlife to escape.

> *'Protecting the canopy is considered paramount in cultural burning because it holds many precious resources – insects, bird nests, bats and shade.'*

Oliver Costello, a Bundjalung man from the Northern Rivers region of New South Wales and chief executive of the Firesticks Alliance, says cultural fire may not be about fuel reduction. He gives the example of a burn near Guyra in New South Wales where Banbai rangers used cultural burning around an art site that contained a painting of an echidna, a Banbai totem. The fire encouraged the growth of native grasses and reduced the density of vegetation so that echidnas could move around the area more easily and find food. Rangers saw more evidence of echidnas after burning, and more growth of a local endangered species, the black grevillea.

'The country has a culture and we're a part of that culture. When you apply the right fire to that culture, you're maintaining your identity with country, maintaining the land,' Costello says.

How do you learn cultural burning?
Despite European colonisation and land theft, Aboriginal cultural lore and knowledge of burning practices endure across Australia.

A revival is being led through initiatives such as the Firesticks Alliance, an Indigenous-led network that undertakes training, on-ground cultural burning and scientific monitoring of its ecological effects.

Fire knowledge has been handed down through generations of Aboriginal families. Costello learnt from his stepfather, a senior Dalabon man from Arnhem Land, who knew how to use fire the traditional way. When his stepfather died, Costello realised how much knowledge had gone with him. It motivated Costello to go to university and focus on Indigenous knowledge systems and sustainability in an era of climate change. 'In New South Wales land management, no one was using cultural burning methodology and protocols, and no one was supporting people to burn their country,' he says.

Over the past decade, the Firesticks Alliance has organised fire workshops in Cape York with Dr Tommy George, a Kuku Thaypan elder. George and his brother Dr George Musgrave (now both deceased) were granted honorary doctorates for their knowledge of fire management and ecology. Fire workshops, such as those held on the south coast of New South Wales and on Yorta Yorta country at Barmah on the Murray River, draw participants from around the country.

Firesticks Alliance practitioners burn on both private and public land, including in New South Wales national parks. Since the 2019–20 summer bushfires, the alliance has fielded a huge increase in inquiries from private landholders and public land management agencies. One landowner in New South Wales credits cultural burning with saving structures on his remote bush property during the Gospers Mountain fire.

Does cultural burning work?

There is a small but growing body of Western academic research on cultural burning and it chimes with what Aboriginal experts have always known. For example, scientists analysing data on fire-scarred land in Northern Australia on behalf of the Nature Conservancy, an environmental organisation, found that early dry-season cultural burning reduced the extent of destructive late-season fires by about 30 per cent compared with the four years before the burning program began.

In Victoria, traditional owners have also noticed a change. There have been more than a dozen cultural burns on Dja Dja Wurrung country, and Nelson says there has been healthy plant and grass regeneration, including kangaroo grass, a traditional dietary staple, and yam daisy, which is used for fibre. Cultural burning is being brought into Victoria's existing burning program, with more planned in addition to 'fuel management' burning done by Forest Fire Management Victoria. They will be conducted in areas nominated by traditional owners, who will lead the burns.

The CSIRO has published a number of papers that find cultural burning delivers a range of social and economic benefits for Aboriginal people, including the protection of heritage, the retention of language and identity and career development opportunities.

Can it help against climate-fuelled bushfires?

Aboriginal people have been devastated to see the damage wrought by the summer bushfires, says Costello. 'We have this knowledge about land management ... and we're really sad because people haven't been listening to us,' he says. 'We have been saying this is going to happen: this country is really thick and it will burn.'

Prime Minister Scott Morrison has argued that hazard-reduction burns are at least as important as cutting carbon emissions in Australia's fight against bushfires, although the Climate Council and federal Opposition say this is a distraction from the government's lack of action on climate change. But analysis from forest scientists at the University of Melbourne found hazard-reduction burns had little to no effect in slowing the severe fires that devastated more than 5 million hectares across New South Wales. It would be best used around assets to protect them from less intense fires, the research found.

Victoria's former emergency management commissioner Craig Lapsley describes cultural burning as a 'holistic land management strategy' and the huge summer bushfires showed that land management agencies need to test new approaches. 'I don't think we valued Indigenous people, and what they believed as a long-term, well-tested strategy, I don't think we have taken that seriously at all,' says Lapsley.

Costello wants land management agencies to support the Firesticks Alliance to develop a national mentoring program so there can be one hundred skilled cultural fire practitioners nationwide. 'We are drawing on the oldest living knowledge system around fire and it works for us,' he says. 'But you also need to share some of the resources and power you have.'

'

Cultural burning delivers a range of social and economic benefits for Aboriginal people.

,

5

HOW CAN A RACQUET MAKE OR BREAK A TENNIS PLAYER?

From strings to 'swing weight', every aspect of an elite player's racquet is calibrated for victory. How do the stars fine-tune their key weapon?

Anthony Colangelo

His perfect hair held by a perfect headband against a pressed polo shirt, Roger Federer walked onto centre court at the Queensland Tennis Centre for his first tournament of 2014 to an adoring crowd. A real-life glimpse of Federer was enough to transfix even the most casual tennis fan but, on this occasion, if you were in the know, his equipment was the focus. Federer had broken with a decade of tradition and got himself a new racquet.

The 2013 season had been a career low for the Swiss champion. Usually number one or two in the world, he'd ended the year ranked sixth. A premature second-round Wimbledon exit had marked the first time in thirty-six consecutive grand slams that Federer had not made a quarterfinal. He'd lasted until just the fourth round in the US Open, a tournament he'd won five times before. These results represented, for some, the start of a career plateau for the then 32-year-old, with back injuries among factors blunting his dominance. But Federer arrested the slide. He hired a new coach – his childhood hero, six-time grand slam winner Stefan Edberg. He set about mending his body. And, perhaps less obviously until he appeared in Brisbane, he changed his magic wand – the racquet he'd wielded through his rise to tennis legend.

For a certain weekend-warrior-type player, changing racquets might offer a seductive solution to a subpar game. After all, it can be easier to spend a few hundred dollars on new equipment than to improve a weak backhand or sluggish legs. At the very least, a change can't do much harm, right? But at the pinnacle, there is nowhere to hide. And just as a player's game is constantly under the microscope, so every gram, inch or centimetre of their racquet is scrutinised. The racquet is the player's key weapon and one with which they have a symbiotic relationship. Even the tiniest change to it will be made only for a very good reason – but then even a 1 per cent improvement is a very good reason in elite tennis.

So, for Federer, in 2014 in Brisbane, the stakes were high. His racquet tweaks marked a recalibration of his game, his new 'specs' offering an insight into a reshaped destiny.

But just how do Federer and other players, such as Serena Williams, Rafael Nadal and Ash Barty, tweak their racquets to boost their games? And how have changes in racquets changed the game itself?

What are the rules on racquets?

There is nothing in the International Tennis Federation's rules restricting what a racquet can be made from, only that it cannot use batteries. 'No energy source that in any way could change or affect the playing characteristics of a racquet may be built into or attached to a racquet.' In principle, that seems to open the way for all sorts of materials – bamboo? titanium? – and customised touches – diamond-encrusted head? fluffy handle? – that make prevailing racquet technology, and players' choices, seem relatively streamlined.

There are some other limits on how much players can soup up their equipment. A racquet can't be longer than 29 inches (73.66 centimetres) overall. The hitting surface (the head) cannot be above 15.5 inches (39.37 centimetres) in length and 11.5 inches (29.21 centimetres) wide. (Players and racquet technicians tend to talk in imperial measures with a smattering of metric – to quantify weight, for example.) Strings must be laid 'flat and consist of a pattern of crossed strings, which shall be alternately interlaced or bonded where they cross. The stringing pattern must be generally uniform … not less dense in the centre than in any other area … and strung such that the playing characteristics are identical on both faces.' But within these parameters, even the slightest variation makes an enormous difference.

How does a racquet reflect a player's style?

Before his 2014 change, Federer used a Wilson Pro Staff 90, with a smaller head than most modern-day equivalents. It was considered

'

The racquet is the player's key weapon and one with which they have a symbiotic relationship.

,

to be the closest thing to the classic, smaller-framed racquets of yesteryear. This had been perfect for his controlled and meticulous game – perfect, in the sense that he had used it to lift seventeen grand slam trophies. Yet it was not built for power.

Bigger racquet heads, such as Spaniard Nadal's 100-square-inch (645-square-centimetre) frame, packed more punch. Federer's 90-inch (581-square-centimetre) head, combined with back injuries, meant he was getting overpowered, particularly on his backhand and even more particularly by the monstrous top spin inflicted by Nadal, who had become the world's number one. Recognising the weakness, Federer tested a new racquet at a German tournament in mid-2013 but reverted to his Pro Staff 90 to end the season, wanting to test more equipment in practice before changing permanently.

After some off-season trial and error he was ready to step out. His updated model, Wilson's RF97 Autograph, had a 97-square-inch (626-square-centimetre) head, designed to help him hit a heavier shot more easily. A bigger head means a bigger sweet spot, which helps on defensive shots, for example, when a player scrambles for the ball.

In the heat of contest, Federer did not have to give the change a second thought.

'I feel like I am not thinking about it [the new racquet] when I am going out there, which is a great thing,' he said after that first competitive match with the RF97 Autograph in Brisbane ended in a straight-sets win. 'I am hitting the ball really well, so I am very pleased with the racquet.' Federer made the final in Brisbane that year, losing to Australian Lleyton Hewitt in a shock result. Yet his career did not plateau: he has won three more grand slams and has been a runner-up four times since. His racquet change is widely regarded as one of the keys to his post-2014 resurgence.

But what of Nadal, the player who, in part, triggered the change? The world's best players, including Federer, hit with heavy top spin, but Nadal is on another level. He deploys a unique amount of up-and-down 'whip', while Federer's swing is flatter. His Babolat AeroPro Drive has a 100-square-inch head, three inches (7.62 centimetres) larger than Federer's. One reason for the big head size is that Nadal needs extra surface area to impart the extreme spin as the ball momentarily slides down his racquet while his arm flings upward.

Australia's sixteen-time grand slam doubles winner Todd Woodbridge notes, 'If I put Roger's racquet into Rafa's hand, he'd [Nadal] be nowhere near the player that he is. He would still be good but he wouldn't be able to do the things that we see from him – his famous shots, his stock things,' he says.

Then there's twenty-three-time grand slam winner Serena Williams, whose racquet is longer than her male and female peers' at 27.7 inches (70.36 centimetres) – most racquets are 27 inches (68.58 centimetres) – giving her more reach. Certainly, she is as powerful a tennis player as there's ever been. The head size of her racquet (104 square inches, or 671 square centimetres) is gargantuan even by the standards of the women's game. Australian Ash Barty, with a 100-square-inch head, is typical of many women in the game. Williams' power is enhanced by the bigger head size while Barty, whose game is particularly based on craft and guile, uses the more conventional racquet to move her opponent around the court and attack at the net.

Weight is another difference for Federer and Nadal. Nadal's racquet, made from graphite – as are most modern racquets – is 27 grams lighter than Federer's. Given Nadal stands much further behind the baseline than most, he must hit further to land the ball deep in the court. The lighter weight allows him to swing harder and faster with less arm fatigue. Williams plays with a racquet lighter than usual for similar reasons, while Barty's is also a bit lighter because she is small.

Why do players have different string patterns?

Both Federer and Nadal have sixteen strings across their racquet head and nineteen from top to bottom, but Nadal's bigger head size means his strings sit further apart. A wider gap between strings holds the ball better before it is launched off the racquet; Nadal's prolific spin is supported by his open string pattern.

Federer's pattern is more closed which, for a player who hits with a flatter swing, means more control. When strings are closer together, the ball rebounds off them at a flatter angle: their trajectory is more direct. Control helps Federer at the net, where Nadal rarely ventures. Williams plays with an open string pattern inside her big racquet head, too. It has further enhanced her power and her spin in the same way it does Nadal's.

Gut or polyester – what's the difference?

Federer's vertical strings are made of natural gut (cow intestine) and his horizontal strings are polyester. Gut is more springy; a ball pinging off it travels an average of 1 kilometre per hour faster than off polyester, according to data from Tennis Australia and Victoria University's racquet technology firm Tennis Lab. More springiness also means the gut is softer, less jarring on players' arms and hands and produces a softer 'feel' on contact with the ball.

Other gut-string users – unusual on tour – are Williams, Novak Djokovic and Kei Nishikori. All mix the gut with polyester. Djokovic plays with an eighteen by nineteen string pattern but on a 95-square-inch (613-square-centimetre) frame. That gives him two more vertical strings than Federer (sixteen by nineteen) even though his head is smaller, for extreme control through a flatter ball trajectory.

Nadal and Barty use only polyester strings, as do most players. Polyester produces almost 10 per cent more spin, the strings sliding against one another on impact with the ball in a way that causes less friction than grippy gut. Spin is enhanced when strings slide upwards or downwards on each other and 'catch' the ball momentarily. As the ball rebounds off them, the strings snap back into place, catapulting the ball further. For Nadal's heavy top spin and Barty's unconventional slice game this makes sense.

> *'Polyester produces almost 10 per cent more spin, the strings sliding against one another on impact with the ball in a way that causes less friction than grippy gut.'*

Polyester breaks more easily and feels more taxing on the arm, but players see worth in enduring those downsides. It costs an amateur player about $90 to have their racquet restrung with the type of strings Federer uses, while polyester only costs $50.

How big a deal is string tension?

Big. Nadal, famous for his on-court superstitions, never changes his. String tension is measured in pounds: how many pounds of pressure are exerted on the strings when pulled into place in the racquet. No matter the conditions, opponent or surface, Nadal's tension is always 55 pounds. Federer, favouring flexibility, carries racquets strung at different tensions (57 to 59). His choice might be informed by factors such as humidity (tennis balls are heavier when it's humid) or comfort.

Professional players report that their racquets feel immediately different when tension is adjusted by a pound or two. A 10-pound drop can increase ball speed by between 1 and 3 per cent, a Tennis Lab test of thirty-eight players found; while a 10-pound tension increase can produce up to almost 4 per cent more spin. 'We talk about string tension like a rubber band – the lower the string tension, the more elastic the strings will be, which results in more power.

The consequence is more energy is reverted back to the ball,' says Tennis Lab sports scientist Lyndon Krause. A lower string tension resulted in balls landing, on average, 54 centimetres deeper in the court than higher-tension racquets, the lab's testing found.

Barty's most abnormal variable is her super-soft string tension (40 pounds), which improves power and comfort. Extra power is important for Barty so she can defend strongly and hit penetrating shots from the corner, given her smaller stature. There's an aural dimension too. The higher your string tension the more of a high-pitched *ping* it will make when you hit the ball. At a lower tension, the ball will thud, or *pock*. There's some speculation that players grunt or screech so their opponents can't hear what tension their racquet is, but it's more likely that they make such sounds as a way to increase the effort and power they hit with, or as a result of exertion.

What does stiffness mean in a racquet?

A stiffer, or less flexible, racquet absorbs less energy, so more energy is instead transferred into the ball when hit, thus making it travel further. Federer plays with a slightly stiffer racquet than Nadal, amplifying the sweet spot which, for Federer's smaller frame, is helpful. While Federer gains some 'softness' by using gut strings, Nadal may well look for it in a less stiff racquet, which absorbs more energy on impact and so is gentler on the arm.

Do players follow through when data suggests changing?

'The embrace of technology in tennis, with equipment and analytics, has been slow,' says Tennis Australia's head of innovation, Dr Machar Reid. A former player and coach and a PhD graduate in biomechanics, Reid runs Tennis Lab. The lab is part of the Game Insight Group, an initiative comprising data and sports scientists and computer engineers who want more data and scientific analysis in tennis. 'If we are to learn from other highly engineered sports like golf and cycling, individual in nature too, and look to what they do really well in terms of customising and fitting equipment better to athletes, what can we do as a sport to catch up?' he explains.

Thanasi Kokkinakis, twenty-four, is one of his generation's brightest tennis talents but injuries have hampered him – a shoulder problem forced him to withdraw from a second-round clash with Nadal in the 2019 US Open. He had used a Babolat – the same one Nadal uses – since childhood. When his sponsorship deal with Babolat was up he decided to test other racquets. Could a different brand, an alternative tension, a change in string types or stiffness give him something extra and help him unlock more of his potential? He used Tennis Lab's Hawk-Eye technology to measure the depth, speed and accuracy of the balls he hit with various racquets. 'I am happy I did it,' Kokkinakis says. 'I had the time, I thought I might as well do it and see what feels comfortable and go from there.'

He didn't change much, though, despite the data suggesting he was better suited to other racquets. 'I hit with a fair bit of spin and I have learnt to control it because it is a pretty powerful racquet,' he says. 'I don't want to change the way I play by adapting to other racquets.' He did go lighter, by 15 grams – the weight of a CD – hoping this might improve injury recovery and fatigue. 'It doesn't sound like a lot to the general punter but when you swing it in your hand over a long period of time … it does help a lot,' he says.

Australia's 2011 US Open winner, Sam Stosur, thirty-six, had success smashing opponents off the court in her peak. As she's got older and opponents have become more powerful, she's tried to add more nuance to her game. After consulting Tennis Lab, she changed to a racquet with more power and spin; however, she found that although she was hitting the ball faster, the significant increase in her spin caused the balls to arc higher and so land shallower in the court, allowing opponents to edge in over the course of a rally and overpower her. She went back to Tennis Lab and found a racquet that still gave her more power and spin – just, this time, a little less spin. Her shots travelled faster and landed deeper in the court. She could control rallies on her terms.

Mid-career, Todd Woodbridge switched to a less stiff racquet to help an ailing elbow. 'I used a really stiff racquet because I could hit the ball flat and hard,' Woodbridge says. But the softer racquet meant his 'bread-and-butter shot' – the slice backhand – suffered even though his elbow felt better. 'I really started to struggle with the feel of that shot,' he says. 'Once you start to doubt that, your confidence goes, you start to lose matches and, there came a point where I went back to the equipment I felt like I could play my stock game with. I had to get my elbow right and get the stiffer racquet back.'

Could today's players win with an old-style wooden racquet?

John Newcombe, a seven-time grand slam champion and five-time Davis Cup winner between 1964 and 1975, used a wooden, small-head Slazenger racquet as a child and a senior version once he began climbing the ranks. 'I didn't know any different,' he says. 'In the seventies, when Prince came out with the big-headed racquet and a couple of the guys started using it, we'd say to them, "Why aren't you down the beach with that big spade? You'll never be able to play with that." You needed a longer stroke [with wooden racquets] and with today's racquets and the strings you see them hit top-spin lobs by hardly moving that racquet head in their stroke. If you did that with a wooden racquet the ball would flop.'

The game itself has been changed by developments in racquets, Newcombe contends. But too much power is a dangerous thing. 'It's probably the major thing that's hurt the net game,' he says, 'because the racquets and strings are so powerful that ten-year-old kids can play terrific groundstrokes and hit top-spin lobs so they don't come to the net. They don't learn the art of net play.

'I do love watching Ash Barty play, she's not just whacking the ball – I find that style boring and a lot of spectators do, I think. I much prefer players with touch as well as power.'

The players' racquet specs

Head sizes: Typically range from 95 to 100 square inches. Federer's is a petite 97 for added control, Nadal's and Barty's are a standard 100, while Williams' is a huge 104.

Weight: Typically 350 to 375 grams. Federer's weighs 366 while Williams' at 305, Barty's at 300 and Nadal's at 339 are relatively light, reducing arm fatigue.

Swing weight: A machine-derived measure of how heavy a racquet feels in motion. Williams' is the heaviest at 366 kilograms per square centimetre with Nadal a close 365, while Federer's is 340 and Barty's 300.

Strings: Can be made of polyester, synthetic fibres or natural gut. Federer and Williams favour a softer and more powerful gut/polyester mix while Barty and Nadal use only polyester, which enhances spin.

String pattern: Refers to the number of vertical by horizontal strings. Barty, Nadal and Federer all have a sixteen by nineteen pattern while Williams has eighteen by nineteen in a large racquet head.

Tension: The pressure applied to the strung strings, measured in pounds. Federer uses a range, from 57 to 59 pounds, depending on conditions, while Nadal's does not deviate from 55. Williams' is 63 while Barty likes a super-soft 40, adding comfort and power.

Stiffness: How flexible a racquet is when bent, measured by an RA (racquet analysis) rating. Federer's is 68 RA, Nadal's 65, Barty's 63 and Williams' 61.

Balance: Weight distribution – it's higher if skewed towards the head, lower towards the handle. It's a comfort thing. In their 27-inch-long racquets, Federer's is balanced towards his hand at 12.4 inches (31.49 centimetres), as is Barty's at 12.6 (32 centimetres), while Nadal's is more 'centred' at 13.3 inches (33.78 centimetres). Williams has a longer (27.7-inch) racquet slightly more towards the hand at 13.4 inches (34.03 centimetres).

Source: Impacting Tennis. Specifications, current for the Australian Open 2020, are subject to change.

6

WHAT DOES MATE MEAN?

It's a short word with a long history.
How has the term 'mate' evolved in
Australia? And how is it used today?

Tony Wright

I t's such a little word. Mate. Small, but with long Australian legs, having survived and thrived through the convict era, the gold rushes, two world wars and the first two decades of the twenty-first century. 'Mate' can mean many things in Australia, from the tenderest greeting to the whiplash of condemnation. It can radiate great goodwill or the oiliest insincerity. It depends on the intonation, the circumstances of its delivery and who is saying it to – or about – whom.

Academics have expended much time and energy grappling with the word. A prime minister caused a national convulsion when he tried and failed to co-opt mate's conceptually broader companion, mateship, for a preamble to the Constitution. The Australian National Dictionary offers long explanations for no less than four forms of common usage of the word. At least one substantial book has been published exclusively about it.

Mate has functional uses too: it is employed vigorously to fill lapses in remembering names when acquaintances meet. It has long been accused of excluding women from its embrace, yet it was adopted by some bold first-wave feminists and, in some modern settings has become at least somewhat gender neutral. It crosses social and political barriers without drawing breath, and may fall as easily from the lips of a person on the street as from a rich and powerful industrialist; from a prime minister to a blue-collar labourer, and many of those between.

So where did this little word come from? How has it managed to last and become so ubiquitous? And do Australians use it differently from everyone else?

Where does the word mate come from?

Mate made its way in the 1300s to Middle English from the Middle Low German *ge-mate*, meaning the act of eating at the same table. It is related to *maat* in both Proto-Germanic and Dutch, meaning partner, colleague or friend. To make the leap to today, we might think about friends gathered around a barbecue. The old mate in *ge-mate*, after all, meant meat.

Etymologists say sailors and labourers were calling each other mate by the mid-fifteenth century. Later that same century the term had evolved on ships to refer to an officer, the mate, who saw that the orders of the master or commander were carried out. From about the 1540s, the word was also being used in English to mean 'one of a wedded Pair'. Thus, from the very start, it was a word about companionship, of eating and working together and/or meaning a formal partnership. For the most part, it implied an equality among those to whom it referred. Shakespeare used the word mate in a number of his plays, including in the sense of companion, associate and comrade. In *The Two Gentlemen of Verona*, for instance, he has Valentine declare of his friends, a band of outlaws, 'These are my mates, that make their wills their law.'

How did mate leap from the old world to a new Australia?

In the years before British lawmakers began sending convicts to the new colony of Australia, Britons – mainly those of the working class in the cities – were commonly using the word mate. It meant friends of all types and included both men and women. Most of Australia's convicts were drawn from the same classes that used mate as an everyday term. As they made the voyage to Australia, the convicts were surrounded by associates of the ship's officers: the surgeon's mate, the carpenter's mate and all the rest. The word, thus, was everywhere among those imprisoned and transported. They were outcasts, with no choice but to share hardship, and a vast majority were men, just like their jailers. They began assigning the word mate a higher meaning – something that belonged to those who had to rely on each other for not just companionship, but survival.

Mateship might have been about shared experience but it was often short on romantic ideals. In Tasmania, convict mates who escaped sometimes ate each other. On Norfolk Island, mateship was turned on its head. To escape their torture, some mates were said to draw lots to murder the other, guaranteeing the murderer would also get the death penalty, like his mate.

Soon, however, mate was being used in broader social settings, although exclusively among men. Nick Dyrenfurth, the author of *Mateship: A Very Australian History*, writes that by 1826, Australia's first newspaper, the *Sydney Gazette and New South Wales Advertiser*, had noted the peculiar convention of mate being used as a greeting to strangers. Here was the start of a double-edged sword. By calling one another mate, but also using the word to address those considering themselves to be social superiors, the convicts were declaring no one was their better.

Most of those in the colony were still overwhelmingly men, about three-quarters of whom, in the early period, would never find a woman to marry. If one's mate in the old world included the sense of a partner from the opposite sex, it no longer applied for the majority in Australia. 'Masculine public culture grew apace,' writes Dyrenfurth. 'In the absence of formal amusements, gambling and drinking became wildly popular pastimes among both convicts and captors, as did testosterone-filled sporting contests such as cockfighting, bare-knuckle prize fighting, and horse racing. This isn't to argue that such a culture didn't similarly develop in other settler societies, notably New Zealand, but in Australia it acquired a particularly pungent masculine odour.'

The gold rushes in the 1850s supercharged mate. A sudden and massive inflow of hopeful immigrants to the uncertainty of the goldfields meant men teamed up, out of necessity, to dig shafts. This 'teaming up' of pairs of mates was already established among travelling bush workers: shearers, drovers and the like who relied on each other for company, safety and muscle. Log sawyers, for instance, had little choice but to work in pairs, one on each end of a crosscut saw. They were business mates in very lonely places, and to retain that mateship and trust – for both practical and social purposes – each would be prepared to defend the other in a tight spot.

The Cockneys of East London had by then embraced rhyming slang, and this vernacular made the gold-rush trip to the Australian diggings. This form of slang meant only those in the know understood that 'me old China' meant mate (China plate rhyming with mate). However, one's 'China plate' excluded Chinese diggers. The often vicious anti-Chinese sentiment of the time morphed into Australia's long-lasting official White Australia policy.

> 'By calling one another mate, but also using the word to address those considering themselves to be social superiors, the convicts were declaring no one was their better.'

Also excluded, in the main, from white Australia's approval of mates were Australia's Indigenous people. From the late eighteenth century through the nineteenth century, Aboriginal people were treated with violence, contempt and, at best, patronising praise or sympathy. Among the crew accompanying Matthew Flinders on his famous circumnavigation of Australia in 1801–3 was Bungaree, a Kuringgai man from what is now known as the Broken Bay area of New South Wales. Flinders wrote that Bungaree was a 'worthy and brave fellow', but when the explorer came to write a book detailing his adventures, it was about his shipmate Trim – his cat. Statues were raised to Trim but not a single statue to Bungaree exists in Australia.

In the second half of the nineteenth century and into the early twentieth century, with literacy spreading fast, Australian writers embedded the idea of mateship, particularly in the bush, deep in

Australian mythology. Henry Lawson elevated the concept, his much-quoted *The Shearers* from 1901 one example:

> *They tramp in mateship side by side*
> *The Protestant and Roman*
> *They call no biped lord or sir*
> *And touch their hat to no man!*

Here was the idea that religious bigotry and social inequality had no place between mates – who were, of course, understood to be white males. Women rarely made it to such exalted places in bush literature unless they were all-suffering and stoic, like Lawson's *The Drover's Wife*. Left alone with her four children, her husband gone droving (with his mates) and forced to deal with the threat of a snake beneath the family hut, her lonely travails are celebrated.

How is mate connected to digger and cobber?

The trenches of World War I combined all the elements that mateship was supposed to be about: the shared experience of hardship, the need to rely for your life on your mates, all enacted within the company of men. This mateship, which remained virtually unchanged through all the wars involving Australia in the twentieth century, began embracing women in the professional soldiering era of the twenty-first century in Afghanistan, Iraq and other theatres of conflict.

The word 'digger' – still used to identify Australian soldiers – first became interchangeable with mate on the Western Front. Digger, interestingly, is another word that harkens back to the goldfields and the egalitarian ideals of the Eureka Stockade rebellion of 1854. The enduring example of mateship from Gallipoli remains Simpson and his donkey: an ordinary man extending the hand of a mate to anyone in great need. The most revered among the men who took part in Australia's first major action on the Western Front – the battle of Fromelles – remain those who, at great risk to their own lives, carried the wounded, their mates, off the battlefield under fire. A giant statue at Fromelles depicting just such a rescue is named *Cobbers*, another word interchangeable with mates. 'Cobber' probably came from a Yiddish word, *chaber*, meaning comrade, used in London during the nineteenth century, but it is no longer anywhere near as common as mate in Australia or the armed forces.

How did mate get into politics?

By the middle of the twentieth century, mate was so familiar to the Australian ear it could be used in novel ways to mean different things. An embittered Bill Hayden, having been forced out of the leadership of the federal Labor Party, unloaded when speaking at the 1983 Labor Party Conference, recalling that one of the plotters had approached him with the words: 'Oh mate, mate.' 'When they call you "mate" in the New South Wales Labor Party, it is like getting a kiss from the Mafia,' said Hayden.

The reputation of a former Whitlam government attorney-general, then High Court judge, Lionel Murphy, was plunged into scandal over the use of the phrase 'And now, what about my little mate?' He was allegedly referring to a lawyer with questionable connections, and a magistrate – to whom he allegedly uttered the question over the phone – felt that Murphy was trying to get an improper deal for his 'mate'. Although Murphy was later acquitted of trying to pervert the course of justice, the words 'little mate' became forever unsavoury.

'"Cobber" probably came from a Yiddish word, chaber, meaning comrade.'

Paul Keating famously loaded hostility, irony and humour into the word when answering a question from opposition leader John Hewson in the early 1990s. Hewson had inquired why Keating, then prime minister, wouldn't call an early election. 'The answer is, mate,' spat Keating, 'because I want to do you slowly.'

The concept triggered an eruption of passion in the late 1990s when then prime minister John Howard tried to insert the word 'mateship' into a preamble to the Australian Constitution. Howard believed mateship embodied what he called the national character and was a central value in the laconic and egalitarian 'fair go'. But many Australians made clear they didn't want mate or mateship hijacked by a politician, particularly one involved in what was known as the 'culture wars' – an early attempt to undo what conservatives saw as political correctness. Having withstood a hail of derision from political foes, media commentators and feminists (Eva Cox said mateship evoked the 'smell of spew in the pubs … mates going gang bang with some sheila'), Howard finally conceded he'd lost the fight only when the Australian Democrats wouldn't support the legislation.

How is mate used today?

Today, mate remains a favoured greeting among 'blokes' in Australia, including those who might dust it off more in certain contexts, such as at football games. But what of women? Dr Johanna Rendle-Short, an honorary researcher in linguistics at the Australian National University, reported in 2009 that more women aged eighteen to twenty-nine were using mate compared to women over fifty. 'The preliminary study (of 689 women) seems to suggest that instead of mate being characterised as a neutral term used by men to show equality and egalitarianism, young women now see mate as a friendly and fun term that, along with many other address forms, is available to show intimacy,' she wrote in the *Australian Journal of Linguistics*.

This author's own experience and limited inquiry finds that many young women today happily use 'mate' among friends. Part of the fun may well be that mate, by now, is so layered with meanings from the past that some Australians cannot deploy it without a trace of ambivalence, or at least a wry knowing. Or perhaps this most resilient of words in Australia has finally come to mean what it was supposed to have meant in the first place: 'friends around a table'.

7

HOW DOES NETFLIX KNOW WHAT WE WANT TO WATCH?

Like a trusted friend, Netflix always gives you tips on what to watch next. How did this streaming service get to be so helpful? How much should you help it back?

Karl Quinn

Netflix has become such an integral part of our lives it's easy to forget it officially arrived in Australia only in March 2015. Although the company doesn't reveal precise numbers, audience research suggests there are more than 5 million subscriptions in Australia, with close to half of all Australians having access to the service.

To many 'members', as it calls its customers, Netflix has become a trusted friend – always there, always with something new to watch and always, always, willing to recommend a show that might just tickle their fancy.

Willingness to splurge on programming – the company was expected to spend an estimated US$17 billion (AU$25 billion) on content in 2020 alone – the ability of viewers to binge-watch entire series in one sitting and the lack of ads are critical factors in the success of the platform. But so too is its ability to siphon the roughly 4800 movies, documentaries and series available on the Australian service (worldwide, it's more than 13,000 titles) through a funnel that seems specifically tailored for each and every one of us, to make viewing suggestions that, more often than not, are at least in the ballpark of what we might actually want to watch at that moment in time.

That funnel is what's colloquially known as 'the Netflix algorithm', and it kicks in the moment you log in and answer the question 'Who's watching Netflix?' But what is this algorithm? Should you be scared of it? And, in a world where you can't possibly watch everything on television, does it help or hinder your ability to pick the best of what's on offer?

What is this 'Netflix algorithm'?
An algorithm is simply a set of rules or instructions to be followed in a calculation – in this case, the calculation that tries to match program suggestions to a member's tastes with the highest degree of accuracy. In the case of the so-called 'Netflix algorithm' –

It's almost as if Netflix actually knows you.

the company prefers the term 'recommendation system' – the calculation is performed by automated programs, not actual humans, and each time it makes a suggestion and you respond to it by selecting or not selecting that recommendation, by watching or not watching the suggested program all the way through, the algorithm gets a little smarter. It's called machine learning, and yes, being just a little bit scared (especially if you've ever watched a *Terminator* movie) is not unreasonable. Our robot overlords are indeed watching us.

You can see the Netflix algorithm in action on the home page on your screen, where row after row of categorised recommendations appear, all of them tailored to your user profile. To get an idea of how it works, try this simple experiment: if you're in a household with multiple users, log on with someone else's profile and you'll notice their home page probably looks quite different to yours. It's not just that different titles are recommended – that much you'd expect if you're an adult, say, and they're a kid – but there's probably a very different ordering of the rows within which those titles are served up.

So, when one member logs on, they might see the 'Because you watched' row up top, but another member might get something entirely different – 'Top 10 in Australia', say, or 'New releases' or 'Historical TV dramas'. And it's not just the order of the rows, either – it's the rows themselves, which can also differ widely from user to user. That's because there isn't just one 'Netflix algorithm', there's a whole bunch of them.

Each member gets a home page tailored to their 'likes' (as indicated by the thumbs-up or thumbs-down ratings they might assign after watching a show or a movie), their viewing history and similarities between their profile and other members' who share similar tastes and viewing histories, across the entire world.

It's almost as if Netflix actually knows you.

How does it work?

It all starts with that user profile you create. This is the anchor to which all the viewing data you generate is tethered. Every time you watch something while logged in under your profile, Netflix records that and feeds that information into its database in a bid to predict what you might like to watch in the future. If you start watching something but don't finish it, it records that. If you binge-watch a ten-part series in a single day, it takes note of that, too.

Perhaps the most powerful tool, though, is the thumbs-up/down rating system, which in 2017 replaced the five-star rating system Netflix had used for the previous twenty years, all the way from its beginnings as a mail-order DVD service.

The old system was a ranking of what people thought of a title after watching it. In 2006, Netflix began trying to predict what rating a title was likely to receive before people had rated it so as to better recommend titles to them. This was the beginning, in very rudimentary and complicated form (an early version utilised 107 different algorithms to produce a single result), of the recommendation system in place today.

From the simplified ratings system now in place, Netflix claims, 'We get a better idea of what you'd like to watch by looking at things such as the genres of TV shows and movies, your previous ratings, your viewing history, and the ratings of Netflix members who have similar tastes to you.'

But unlike the old star system, the percentage figure is not a rating per se, nor even a prediction of how you will rate it. 'The percentage next to a title shows how close we think the match is for your specific profile,' Netflix says.

Why does the recommendation system even exist?

Two reasons, really: to serve the business, and to serve us. Netflix's business isn't built, like traditional television, on ratings and selling advertising. It's all about subscribers: acquiring new ones, maintaining existing ones and winning back lapsed ones. And the higher the accuracy of recommendations, the less reason a customer has to drift away or question the value of their subscription. And for members, it's all about making the path from option to decision as smooth, simple and swift as possible.

'Humans are surprisingly bad at choosing between many options, quickly getting overwhelmed and choosing "none of the above" or making poor choices,' a couple of Netflix developers wrote in a technical paper published in 2015. 'Consumer research suggests that a typical Netflix member loses interest after perhaps 60 to 90 seconds of choosing, having reviewed 10 to 20 titles (perhaps three in detail) on one or two screens [rows].' In other words, we're easily overwhelmed by too much choice so the job of the recommendation system is to make it easy for us by winnowing the options to a more manageable size. But merely restricting choice won't necessarily produce a great outcome. To keep members happy, the recommendations need to be both manageable in number and right for an individual more often than not.

If you select a show that carries a '96 per cent match' score, you start watching it, and you hate it, that counts as a fail. The system can't wear too many of those or it risks creating dissatisfied customers, who might quickly become former subscribers. So the algorithm will factor in your non-completion of the show, and adjust the next recommendation accordingly.

Netflix's product development teams are continually working on minor tweaks to make the recommendation system simpler, everything from moving billboards to short video 'synopses' to tailored images for titles. They continually carry out 'A/B testing', whereby different options are presented to a percentage of the global audience to see which produces the better outcome. That then becomes part of the relevant algorithm. It's all designed to maximise what Netflix calls the 'take-rate' – the rate of conversion from recommendation to watch.

But all this data doesn't just inform what gets recommended to us, of course. It also helps guide Netflix in deciding which shows to buy for the service, which ones to keep, which genres to back and which actors/writers/directors to invest in. It was data that drove Netflix to sign a four-picture US$250-million deal with Adam Sandler in 2014, and to extend that deal in January 2020 for another four movies. 'Whether you know him as Sandman, the Water Boy, Billy Madison, Happy Gilmore, Nick Spitz or simply Adam, one thing is clear: our members can't get enough of him,' Ted Sarandos, Netflix chief content officer, said of Sandler in announcing the extension. 'They love his stories and his humour.'

They love *Friends*, too, which is why Netflix paid US$100 million for the series in 2015, despite the fact it had been in rerun on free-to-air television for years. By some estimates, it was the platform's second-most-watched show (after the US version of *The Office*). But when Netflix lost *Friends* in 2019 to Warner Media – which was reclaiming its back catalogue ahead of the launch of its own streaming service, HBO Max, in May 2020 – it spent a whopping US$500 million to shore up the rights to *Seinfeld* in its place. It was a clear demonstration of the immense value of good content with a proven audience to a business built on retaining subscribers. Those are big numbers, but they are all about giving people what the data says they want, and giving them plenty of reasons to remain as subscribers.

What about the 'stumble-upon' factor? With everything determined by past behaviour, am I ever going to be surprised and delighted again?

That's what the shuffle feature, introduced in September 2020, aims for, but really the answer is probably not, at least not in the way you might have been back in the days of browsing the shelves of the local video store (remember them?). The more complex answer is that Netflix is aware that the lack of randomness, of the happy surprise, is a limitation, and it is trying to factor in ways to compensate for this. But how exactly do you program the unexpected?

One solution is the 'Top 10' and 'Now trending' rows, which put in front of users titles they might not otherwise have discovered if left purely to their own devices. The trouble with this is it's dictated by the lowest common denominator: a title might be popular not because it's good but purely because a lot of other people have watched it, for any one of a variety of reasons (social media chatter, perhaps, or accidental newsworthiness among them). In effect, that creates a self-fulfilling feedback loop: a show becomes popular for some reason unconnected to its quality, it shows up in the most popular row, curious viewers check it out, and that reinforces its popularity (as measured in views), and so it goes. How else to explain the sudden popularity of the dire Polish erotic film *365 Days* in mid-2020, for example?

The dedicated explorer can, of course, escape the tyranny of recommendations by using the 'Movies' or 'TV shows' buttons at the top of the screen and selecting from the pull-down menu among dozens of genres. Select LGBTQ under Movies, for example, and you'll get a landing page with a whole bunch of new rows, including, perhaps, Documentaries, Romance, European movies, Asian movies, Independent movies and Netflix originals. If you're a fan of Sylvester Stallone action films, chances are none of those would have shown up on your home page. But now you've done this, of course, they just might.

For a serious shot at randomness, you can even type the word 'random' in the search bar. Trust us, you'll get exactly what it says on the box.

Well, *this* is pretty random: I watched *Austin Powers* and then it recommended *The Boy in the Striped Pyjamas*. Why?

True story, this. It's impossible to say with certainty why a comedy about a shagadelic sixties spy might lead to a harrowing tale about Nazi concentration camps, but it's unlikely Netflix thinks the Holocaust was a hoot. It is just about conceivable, though, that the confusion was sparked by something as simple as an image of *Austin Powers* star Mike Myers in a striped Carnaby Street suit, because images have become such a crucial factor in all this.

Since May 2016, different users have been served different images to promote the same title – with those images chosen on the basis of what Netflix knows about them. The reason? Most of us make our viewing choices based on the image, and we do so very, very quickly. Announcing this new approach, Netflix noted 'artwork was not only the biggest influencer to a member's decision to watch content, but it also constituted over 82 per cent of their focus while browsing Netflix'. It added, 'users spent an average of 1.8 seconds considering each title'.

Because it is impossible to know precisely which images any one of us will see, we'll take a hypothetical example to demonstrate how it works. Let's say the Australian-made post-apocalyptic sci-fi thriller *I Am Mother* turns up in your feed because you have watched a lot of sci-fi on Netflix lately; chances are you'll see an image of the movie's robot, Mother (lovingly built by those special-effects wizards at Weta in New Zealand, the same people who gave us all those hobbits and orcs in Peter Jackson's Tolkien movies). But if you've just watched and given the thumbs-up to *Million Dollar Baby*, you might be served an image of Hilary Swank instead (she's one of the stars of *I Am Mother*, and won a best actress Oscar for Clint Eastwood's 2004 boxing movie).

It's ingenious, but it can have unintended outcomes, as some African-American customers noted in 2018 when they were served title cards featuring black actors who only had minor roles in shows. An embarrassed Netflix was forced to once again declare it did not use ethnicity as a filter – presumably it was viewing history alone that produced that tailored result? – but people quite rightly

'

Most of us make our viewing choices based on the film's artwork, and we do so very, very quickly.

,

wondered precisely what information they were handing over every time they declared who was watching.

Do I need to play nice with Netflix on all this?

It's up to you whether or not you want to be an active participant in the whole thumbs-up/down thing, but even if you don't, you should know that Netflix is harvesting an awful lot of data on your viewing behaviour anyway. The company swears it does not share this information externally but, as we've discussed, it does use it to determine what sort of programs it commissions and who it gets to direct them and act in them, as well as what it serves up to you. So frankly, unless you just don't trust them with your data, you might as well get in there and get involved.

The recommendation system is powered by machine learning, but the algorithms that drive it are only as good as the inputs they receive; garbage in, garbage out, as they say in the computing world. If you watch a show and don't rate it, a crucial piece of data is missing from the feedback system (although if you only watched the first seven minutes, say, of a two-hour movie, that still tells the AI something).

Not everybody wants to have their decision-making 'guided' in this way. But if the recommendation system may never be able to fully replicate that serendipitous sense of discovery that physical shelves of DVDs (and VHS tapes before them) afforded us, what is clear is that the more accurate data it is fed – from the system, from the individual user, from a global community of like-minded members – the more efficient it will become at scouring those virtual shelves on our behalf.

8

WHAT IS QUANTITATIVE EASING?

It's unconventional, it's not
for the faint-hearted and it's being
deployed around the world.
How does 'QE' work – and does it?

Shane Wright

Before anyone had even heard about a new disease spreading in the Chinese city of Wuhan, the concept of quantitative easing was being floated. Interest rates were at record lows and the classic levers for boosting the economy were no longer working.

Reserve Bank of Australia (RBA) governor Dr Philip Lowe, in the immediate wake of the 2019 federal election, had signalled using some unusual economic measures in his desire to see the economy grow much faster so as to drive down unemployment and lift wages. In June of 2019, official interest rates were cut to 1.25 per cent. By year's end, they were at 0.75 per cent. But Lowe also revealed the RBA was starting to war-game other policies to get the economy moving. And then came the coronavirus, killing hundreds of thousands of people, making millions more ill and causing the biggest economic downturn since the Great Depression. The RBA took official interest rates to a record low of 0.25 per cent to deal with the pandemic but also embraced those other policies it had foreshadowed – known by some as 'quantitative easing' or 'QE', but more broadly as 'unconventional monetary policy' – to protect the economy from the financial disaster.

These have been unprecedented times for the Reserve Bank. When it announced its policy plans in March 2020, it was done via a 'virtual' speech given by Lowe who then held an online press conference facing the nation's finance journalists. The press conference itself was a first for the bank, necessary to explain the extraordinary steps being taken.

So what are the steps? What is quantitative easing? And does it work?

What does the Reserve Bank usually do to help the economy?

The Reserve Bank's number one weapon to manage the economy is via interest rates: cuts, to get the economy growing faster – and which are a form of 'easing' – or increases – to stop inflation getting out of hand – are what most people know as monetary policy. The official interest rate, also known as the cash rate, then sets the level of all other interest rates, such as the one that applies to your savings account.

CASH RATE TARGETS SINCE 1990

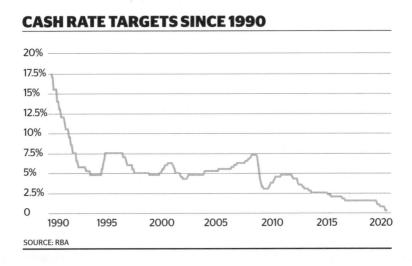

SOURCE: RBA

Graphic: Jo Gay

In challenging times, such as during the coronavirus pandemic, interest rates are also pivotal in preventing an utter collapse in economic activity. Going into the pandemic, official interest rates were already at record lows, with the federal government pumping extra money into infrastructure projects. That was due to the economy growing well below trend, with close to 2 million people either out of work or who wanted to work more hours.

But the economic shock delivered by the coronavirus was unlike any ever seen by a central bank. Slightly lower interest rates cannot deal with the forced closure of large parts of the economy, shutting the country to international visitors, a collapse in immigration and the very real fear among consumers that time with family or friends could give them a potentially deadly disease. The RBA has been urging the federal and state governments to embrace a new round of economic reforms in areas from taxation to regulation while calling for even more public expenditure on infrastructure and income support programs. But unconventional monetary policies, on top of very low interest rates, are the only ways the RBA itself can boost the economy.

Quantitative easing is one form of unconventional monetary policy – there are several that the RBA has deployed while shunning others. The most unconventional of policies for a central bank is to take its official interest rate below zero. The Swiss National Bank actually forced its commercial banks in the 1970s to charge −2 per cent interest on accounts held by foreigners. But the negative interest rates of recent years are broader, as central banks have sought to make it very unappealing for a person with money to simply leave their cash in an account.

In Australia, the RBA took the official cash rate to an all-time low of 0.25 per cent, which brought down mortgage and general borrowing rates to their cheapest levels on record. Factor in inflation, and anyone with money in a savings account was going backwards in real terms.

Central banks can manage expectations by engaging in 'explicit forward guidance', stating publicly they are going to keep interest rates very low for a set number of months or years or until they see unemployment at a particular level. The RBA, announcing its quantitative easing package, adopted this particular measure by signalling no move in interest rates for several years.

Quantitative easing, as used by the United States and Europe during the global financial crisis (GFC), is another tool in the unconventional monetary policy kitbag. This is where a central bank effectively prints money that it uses to buy government bonds. Bonds are debts issued by the government (for instance, the federal government currently owes almost $700 billion to investors who have bought Australian bonds over the years). They are considered the safest form of investment because governments don't have a habit of going bankrupt. As demand for government bonds goes up, the interest rate on them falls. By the RBA buying as many government bonds as possible, it would hope to push down interest rates to such a low level that banks are better off lending money to businesses and households than holding on to it. In other words, it is spending large quantities of new cash to ease monetary policy. The RBA has used this mechanism to buy more than $50 billion of state government bonds, keeping a lid on the interest rates on this form of debt.

A twist on this is that a central bank could offer low-interest loans direct to commercial banks (which, effectively, happened in Australia during the GFC) or buy private debt such as mortgage-backed bonds. Even shares, in extreme cases, could be on the central bank's shopping list.

One option for the RBA in dealing with the coronavirus was to offer low-interest loans to banks on the proviso they pass on that cash directly to businesses. This formed a part of its policy prescription, offering commercial banks cheap access to $90 billion as long as that was offered to small- and medium-sized firms.

The RBA, which wouldn't mind seeing a lower Australian dollar, could buy and sell the currency. Intervening in the currency market would require deep pockets to make a material change in the value of the Australian dollar. It would also risk retaliation from other central banks as they sought to keep a lid on their own currencies.

What is helicopter money?

A final part of the unconventional policy suite involves the central bank printing money and giving it to the federal government so it can send out cheques to the nation's taxpayers. This 'helicopter drop' of money idea was first raised by noted economist Milton Friedman in 1969 in a famous paper about ways a central bank could quickly boost a sagging economy. Friedman suggested a chopper dropping $1000 notes from the sky, which would be collected by consumers. His idea rested on the notion that it would be a 'unique event' that would never be repeated. Hence, consumers would go out and spend their windfall gain, boosting a struggling economy. The helicopters would be flying only if interest rates had already fallen to zero. Friedman also argued the cash drop would work much quicker than anything a government might provide.

Former chairman of the US Federal Reserve during the GFC, Ben Bernanke, was known as 'Helicopter Ben' after using Friedman's metaphor in a 2002 speech about ways to prevent deflation. It's slightly different to the way the Rudd government sent out cheques to millions of Australians during the GFC and the money the Morrison government handed out to people during the pandemic. In both of these cases, the money was raised by borrowing on debt markets. Pure helicopter money is actually the central bank creating the cash out of thin air. They don't even need a printing press – just a few keystrokes on a computer generates the money.

Some economists, over the years – worried that helicopter cash may be put into bank accounts or under the mattress rather than spent – have advocated an even more exotic concept: cash would be issued to people with an expiration date. You might have six or nine months in which to spend the money. After a set period, any cash sitting in a person's bank account with an expiration date would simply cease to be legal tender.

But don't get excited if you hear a helicopter pass overhead. Given the huge injections of cash seen in Australia in schemes such as JobKeeper in 2020, the chances of the government using this tactic are just about zero.

Why are we talking about quantitative easing?

Quantitative easing has been forced onto the world's central banks by the pandemic and the measures put in place to stop its spread.

But even before the virus, quantitative easing was on the global agenda for three key reasons.

Firstly, inflation has been well short of the mandated targets of central banks. The RBA is supposed to have inflation sitting between 2 and 3 per cent but it is expecting prices to actually fall in the wake of the virus.

Secondly, global economic clouds have been gathering and central banks around the world have already taken their interest rates lower (or have been beefing up their quantitative easing policies). The coronavirus outbreak became an economic existential threat. The virus, and its economic impact, spread faster than treasury departments could model the financial fallout.

And finally, the RBA has run out of interest rate ammunition to boost the local economy and take unemployment lower. With official interest rates at 0.25 per cent, cutting rates even further has little effect as commercial banks have to reduce both lending and deposit rates. While low lending rates are great for those who want to borrow money, zero or (as has occurred overseas) negative deposit rates hurt those with money. Average savings account interest rates are already between 0 and 0.1 per cent.

Is quantitative easing working?

We've already seen some elements of the unconventional monetary policy battle plan put in place. The RBA has made clear that low interest rates are going to be with us for a long period, saying it believes inflation won't start increasing until the jobless rate gets down to at least 4.5 per cent – Lowe has suggested we should expect low rates 'for decades'.

It would be unlikely the bank would try to deliberately drive down the Australian dollar – partly because of the immense cost and because if other central banks did the same then the dollar may go nowhere.

When stimulus packages, such as the ones we've seen during

the pandemic, come to an end, the 'fiscal cliff' has to be offset by monetary policy support. But there are legitimate concerns about quantitative easing, especially if it remains entrenched. Experienced economist Dr Stephen Kirchner, in a research paper on the issue for the United States Studies Centre at the University of Sydney, has noted that if the Reserve Bank went down the quantitative easing path, it would not be for the faint-hearted. He found if the RBA's scheme was to be of the same size put in place by the US Federal Reserve it would have to buy bonds worth about 1.5 per cent of GDP to achieve the equivalent of a 0.25 percentage point decline in interest rates. Kirchner estimated that, in dollar terms, it would mean buying up to $550 billion worth of debt.

> *'When stimulus packages, such as the ones we've seen during the pandemic, come to an end, the "fiscal cliff" has to be offset by monetary policy support.'*

The total value of federal and state government debt at the moment is approaching $1 trillion so trying to find enough bonds to buy would be difficult. That might force the bank into every corporate nook and cranny looking for business debt to buy. Unlike governments, businesses do have a track record of going under, potentially leaving the RBA with corporate bonds that may never be repaid.

But Kirchner found that quantitative easing in an Australian context was likely to be much more effective than in the United States, especially if it did not make some of the mistakes the US Federal Reserve made during its five-year debt-buying program – the so-called 'taper tantrums', for example, occurred when equity markets reacted negatively to the bank's plans to start winding back the program.

What are the risks around quantitative easing?

The avalanche of money thrown at the world's economies in the wake of the GFC certainly avoided a repeat of the Great Depression. Before the pandemic, unemployment rates in Europe and the United States had fallen and there were signs of upward pressure on wages (particularly in the United States and Britain). But there's also been criticism of how quantitative easing appears to have benefited high-income earners who have been able to borrow money more cheaply, pumping up property and share markets.

The rise of political populism and extremists on both the left and the right has been aided and abetted by some of the economic policies – including ones such as quantitative easing – used over recent years.

In the wake of the banking royal commission, tighter lending standards and risk aversion has forced lenders to adjust the way they lend. The pandemic is something else. It destroyed supply chains and depressed demand (except perhaps for toilet paper); the RBA believes it may cast a shadow over the economy for years.

The globe's central banks have ended up in the world of unconventional monetary policy. That points to one unavoidable fact – the economy is in trouble.

9

WHAT IS RAMADAN?

A quarter of the world, and about
600,000 Australians, observe Ramadan
every year. What is this festival for?
What are the dos and don'ts?

Maher Mughrabi

Most of the world's 1.8 billion Muslims – roughly a quarter of the Earth's people – observe the rites of Ramadan annually, from the new (crescent) moon of the Islamic calendar's ninth month until the next new moon, twenty-nine or thirty days later.

According to the last census, there are 600,000 Muslims in Australia, with backgrounds ranging from Middle Eastern to South-East Asian. Every Muslim who has reached the age of responsibility (puberty) and is mentally and physically capable is expected to observe Ramadan. But what does this mean in practice? What kind of activities are Muslims allowed to take part in and what must they abstain from? What is the thinking behind this festival? And can you apply for an exemption?

What is Ramadan and what is it for?

Ramadan is a kind of 'spiritual training ground', says Islamic Council of Victoria vice-president Adel Salman, the 'main game' of which is to improve your relationship with God and improve yourself. It may last for just a month but the idea is to develop new and better habits long term, Salman explains. 'It's a bit like New Year's resolutions,' he says.

'Ramadan is a kind of "spiritual training ground".'

Ramadan is the word in Arabic – the liturgical language of Islam – for the ninth month in the Islamic calendar, sometimes rendered as Ramzan or Ramazan in other languages. As the Islamic calendar is lunar (organised by the cycles of the moon) and the Gregorian calendar introduced in the West and now used globally is solar, Ramadan's timing in the Gregorian year shifts by roughly eleven days each year.

The timing is much discussed among Muslims, says Salman, with some Muslims simply looking to the Bureau of Meteorology or phone apps for advice on the new moon, while traditionalists prefer to wait for an authority to actually see the moon in the sky the night before it becomes 'new'. In any case, the month has a special status because Muslims are taught that the Koran – which they revere as the word of God – was revealed to the Prophet Muhammad during this month, beginning in the year 610 CE. During this month, Muslims are expected to undertake prayer and abstinence in thanks for God's revelation and his creation, as a result of which they will emerge spiritually purified.

But that's not all. The Koran tells Muslims that on the holiest night, Lailat al-Qadr (The Night of Power or Destiny or Decree), which falls during the last ten days of Ramadan and marks the beginning of God's revelation to Muhammad, any prayer they make will be better than the prayers of 1000 months and that angels descend to Earth to carry out God's wishes.

Fasting, which Ramadan is best known for, is one of the five pillars of Islam, the practices that are intrinsic to being a Muslim. The others are the testament of faith – a short verbal declaration of adherence to Islam, which is repeated whenever Muslims are called to prayer; prayer itself – at five ordained times every day throughout the year; charitable giving; and the Haj pilgrimage, when thousands of pilgrims from around the world converge on the ancient city of Mecca for five days of worship. Muslims are expected to undertake the Haj – which includes a visit to what is said to be the world's first mosque, a small stone building known as the Kaaba, which Muslims turn to in prayer – once in their lifetimes if they have the means to do so.

What is not allowed during the month of Ramadan?
Between sunrise and sunset, Muslims have to abstain from eating, drinking, ingesting medications, smoking (which is generally

frowned upon in Islam) and sexual intercourse. During daylight hours, a single sip of water or coffee, or a puff of a cigarette, is enough to invalidate the fast. This is as true in Australia as anywhere.

To prepare for their daily fast, Muslims wake for a pre-dawn meal called suhoor: vegetables and fruits, tea, yoghurt, dates and foods that offer lasting sustenance such as beans and lentils. In many cities in the Muslim world, volunteers wake the faithful for suhoor by marching through the streets chanting and beating drums.

Many Muslim-majority countries curb the sale of alcohol during the month. In countries such as Saudi Arabia, the United Arab Emirates, Pakistan, Tunisia and Brunei, people who eat in public during the day can be fined, jailed or even deported.

In the UAE, which has large Western expatriate populations in Dubai and Abu Dhabi, restaurants use curtains to conceal customers who eat during the day. In Saudi Arabia, restaurants simply close until evening.

The fasting acts as a reset for the mind, body and soul. Ramadan is also a month of gratitude. By abstaining from food and water during the day, the faithful are reminded of those less fortunate. Muslims are also expected to refrain from misdeeds, idleness and hateful speech.

'I find myself restraining my inclination to road rage,' says author and broadcaster Tasneem Chopra, '[or to] snap at my kids while preparing dinner, or whinge to a colleague about someone or something during an intense work day – all of these scenarios require a greater presence of mind than forgoing my 11 a.m. coffee over the holy month,' she confides. 'They say that for some people, the only thing they receive from Ramadan is hunger. [But] fasting is less concerned with hunger and more about nourishing good conduct.'

As for idleness, watching television seems to be okay. In fact, in the Middle East in particular, people who are less active because of fasting are a captive audience for broadcasters, who will schedule soap operas or historical dramas to run in the evening throughout

Ramadan. Having said that, Islamic authorities have criticised these shows for distracting people from the holy month's primary purpose.

What should you do during Ramadan?

Once the start of the holy month is declared, Muslims share holiday greetings such as *Ramadan Mubarak*, or 'Blessed Ramadan', and *Ramadan Kareem*, 'may Ramadan be generous [to you]', via text messages, calls and emails to family and friends.

Ramadan is a month of worship. Muslims are expected to show self-control and deeper spirituality, spending time in contemplation and prayer – although they can also go to work. Year-round, Muslims pray throughout the day but during Ramadan there is another ritual: Tarawih prayers are observed after the evening meal, or iftar, either at home or in congregations at mosques.

Muslims can shop for food during the day but just can't eat it. At sunset, they traditionally break their fast, as the Prophet Muhammad did some 1400 years ago, with a sip of water and some dates. After sunset prayers, a large feast is shared with family and friends. Iftar is a social event as much as it is a gastronomical adventure. Across the Arab world, apricot juice is an iftar staple. In South Asia and Turkey, yoghurt-based drinks are popular.

> 'After sunset prayers, a large feast is shared with family and friends. Iftar is a social event as much as it is a gastronomical adventure.'

'Every evening of Ramadan was like a festival, playing at night as children … breaking fast with all the family,' remembers former Victorian of the Year and social activist Berhan Ahmed, who grew up in Keren, Eritrea. 'We shared any leftover food with our neighbours and the homeless. Food doesn't go to waste.

'The month of Ramadan was like a map … [so that] all the mistakes made before Ramadan could be avoided in [the holy month] and beyond.'

Mosques and charitable organisations will open their doors to feed the poor and needy – particular merit is attached to performing charitable works during the month. In Australia, this can include volunteering at the local mosque, helping with aid groups or donating to charities, says Salman. 'Even a smile to someone is considered an act of charity.'

Don't people get hungry and tired?

Yes. In some countries where Islam is the chief religion, the working day is shortened for Ramadan. It's particularly onerous when it falls during the summer months. Muslims living in countries with excessively long daylight hours (in Scandinavia, for example) are advised by religious scholars to adhere to the fasting times of the nearest Muslim-majority country.

Just as Christian holy seasons such as Christmas and Easter have become commercialised, Ramadan is increasingly associated with night-time festivities and binge eating. While, traditionally, the fasting day ends with a domestic feast, in modern times people often attend Ramadan events at hotels and restaurants and, combined with the lower activity of fasting days, can even find themselves gaining weight during the holy month. In the Gulf states, a spike in attendances at hospitals has been reported, with problems ranging from dehydration to uncontrolled diabetes, as well as injuries from traffic accidents attributed to drowsiness.

Can you 'apply for an exemption'?

Children, the infirm, pregnant or breastfeeding women and those with chronic health conditions are all understood to be exempt from fasting. Women who are menstruating or people who are ill or travelling on long journeys can also fast at alternative times of the year.

The Koran makes it clear that the point of fasting is self-discipline and not to put oneself through unnecessary suffering and hardship. 'Allah intends for you ease and does not intend for you hardship,' it says. The Prophet Muhammad is said to have fasted two days in every week – something television journalist Michael Mosley cited when he popularised the 5:2 diet.

In recent years, questions have been raised over the assessment of students and examinations during the fasting month. 'They struggle to concentrate and their energy levels are low,' said one school principal.

How does Ramadan end?

Traditionally, Muslims rely on an authority to sight the new moon to determine the beginning and the end of Ramadan. For example, some Sunni Muslims wait for the Saudi Arabian religious authorities to declare the end of Ramadan. Shia Muslims and other denominations will prefer their own religious authorities. In Nigeria, where more than 80 million Muslims live, the Sultan of Sokoto – a hereditary religious authority – formally asks Nigeria's Muslims to look for the moon so that the beginning and end of the holy month can be determined.

Muslims mark the end of Ramadan with a celebration and feasting known in Arabic as Eid al-Fitr, the Festival of Breaking the Fast. In Indonesia this festival, known locally as Lebaran, is the most important of the year and sees all employees get a legally mandated salary bonus. Millions of Indonesians return to their home villages to celebrate and seek the blessings of their elders, a ritual known as mudik.

In Australia, there is a lot of buzz, including giving presents to children, visiting family and friends (or saying hello on Zoom, if you are in the midst of a pandemic) and eating lots of special sweets and pastries. Women dress in colourful clothes and men spruce up, too. 'It's quite a celebration,' says Salman.

10

HOW DO YOU CONQUER CRYPTIC CROSSWORDS?

They're a daily ritual for some people, a complete mystery to others. Who on earth invented these devious puzzles? And how do you crack their code?

David Astle

Explain cryptic clue I see (9)

Rookies will be thrown by this clue. Even veterans might hit the wall – but that's half the fun. To crack the cryptic code you need to be rubber-minded. While quick crosswords surrender their secrets in a rush, cryptics involve a few more twists.

Cryptic, the word, comes from *kryptos* in Greek, or hidden. That's the challenge. To look past the camouflage, the so-called 'surface sense of the clue' and find the truth hiding below the surface. But how do you play the game? Who came up with cryptic crosswords in the first place? And how do you know what kind of clue you're looking at?

Who invented the crossword?

Arthur Wynne is the scapegoat. Born in Liverpool, Wynne earned a quid in America as an onion-planter then as a violinist in Pittsburgh and, later, as a section editor for the *New York World*. His baby, in fact, was a weekly lift-out called 'Fun'. Aimed at kids, the supplement combined comics and games plus a few picture puzzles. Yet in 1913, just before Christmas, one page had a nagging gap with no cartoon to fill it. No ad, no jokes, no riddles – nothing.

Rather than panic, Wynne invented the 'word-cross', as he called it – a diamond-shaped diagram with FUN inscribed across the top line of squares. The rest was up to the reader to complete, using numbered clues below the grid: quick clues, such as 8–9 *To cultivate* (FARM) or 4–26 *A daydream* (REVERIE).

The numbering system was part of Wynne's revolution. While word squares existed before 1913 – as simple boxes of four-by-four entries – the word-cross introduced internal navigation, with inbuilt numbers and blackened squares. Obvious in hindsight, but those tweaks proved game-changing. And addictive. Soon the puzzle's name flipped into cross-word, the hyphen lapsing as the fad swept across and down the United States.

Chequered fashions, pocket dictionaries – the craze ran amok. Crossword musicals appeared off-Broadway. By 1924, two Columbia grads named Richard Simon and Max Schuster published the world's first crossword book, generating the capital to seed their own publishing empire.

Jealousy, in a word. Think about it. Here was America, smitten by a gimmick, contorting English into fresh shapes while London looked on, one part curious and two parts peeved they hadn't hatched the idea first.

In 1924, a *Times* editorial characterised crosswords as 'a menace … making inroads on the working hours of every rank of society'. A moral scourge. A blight upon society. But that didn't stop the Poms from adopting the novelty, on the proviso they could tweak the rules.

This time the culprit was Torquemada, an alias borrowed from one of the Spanish inquisitors who tormented non-Catholics during the 1400s. The compiler's real name was Edward Powys Mathers, a literary critic with a flair for word-bending. His maiden puzzle, appearing in the *Observer* in 1926, was entitled 'Feelers', a weevil-shaped grid declaring itself as: 'A putting out of feelers from setter to solver, and from solver to setter. A beginning has been made with an unusual number of varied lights.' 'Lights' is British slang for answers, the inspiration flashes to fill a diagram. Instead of quick clues, Mathers had ransacked parlour games to create a range of deceits: *Money made out a rail accident* (LIRA). Or: *You get this measure from a bill* (PECK).

The first clue is an anagram; the second, a double-meaning. Neither trick is as concise as listed in the modern playbook, but only because Torquemada was drafting the rules in real time, forging a British innovation out of an American inception.

'Feelers' heralded a swarm of novelty patterns in subsequent puzzles – a peacock, a doll's house, a chess knight – as Mathers refined his own rules towards the modern cryptic genre.

Rules? What rules?

Yes, cryptic clues have rules. What did you expect? Where Mathers splashed ideas on a blank canvas, other setters followed to codify the art form. One was Alasdair Ferguson Ritchie, a crossword maker for the *Listener* from 1932. Better known as Afrit – after his condensed name and an Islamic demon – the Norfolk curate composed a maxim still relevant to clue-makers: 'You need not mean what you say, but you must say what you mean.' Clues, in other words, can conceal their answers just like our opening clue – but they must conceal fairly. Hence the call for guidelines.

Boiled down, the rules insist most clues own two parts. One part is the definition (just like Wynne's quick clues) while the other is the mind game providing the same solution. The art of solving is to pick which part is which – where to split the clue, and how to read each fragment.

As for the mind games, the so-called wordplay elements, check the clue box on page 111, 'Twelve ways to "clue" DEAR', to see how the one answer can be clued twelve different ways, according to each formula. Later on, I'll give you some bonus hints to help you intuit what formula you might be facing. But first, let's take a whirlwind tour of puzzle pages around the world.

Are cryptic clues exclusively in English?

Before I wrote *Cluetopia* – my book to mark the crossword centenary – I'd presumed cryptics were uniquely English. Our language seems tailor-made for tampering. Layered by history, from classic Greek to Viking verbs, from Norman French to web slang, English alone felt fit for such elasticity.

Turns out the French adore similar hijinks, with novelist George Perec a notable pioneer for *Le Nouvel Observateur*. Over the border, Netherlanders revel in double meanings while the Swedes devour visual puns, building a cartoon into their open grids – no black squares but heavy bars and arrows. Chinese constructors craft

'

You need not mean what you say, but you must say what you mean.

,

a mahjong version of cryptic subterfuge just as Arabic speakers delight in semantic sleight of hand, with solvers entering their script right to left, from base to top.

If only Wynne could see how far his FUN has spread. All evidence suggests that *Homo faber* (man the maker) is hugger-mugger with *Homo ludens* (man the mischief-maker). That experimental bug, first devised by Mathers in 1924, has clearly bitten, sharpening an appetite for cryptic play from Pago Pago to Woop Woop.

To solve a cryptic clue, you need to read the words in two ways. The first is the orthodox way, to grasp the story the language is presenting. Let's try that: *Get waves in boat* (6). The picture is dramatic. Vivid. A glimpse of high-sea drama. But now try reading the clue a second way, separate from the story. Because the story is a lie, a fabrication designed to hide two elements – the definition and the wordplay (or vice versa). The sooner you leave that sodden boat in your wake, the quicker you'll see how the clue is built.

The answer has six letters. So does the phrase 'in boat'. There's a hint. Another observation is how 'waves' can apply to surf as well as being a verb, meaning to waggle or flap. In the trade, such words are anagram indicators – or anagrinds. I prefer the label of signposts, as they signal the solver to juggle the adjacent set of letters, the cluster whose amount matches the answer's length.

Anagram signposts can be any word or phrase denoting change or upheaval. Rock or roll. Break or shake. Or slyer candidates such as fluid or derelict, rent or doctor. Obey their command and get rending, start doctoring, rock and shake those six letters: INBOAT. Notice how I've clumped the phrase into a block. That's because I've dumped the story for the clue's deeper truth, waving INBOAT to make … what? The clue's remainder is telling you, the definition sitting apart from the wordplay. We're after a synonym of 'get'.

Did you obtain it? Well done. That's how anagrams work, their signpost a handy way to spot them, adjoining a letter-batch that corresponds to the answer's length. A similar trick is observed in the DEAR example (see the box 'Twelve ways to "clue" DEAR'), just as every other recipe has its own giveaways.

So which clue is which?

Double meanings are often short as they need no signpost. *Narrow light*, say, equals TAPER, both words defining the one answer. Brevity can betray this style, making this recipe a useful starting place.

Containers put RAM inside MACE to make MACRAME; or MACE around RAM to spell the same result. Depending on which choice of action, inserting or enclosing, the clue's signpost will ask you to put the burger in the bun, or the bun around the burger, so to speak. Look for words implying entering (insertion) or holding (enclosure). No surprise, containers are known as sandwich clues.

Homophones ask you to utter one word ('deer') to hear another: DEAR. Hence the signpost denotes the audio domain, suggesting speech or soundwaves, using markers such as 'say', 'on the phone' or 'vocal'. In the DEAR box, the classic 'we hear' is used.

Charades link FRO and ZEN to make FROZEN, à la the parlour version of charades. No jumbling involved, no sandwiching or speaking – charades shirk signposts as their action is sequential. This can make them trickier to isolate but sometimes a lack of signpost serves as its own signpost.

Hidden clues bury the solution inside its wording. AVIDLY, for instance, lies within 'David Lynch', so a hidden clue could read: *David Lynch screens with gusto* (6). Take note of 'screens', a signpost implying hiding, prompting the solver to seek a word that means 'with gusto'.

Any more tips?

Yes – be kind to yourself. Rookies, avoid my crosswords – for now. Crosswords come in all degrees of difficulty. Turning to *The Age* and *The Sydney Morning Herald*, Nancy Sibtain (NS) on Thursday is ten times kinder than me, as is David Plomley (DP) on Wednesday, while Liam Runnalls and Rose McGinley – sharing Monday and otherwise known as LR and RM – err on the lenient side of playful.

Checking answers is valuable, or learning answers for the clues that stumped you. There's a reason 'cheating' draws on 'teaching'. Reverse engineering, as boffins call it, allows you to recognise the traps for next time.

Try reading a tricky clue aloud. Slowly. This highlights the language. Ask yourself what role is each word playing, as good clues waste nothing. And remember: words can have several meanings, just like 'waves' in our boat outing, the setter adapting a word that's distinct from its role in the clue's story.

> *'There's a reason "cheating"*
> *draws on "teaching".'*

Another tip: if you can't crack 1-across, move around. Look for the clue that murmurs its own formula. Every fortress has an open window to grant you access.

And lastly, remember the two-part rule. Namely, if a clue has two parts, the definition lurks in the first word (or words) or the last word (or words). Sounds a useless hint until you try it.

Hang on, what about that opening clue?

Oops. Here it is again: *Explain cryptic clue I see (9)*. Following that two-part tip, 'explain' is the answer's definition, assigning the rest

Take note of the tricks as you travel and soon the hybrids will also unravel.

as wordplay. Yet, unlike every clue you've met so far, this gnarly customer combines two formulas – anagram plus charade. These fusions are called hybrids, the tougher level of clues awaiting rookies in the long run.

Don't panic. Go slow. Walk before you can run. Take note of the tricks as you travel and soon the hybrids will also unravel. Here we need to make a 'cryptic' version of CLUE, those four letters: the combo's anagram element. After that – 'I see' – warrants the charade treatment. To see a special friend is to date. Can you see what I'm seeing, forging a synonym of explain? If you need more insight, diving into cryptics with time – with special friends – will only go to ELUCIDATE. Have fun.

Twelve ways to 'clue' DEAR

- *Sweetheart spilt a red* = DEAR (anagram)
- *Pricey sugar* = DEAR (double meaning)
- *The German hugged a favourite* = DE(A)R (container)
- *Beloved caribou, we hear* = DEAR (homophone of deer)
- *Steep side around nest* = DEAR (hidden inside 'side around')
- *$500 hearing aid isn't cheap* = D-EAR (charade)
- *Babe repulsed ringleader and a journo* = DEAR (reversal of R-A-ED)
- *Dismal redhead leaves pet* = DEAR (deletion – R from DREAR)
- *Expensive letter-opener?* = DEAR (pun)
- *Precious Shakespearean king left for dead* = DEAR (manipulation – L for D in LEAR)
- *Regularly I'd repair valuable* = DEAR (alternation – even letters)
- *Drake expedition across river leads to treasure* = DEAR (code – initials)

For handy sources, my own Rewording the Brain *is a step-by-step manual through each formula, including some omitted here. Websites such as www.solving-cryptics.com will also lend you nerve; solvers of Friday's DA can consult www.datrippers.com for a boost.*

Stop & Stare, 2019 by Dylan Mooney

11

WHAT IMPACT HAS SLAVERY HAD IN AUSTRALIA?

The enslavement of Indigenous and South Sea Islander people is a painful part of our nation's history. What forms did this slavery take? And what are its legacies today?

Ella Archibald-Binge

Waskam Emelda Davis was sitting in her favourite orange armchair in her loungeroom on a cool winter's day when her phone rang. 'Did you just hear this?' came her friend's voice down the line. Prime Minister Scott Morrison had just been on live radio, her friend informed her, claiming there was no history of slavery in Australia. 'I was enraged,' says Davis. The fifty-eight-year-old has spent her life advocating for the rights of Australian South Sea Islander people – the descendants of men, women and children known as 'sugar slaves' who were taken from the Pacific Islands and forced into hard labour in Australia. She chairs the Australian South Sea Islanders Port Jackson organisation in Sydney. 'Slavery is slavery. You can't dress it up or dress it down,' Davis says. 'The kidnapping, the coercing, the stealing and the serious abuses that happened to our people … this is something that's handed down through generations.

'It's very emotional and it's very challenging to find the balance in trying to deal with a lot of these atrocities that have occurred, and especially when you hear the highest order of your government speaking out and dismissing it.'

The Prime Minister later apologised and clarified his comments. But his words prompted a fresh examination of Australia's colonial history, at the height of a reinvigorated global Black Lives Matter movement. So how did slavery operate in Australia? How long did the practices continue? And how has it made a lasting impact on the nation?

What forms of slavery were in Australia?

Article 1 of the United Nations Slavery Convention defines slavery as 'the status or condition of a person over whom any or all of the powers attaching to the right of ownership are exercised'.

Around the time of colonisation in Australia – the First Fleet arrived in 1788 – an anti-slavery movement was growing in Britain. The British Parliament abolished the Atlantic slave trade in 1807 and passed the Slavery Abolition Act in 1833. As such, there was to be no slave trade in Australia. However, numerous historians, legal experts and government officials have found that the controls imposed on First Nations and Pacific Islander peoples essentially amounted to slavery.

'It is true that Australia was not a "slave state" in the manner of the American South,' writes Stephen Gray in the *Australian Indigenous Law Review*. 'Nevertheless, employers exercised a high degree of control over "their" Aboriginal workers, who were, in some cases, bought and sold as chattels ... Employers exercised a form of "legal coercion" over their workers in a manner consistent with the legal interpretation of slavery.'

What was blackbirding?

Davis says her grandfather was twelve when he went for a swim at the beach near his home on the island of Tanauta (formerly Tanna) in Vanuatu and never returned. He was kidnapped in the late 1800s, she says, and taken to Bundaberg, in North Queensland, where he was put to work on cane fields.

As many as 60,000 people, mostly men, from eighty Melanesian islands were brought by boat to work in Australia's agriculture, maritime and sugar industries. Some went voluntarily but many were coerced or kidnapped. Their wages were less than a third of other workers'. The practice, known as blackbirding, was sanctioned by various Queensland laws from the mid-1860s to 1904. Several members of parliament grew wealthy through this system.

Those who chose to leave the islands signed three-year indenture agreements, explains University of Queensland historian Professor Clive Moore, but few knew what awaited them in Australia. He says the indenture system has often been called 'a new form of slavery'. 'Just think, you're a capitalist in the 1830s and 1840s and they've just abolished slavery and you want cheap labour, so you scratch your head and you say, "Well, how can I get cheap labour?"' Moore explains. '[Islanders] were legally indentured, but then you've got to ask, did they understand the indenture system? Often no, they wouldn't have had a clue what it really was ... therefore you might say the contract's invalid.'

Moore estimates around 15,000 South Sea Islander people, around a third of the workforce, died from common diseases during their first year in Australia due to low immunity levels. 'The mortality figures are horrific,' he says. 'The government must have known, and yet it did absolutely nothing to try to stop it.'

When the White Australia policy was enacted in 1901, the government ordered the mass deportation of all South Sea Islander people, sparking outrage among those who had built lives on the mainland and wished to stay. Ultimately, around 5000 workers were forcibly deported. In a cruel twist of fate, their deportations were funded by the wages of deceased South Sea Islanders, whose estates were controlled by the government. Those who remained were subject to racial discrimination and embarked on a long journey to carve out their own place in Australian society.

How did 'protection' usher in a new form of slavery?

It could be argued that what happened to South Sea Islander workers was a precursor to the systematic wage controls imposed on Aboriginal and Torres Strait Islander groups from around the 1890s, notably in the pearling and cattle industries.

In the late nineteenth century, every mainland state and the Northern Territory enacted laws, known as the Protection Acts, to control the lives of Indigenous people. Prior to this, Aboriginal and Torres Strait Islander workers were routinely exploited.

Historian Dr Ros Kidd says there is evidence that women were used as sex slaves, children were kidnapped and Aboriginal stockmen were encouraged to form opium addictions to make them reliant on their employers, who supplied the drug. Kidd says the Protection Acts were largely introduced to ensure industries remained profitable rather than to protect the welfare of Indigenous people. 'Part of the problem, as the authorities saw it, was the rise of interracial children and the fact that we, as the whites, needed to assert some authority and regulation over all of this,' she says. 'It wasn't so much ... for the benefit of Aboriginal people necessarily, it was more to protect the whiteness of white Australia and to regulate these illegal trades in order to preserve the cheap workforce.'

Under the Protection Acts, most Aboriginal people were removed from their homelands and forced to live on missions or reserves run by the church or government, respectively. Some South Sea Islander people were subjected to the same controls. Aboriginal people were forbidden from speaking their native language or practising their culture, and children were separated from their families and placed in dormitories.

Employment laws varied from state to state but, for the most part, the wages of Aboriginal people were diverted to government-managed trust funds, while local protectors managed the residue as legal trustees. Official documents reveal protectors habitually defrauded Aboriginal workers during much of the twentieth century.

For most Queensland workers, the minimum monthly wage was set at five shillings (around $24), less than one-eighth of the non-Indigenous wage. Sometimes, the worker would receive a small portion of that amount as pocket money but, in many cases, they received nothing. Workers could, in theory, withdraw from their trust account for necessities but only with permission from the local protector. Requests were often refused, or workers were falsely told they had no money.

Roy Savo is a former stockman who spent a decade working on Queensland cattle stations from the age of thirteen. He says he didn't see physical money until he was almost twenty. 'When we wanted to go to the shop, they'd just write us a note and say, "Take that to the shop,"' he says. 'That's how we got through life.'

The eighty-year-old says the bosses would not call the Aboriginal workers by their names, referring to them only as 'boy'. 'They made you feel so low. When I think back, we were just no one, nothing. We had no chance against the white people, they just ruled our lives. We were one step from being an animal. In some places you were told to sit out and eat with the animals anyway, out in the wood heap.'

When he was about nineteen, Savo ran away from his 'job'. Dodging authorities, he continued to work at various cattle stations and railways across Far North Queensland and the Torres Strait, before meeting his wife and starting a family in Silkwood, south of Cairns.

In Western Australia, most employers weren't legally required to pay Aboriginal workers at all until the 1940s, as long as they provided rations, clothing and blankets. Many workers in the Northern Territory died from starvation in the 1920s and '30s due to poor rations, records show. One anthropologist reported that on one station, only ten children survived from fifty-one births during a five-year period. The government declined to intervene. The chief protector in the Northern Territory said in 1927 that Aboriginal pastoral workers were 'kept in a servitude that is nothing short of slavery'. Those who absconded from a work contract could be whipped, jailed or arrested and brought back in chains.

'The chief protector in the Northern Territory said in 1927 that Aboriginal pastoral workers were "kept in a servitude that is nothing short of slavery".'

Aboriginal children were routinely indentured into service, with boys sent to farms and pastoral stations and girls to domestic service for non-Indigenous families. Their wages were supposed to be administered similarly to the adults' but there was little to no regulation to ensure employers complied with the law.

Protectors themselves described Queensland's Aboriginal wage system as a 'farce' in the 1940s, says Kidd, with workers 'entirely at the mercy of employers who simply doctored the books'. She notes the broad lack of oversight prompted one protector in the Northern Territory to remark, 'I think it is about time that slavery is put a stop to among the natives of Australia.'

When did this kind of slavery end?

The Protection Acts were gradually amended and replaced throughout the second half of the twentieth century but some controls endured until at least 1972 – the year Gough Whitlam was elected prime minister.

And yet when the laws were repealed, the money held in trust was never returned to Aboriginal workers. The unpaid funds have become known as the stolen wages. In Queensland, Aboriginal trust funds were used to cover government revenue shortfalls. Millions were spent on regional hospitals. Hundreds of thousands of dollars were used to facilitate the forcible removal of Aboriginal families from their traditional land. In today's money, Kidd conservatively estimates the missing or misappropriated funds to total half a billion dollars in Queensland alone. 'The government made a lot of money exploiting the savings accounts for its own profit,' she says. 'This is while people were starving and dying in need of these payments.'

For decades, Aboriginal and Torres Strait Islander people have been fighting to get that money back. In Queensland, thousands joined a class action to sue the government. In 2019, the state government agreed to a landmark $190 million settlement. It was the largest settlement for Indigenous people outside native title and the fifth-largest class action settlement in Australian history. But it was less than half what the workers were owed and by the time the settlement was reached more than half of the claimants had died. Similar class actions are being investigated in New South Wales, Western Australia and the Northern Territory. Australian South Sea Islanders are also fighting for reparations for an estimated $38 million in misspent wages of deceased workers.

A year after Queensland's class action was settled, Savo still doesn't know when, or how much, he will be paid for a decade's hard labour. He fears it will be much less than he had hoped. 'I wanted to buy a home,' he says. 'But looking at what I'm going to get now, I'm thinking it would be better putting it into some trust or something for my funeral. I come in with nothing, go out with nothing, I suppose.'

What is the legacy of slavery in Australia?

As fate would have it, Davis's housing unit in the inner-Sydney suburb of Pyrmont looks out to the sugar refinery where the raw sugar harvested by South Sea Islanders was once processed. It's widely acknowledged that much of Australia's wealth across the sugar, pastoral and maritime industries was built on the backs of Indigenous and South Sea Islander labour. 'The contribution of the sixty-odd thousand [South Sea Islanders], coupled with our First Nations families, is quite significant in establishing what we call today the lucky country,' Davis says. 'Our legacy is what people are thriving off today.'

At the Redcliffe Hospital, north of Brisbane, there is a plaque to acknowledge that it was built, in part, with a $1.7 million loan from Aboriginal trust funds in the 1960s. Similar plaques have been installed across Queensland, at the recommendation of a 2016 taskforce, to recognise the labour and financial contributions of Aboriginal and Torres Strait Islander people. Yet many within these

'Plaques have been installed to recognise the labour and financial contributions of Aboriginal and Torres Strait Islander people.'

communities still live in poverty. Disparities in health, education and employment between Indigenous and non-Indigenous people are well documented.

Kidd says this disadvantage is 'inextricably linked' with historical practices. She says Aboriginal and Torres Strait Islander people were excluded from the capitalist society. 'They trapped people in what I would call engineered disadvantage – because it didn't happen by coincidence, it didn't happen through an unfortunate set of circumstances. All of these conditions and this poverty was specific government policy and practice.'

Australian South Sea Islanders, too, have inherited generations of trauma and disadvantage. The community was officially recognised as a distinct cultural group in 1994, but without targeted policies Davis says they often 'fall through the cracks', missing out on support programs tailored for Indigenous Australians. 'We're at a point where it's completely desperate. There's no hope in looking to our government for anything. It's just constant hoop-jumping and lining up against everybody else in the queues for rations,' she says.

The legacy of trauma is also felt in the Pacific Islands. On a beach in Vanuatu, there's a spot called Howling Rock, where mothers would mourn their husbands and children who disappeared. There are songs, passed through the generations, warning not to go to certain beaches for risk of being taken.

But new generations in Australia have inherited something else from their ancestors, too: strength. Queensland artist Dylan Mooney, twenty-four, has Aboriginal, Torres Strait Islander and South Sea Islander heritage. His paternal great-great-grandparents were blackbirded from Vanuatu. His great-great-grandfather worked on sugar plantations in northern New South Wales while his great-great-grandmother was sold as a house servant in Sydney. Mooney says knowing what his ancestors went through has only strengthened his sense of identity and pride. 'I carry that with me every day – that strength, that resilience, that story of survival.'

'I carry that with me every day – that strength, that resilience, that story of survival.'

12

WHAT CAN DREAMS TELL US ABOUT SOCIETY?

Many of us have vivid dreams but how are they shaped by world events? Do dreams offer glimpses of the zeitgeist? Can they even help us shape our future?

Felicity Lewis

It was January in the northern Italian city of Turin and Franca Fubini, a psychotherapist and organisational consultant, was unsettled. She had been engaged in a long-running project where people share their dreams – a practice called social dreaming. But this group had spoken of nightmares: an asteroid hurtling towards Earth; a truck falling from the sky; people jumping from the balconies of a skyscraper ...

'In January we didn't know yet,' says Fubini of the coronavirus pandemic. 'It was moving in the Far East, it would not touch us. But the dreams were all talking of losing control, of unexpected disaster of major magnitude.' By February, Italy was in a state of emergency, and the social dreaming group was a different mix of people but 'that thread, which started to be woven [in January], was there,' says Fubini. In the following months, with the country in lockdown, other dream themes emerged: genetically modified insects, alien attacks, disconnected body parts, locked-up eyes and legs, dreamers unable to recognise themselves in mirrors – white-haired or unkempt, all dressed up but in ill-fitting clothes. 'They take a life of their own,' says Fubini of the dreams, 'and we are no longer in control, [in the same way that] we are not during the pandemic.'

Since ancient times, cultures have tuned into dreams as messages from the gods, nature or their souls; since last century, dreams have been viewed as a coded language of the psyche; and today, some doctors, scientists and citizens also collect people's dreams as data on, among other things, how we share responses to significant events and widespread crises.

'Since ancient times, cultures have tuned into dreams as messages from the gods, nature or their souls.'

Trump dreams are a genre. Brexit dreams have been documented. Amid pandemic lockdowns, COVID dreams became virtual-watercooler fodder; and you only had to look on Twitter to see a sample of postcards from the land of nod (#CovidDreams).

What does it all mean? How is dreaming a social activity? What glimpses of subterranean zeitgeists might a group's dreams offer? And what would be the use in knowing?

What is social dreaming?

It's a Sunday evening in Australia and the faces of sixty-five (mostly) strangers from Europe, South Africa, the United States and Asia form an onscreen mosaic as they join an online video meeting. After a brief introduction, cameras are switched off and only voices remain. There is a sea of black squares. 'The matrix is now open,' says a woman's voice. 'And what will be the first dream?'

In the dystopian science-fiction film *The Matrix*, humans unwittingly exist in a simulated reality. In this matrix, humans are well aware they may be in the dark about the desires and impulses that move cultures and the systems in which they operate – but, through creating a network of associations about one another's recent dreams, they can start to see a bigger picture. One social dreaming expert likens this network to mycelium, the delicate filaments that underpin fungi and transmit nutrients and information across vast forests. Another adds that 'we're talking about deep, subterranean, murky, in-the-mud sort of stuff'.

So what will be revealed by these dreams dreamt all over the world overnight? Over the hour-long matrix, the Roosevelts appear twice (New Deal or new normal?); a dreamer is annoyed to discover she is married to pop singer Ed Sheeran (intimacy can be problematic during a lockdown); another dreamer is in the ocean trapped in a plastic bag full of water (a bit like a goldfish for sale, a bit like all of us during this pandemic, blinking out from our self-contained little worlds).

One of these goldfish is Mannie Sher, an organisational development and change consultant and executive coach with the Tavistock Institute of Human Relations. The institute has been at the cutting edge of research into group dynamics since World War II when it worked with the British Army on matters such as improving morale and developing better methods for recruiting officers. Central to its thinking is that a group, as well as an individual, has a life of its own.

'Social dreaming is like a megaphone from another world and we ought to listen to it,' says Sher. 'It's not miraculous, it's not mysterious. The unconscious is an unexplored continent and there are links and connections that float around, looking for dreamers.'

Sher, who trained as a social scientist and psychotherapist, has used social dreaming as 'a diagnostic tool' for years, including in boardrooms and at conferences to loosen minds – after all, the focus is on the dreams and not the dreamers. 'If the matrix is run skilfully, you'll find that it's not just the dreaming that gets freed up ... the organisation too somehow gets freed up to think new thoughts. And that's what we're after.' He and colleagues, including in the Social Dreaming International Network, watched for patterns emerging in dream matrices as the pandemic made 'social trauma' a 'global trait'.

At first blush, the many dreams and associations seem to be a jumble of signs and symbols. Tigers and Tiger Kings, for example, appear in matrices run by the Tavistock Institute from April to June 2020, along with an exploding Brooklyn Bridge and people evacuated from Manhattan Island; a lieutenant on the Western Front with 'Trump-like red hair that looks fake'; and then a house that looked beautiful on the outside but that had no 'bone structure' within – just a rear room wallpapered with the face of George Floyd, whose death at the hands of police sparked riots in the United States and protests around the world.

But over time, the dreams begin to kaleidoscope into a chronicle of the milieu in which they were dreamt. 'Dreams can mean

'

Social dreaming is like a megaphone from another world and we ought to listen to it.

'

many, many things,' says Sher, and in social dreaming, a group's free associations about the dreams are as important as the dreams themselves. 'What we're looking for is the drift. What direction is it going? What's emerging out of the associations – rather than saying "your dream means this or that."

'People don't come to social dreaming because they're having bad dreams or difficult lives,' he says. 'They're invited to join what you might call a social experiment – namely, what are our dreams able to tell us about the society we're in?'

So, what are our dreams able to tell us about the society we're in?

This was the question Scottish sociologist, organisational consultant and educator Gordon Lawrence wanted to investigate when he developed social dreaming as a tool of organisational dynamics in the early 1980s, influenced by the work of Jewish journalist Charlotte Beradt, whose book *The Third Reich of Dreams* made his 'skin tingle'. Beradt covertly collected 300 dreams from Berliners from 1933, when the Nazis came to power, until she fled Europe in 1939, and detailed some of them in her book. A factory owner, for example, dreams he is visited by propaganda minister Joseph Goebbels; as he lifts his arm in the Nazi salute, his back breaks. Another man sees only rectangles, triangles and octagons in his dreams because dreaming itself is 'forbidden'.

It was not personal issues that fuelled these dreams, Beradt contended, so much as 'conflicts into which these people had been driven by a public realm in which half-truths, vague notions and a combination of fact, rumour and conjecture had produced a general feeling of uncertainty and unrest'. The dreams, collected before war had broken out, offered the warning 'that totalitarian tendencies must be recognised before they become overt'. Beradt's book has quite possibly been referenced more in discussing COVID dreams than at any time since it was first published in the 1960s.

Both Fubini and Sher worked with Lawrence. Over the years, Sher and colleagues have collected dreams during a range of major events: from tent dwellers during the London Occupy movement ('murder, cutting up bodies, rotting bodies – awful stuff'); at public sessions in a library during the Brexit vote ('parents divorcing, chaos, the piling up of rubbish') and after the 2016 election of Donald Trump ('triumph of the win, not binding together, insulting a woman'). But while the pandemic has again focused attention on dreaming en masse, dreams can also shed light on smaller group dynamics – including in the workplace.

What happens when you take dreams to work?

Dame Ruth Silver had been the principal of Lewisham College, in London's south-east, for several years when she offered social dreaming sessions to staff at the start and end of each term. A trained psychologist (twice honoured for her services to further education), she also worked with Lawrence, and regards dreams as data that offer 'the opportunity, among other things, to construct an agenda for change'.

'The challenge for me, as the principal, was to say, "How do I keep on supporting the staff to be creative in raising students' success?"' says Silver. 'We had dreams of ... lost staff looking for students, students looking for staff, people not getting the right textbooks.

'There was a whole system of dreams that talked about, actually, we need to do more. There were also things going on in society – black kids getting beaten up, the Stephen Lawrence murder [in south-east London in 1993]. What we were doing was terrific curriculum learning but actually it didn't help them deal with the issues in their housing estates so colleagues encouraged and legitimised social justice work from students, not just to them.

'So it's how the dreams are made meaning of by the institution – and that wasn't for me alone to do, it was for all of us, saying,

"What do you think that's about?" and, "If it is about that, what could we try?" So, to authorise teachers to be free experimenters, not just experts.'

After the dream conversations, the college set up a sector first: a 'quality unit' with a data analyst, researcher and head of learning and development for all staff. Out of that came a confidential teacher's help desk that was 'off system' so staff could flag issues without fear of their appraisals being affected. 'They had a place to go that was for increasing and sharing their expertise because that helped the students,' says Silver. 'We prototyped a lot of new structures that are still around.'

Silver, who now runs a think tank and sits on the board of the Jamie Oliver Foundation, has advised prime ministers on further education but stopped short of conducting a dream matrix at Number 10. '[Tony] Blair had a curiosity about it but he didn't manage to do it,' she laughs.

What do we make of all this?

Back in mid-2020, as the early pandemic lockdowns were initially eased around the world, dreams of (second) waves and of nature emerged in local and international social dreaming matrices, says Susan Long, research director of the National Institute of Organisation Dynamics Australia. Whether in Italy, Israel, England or the United States, says Long (who also co-edited *Social Dreaming: Philosophy, Research, Theory and Practice*), group dreams were showing that people had not forgotten the plight of the natural environment even as the pandemic had eclipsed talk of it. But if our nocturnal visions can act as stealthy reminders of our abiding concerns, Long also contends they can be 'memoirs of the future' – not in a psychic way but in the sense that they help us to imagine what's next. 'In our daily lives we constantly anticipate what we will do in the future, whether in the next hour or the next year,' she says.

'Our dreams do this also but they do it from an unconscious level. Social dreaming brings together the unconscious anticipations of all the participants and allows thoughts that we individually would not dare to think in our waking lives because they seem weird, risky or dangerous – but are there in the back of our minds.

'The associations of others turn the oblique and dissociated ideas in the dreams into comprehensible narratives, linked to everyday experiences.'

Sher says talking together about dreaming enables new things to happen, even if, in organisations, these are mostly in the form of 'baby steps'. But it seems that making sense of our COVID dreams, or of any dreams for that matter, will take time; there's a slow-burn aspect to the epiphanies they offer. 'You go to a matrix, you hear these dreams, and you can't make sense of them,' says Sher. 'That's a state of mind that you have to accept, that sometimes you just don't know what's happening. Later on, you may find out, oh, we did know something – but we refused to acknowledge it.'

13

WHAT IS A THINK TANK?

There are more than 8000 think tanks
in the world, including 42 in Australia.
What do they do? How? And for whom?

Nick O'Malley

The most prestigious think tank in the world, the Brookings Institution, once annoyed then president Richard Nixon so much that he proposed firebombing its headquarters in Washington, DC. One of his aides, John W. Dean III, described how in recordings from the Oval Office Nixon could be heard, 'literally pounding on his desk, saying, "I want that break-in at the Brookings."' He figured that during the blaze his operatives might be able to sneak past the firefighters to steal files from its safe, Dean later told *The Washington Post*.

The firebombing never happened and Nixon later resigned in disgrace (over other scandals) but Brookings has thrived. It was named think tank of the year in 2016, 2017 and 2018 by the University of Pennsylvania's Think Tanks and Civil Societies Program, a kind of think tank think tank, which elevated Brookings to a Centre of Excellence after its triple top billing, giving other think tanks a chance to take the top spot.

Though think tanks are constantly cited and quoted in media, and often even in policy documents, confusion remains about what exactly it is that they do, why and how they do it, and for whom.

According to the Think Tanks and Civil Societies Program's 2019 report, there are 8248 think tanks in the world, including forty-two in Australia. The highest-ranked Australian outfit is the Lowy Institute, which comes in at number sixty-four in the world, followed by the Australian Institute of International Affairs, at seventy-one. So what do these think tanks do? Who are they? And what effect do they have?

What's the difference between a think tank and a lobby group?

A lobby group typically acts as a hired gun, prosecuting the interests of its members – which may be major commercial interests – while a think tank conducts and presents the research of its scholars and experts. In practice, the line becomes blurred, especially when think tanks undertake work for clients on commission. Some think

> *A think tank conducts and presents the research of its scholars and experts.*

tanks in Australia are viewed by critics as acting like lobby groups, pushing industry-friendly research or junk science in support of interest groups.

There are other distinctions. According to the University of Pennsylvania, think tanks are structured as permanent bodies rather than as ad hoc commissions or research panels; and they devote a substantial portion of their resources to commissioning and publishing research and policy analysis in the social science areas such as political science, economics, public administration and international affairs.

The term itself surfaced during World War II, according to *Britannica*, to describe a safe place where plans and strategies could be nutted out. It was in the 1960s, though, that 'think tank' hit its stride when used to refer to private, non-profit policy research organisations.

By 1971, *The Canberra Times* was reporting on a think tank set up by Don Dunstan's Labor government in South Australia, noting the term 'has tended to conjure up visions of a small army of long-haired, ideologically motivated, faceless backroom intellectuals … spawning brilliant theoretical ideas like mushrooms in a rainforest'. Yet, the report went on, the South Australian premier's think tank, consisting of an army of 'five hand-picked public servants, has just celebrated its first birthday and is in pretty good shape'.

How do think tanks work?

The Lowy Institute was founded in 2003 with a gift from shopping-centre mogul Frank Lowy and his family and instructions to academic Michael Fullilove, who wrote the original feasibility study, to help create an organisation that would 'deepen the debate in Australia about the world, and give Australia a greater voice abroad'.

The billionaire's philanthropic gesture vaulted the Lowy Institute to the front rank of Australian think tanks when it

Some progressive Australian think tanks

The Australia Institute: Though not party aligned, the most prominent progressive think tank was founded largely with donations from an offshoot of Rupert Murdoch's family, the Kantors, through two private organisations, the Poola Foundation and the Treepot Foundation, and prosecutes research on a broad range of public policy areas.

Per Capita: Per Capita was founded in Melbourne in 2007 as a centre left organisation with a focus on the causes and impacts of inequality.

Chifley Research Centre: Named after reformist post-war prime minister Ben Chifley, the centre is the official think tank of the Australian Labor Party, designed to help 'renew Australia's progressive values and to rebuild the progressive movement'.

Evatt Foundation: Founded in 1979 as a memorial to Dr Herbert (Doc) Evatt, the former Labor leader, attorney-general and High Court judge, the foundation seeks to uphold the 'highest ideals of the labour movement', promoting research, debate and discussion of social and economic issues.

launched. Today it functions as a model think tank. Its experts produce original research in fields run by program directors who report to research director Alex Oliver and Fullilove. Fullilove also serves as an executive director answering to a board made up of Lowy family members as well as business, political, academic and retired military heavyweights.

Think tank directors generally agree that their key role is to bridge the gap between other sources of information – such as media and academia – and policymakers.

Ben Oquist, director of the Australia Institute, says that even the best academic research can be slow to produce and difficult to digest, while journalists often produce timely information that is not deeply enough researched to inform policymaking. The work of a think tank takes up the middle ground.

Normally, that research is made freely available to anyone who wants to use it and it is often presented in talks and conferences hosted by the institutions. The Lowy Institute publishes its flagship papers commercially and some of its most significant research is crafted as digital interactives that compare aid spending and diplomatic influence in Asia and the Pacific. This information is used widely in diplomatic, political, military and media circles around the region and the world.

Who sets a think tank's agenda?

Most think tanks are transparent about their core values. Both the Labor and Liberal parties run affiliated think tanks to inform their policymaking, though these think tanks' influence surges and recedes over the years.

Because they are expensive to run, think tanks can have a tendency to amplify the voices of those individuals and organisations – public or private – that fund them.

According to Oquist, fundraising takes up a substantial amount of time that could better be spent on research and the task has become harder since the global financial crisis. As a result, large donations, either corporate or philanthropic, are crucial.

The right-leaning Institute of Public Affairs (IPA) has been accused of championing policies to reduce the wages bills, taxes and regulations on some of its biggest donors, including tobacco companies and Gina Rinehart, the chairman of Hancock Prospecting. Liberal Party politician Tim Wilson, a former policy director at the IPA, says the suggestion that corporate donors shape the IPA's policy outlook is unfounded as its public positions remain in line with its values. 'Look at the consistency of our work, there is no inconsistency,' he says.

In 2016, *The New York Times* published an investigation critical of leading US think tanks, which it said had allowed their research and even their internal appointments to be influenced by donations from foreign governments and corporations. Democrat Elizabeth Warren said at the time, 'This is about giant corporations who figured out that by spending, hey, a few tens of millions of dollars, if they can influence outcomes here in Washington, they can make billions of dollars.'

Martin Indyk, the Australian-born diplomat and academic who was then serving as Brookings' executive vice-president (and who is now on the Lowy Institute's board) said at the time, 'We do not compromise our integrity. We maintain our core values of quality, independence, as well as impact.'

Asked why the Centre for Independent Studies does not publish details about its funding, its executive director, Tom Switzer, says public debate has become so toxic that to do so would be to invite a needless barrage of criticism upon the organisation's supporters.

Fullilove says while the Lowy Institute's outlook is determinedly international, the views of its scholars are their own and they often disagree with each other. 'There are no house positions,' says Fullilove. 'We are host to a range of opinions but the advocate of none.' He says what influence Lowy has it retains

Some conservative Australian think tanks

Institute of Public Affairs: Founded by businessmen during World War II to champion neoliberal ideas such as deregulation, free speech and tax cuts.

Centre for Independent Studies: Created in 1976 by a schoolteacher influenced by the libertarian ideas of Milton Friedman and Friedrich Hayek and classical liberal philosophers such as Adam Smith, David Hume and John Locke.

Menzies Research Centre: Named after the Liberal Party's founder and Australia's longest-serving prime minister, Sir Robert Menzies, the centre was founded in 1994 with the support of the Liberal Party, funded by corporate and philanthropic sponsors. It seeks to promote 'individual liberty, free speech, competitive enterprise, limited government and democracy' through its research, publications and conferences.

through the quality of its research and by positioning itself as the chosen venue for powerful people to introduce big ideas. In 2019 Scott Morrison became the third sitting prime minister to deliver the Lowy Institute's annual address.

How much influence do they have?

In his book *Masters of the Universe: Hayek, Friedman, and the Birth of Neoliberal Politics*, Daniel Stedman Jones traces the ascendancy of neoliberal politics in the West after World War II. He argues that politicians in the United States and Britain came to accept the primacy of free markets, deregulation and limited government not by chance, but due to the work of a network of advocates supported and informed by think tanks founded for the purpose, particularly the Atlas Foundation and the Mont Pelerin Society. He quotes correspondence between two of the intellectual fathers of the movement, Friedrich Hayek and Antony Fisher, in which Fisher writes, 'You mentioned "luck"! … No doubt, luck is important … Was there not an intention on both our parts and consequent action? [to start a think tank] How much is luck?'

In Australia, Switzer says the liberal reforms prosecuted by the Hawke, Keating and Howard governments were championed by the work of the Centre for Independent Studies.

In *Political Troglodytes and Economic Lunatics*, author Dominic Kelly argues far-right ideologues in Australia used think tanks to lend credibility to dubious research to shift public debate and government policy. His book, its title a quote from Bob Hawke himself, argues that a small handful of men led by conservative business leader Ray Evans was able to shift Australian political thinking on industrial relations, constitutional change, Indigenous affairs and climate change to the hard right through the creation of a clutch of think tanks, some funded by the mining sector – namely, the H. R. Nicholls Society, the Samuel Griffith Society, the Bennelong Society and the Lavoisier Group.

The IPA is known for the influential roles its members have secured outside the organisation in support of its mission. Tim Wilson advocated for free-speech reforms – which critics fear may serve to protect racial vilification – in line with IPA positions as the Australian Human Rights Commissioner from 2014 to 2016, before he was elected to parliament. Other IPA current or recent members or staff who serve or have served in parliament include James Paterson, David Leyonhjelm and Bob Day. Its director, John Roskam, has twice sought Liberal Party preselection.

Fullilove notes that the reforms and changes advocated by think tanks need not be ideologically driven or partisan. In 2009 and 2011, the Lowy Institute published research showing that the reach of Australia's diplomatic network was falling behind that of comparable OECD and G20 nations. When Julie Bishop became foreign minister in 2013 she ordered a review of Australia's diplomatic footprint and two years later announced that five new overseas missions would be opened – the largest expansion of our diplomatic network in forty years. She said that the institute's research had been 'ringing in her ears' when she ordered the review. 'Since Bishop's announcement,' says Fullilove, 'ten posts have opened and a further five have been promised in the Pacific.'

Wilson says that the IPA has done much to support sometimes controversial free-speech laws and extend freedom of religion protections.

When are think tanks most effective?

Oquist says think tanks are at their best when they dramatically shift stale policy thinking. He says the political consensus that Australia needs a federal anti-corruption commission was driven in part by Australia Institute research and advocacy, as was the acceptance that superannuation tax concessions needed to be reined in. He says the Australia Institute was able to shift the

Some specialist or centrist Australian think tanks

Australian Institute of International Affairs: This think tank was formed in the 1920s in the wake of the Paris Peace Conference in order to foster public debate on foreign policy.

Lowy Institute: The dominant foreign affairs think tank in Australia, founded by shopping-centre billionaire Frank Lowy in 2003.

Australian Strategic Policy Institute: ASPI was created in 2001 by then prime minister John Howard to provide policymakers with research and analysis on strategic and defence issues.

Institute for Economics and Peace: A global think tank headquartered in Sydney and founded by Australian tech billionaire Stephen Killelea in 2007, its research focuses on the economic cost of violence.

Grattan Institute: The institute focuses on policy it views as contributing to liberal democracy in a globalised economy, having been formed in 2008 with contributions from the federal and Victorian governments and BHP.

needle on these issues by presenting compelling evidence of the benefits of change consistently over a prolonged period.

Trent Hagland, an adjunct professor at the University of Sydney who is undertaking doctoral studies on the role and impact of think tanks, agrees, saying that think tanks have the luxury of long-term thinking that political parties no longer enjoy. In think tanks, he says, unpopular ideas can be kept alive over decades rather than election cycles. 'Look at the debate over nuclear weapons,' he says, referring to the suggestion by ANU professor Hugh White in 2019 that Australia might need to consider their development in the possible absence of US power in the Pacific. 'No one was talking about nuclear weapons before he wrote about them in his book. Now ASPI [the Australian Strategic Policy Institute] is discussing it.

'It would be politically toxic for any party to go to an election today proposing to develop nuclear weapons. But over time, if the public debate is held for years, the public becomes desensitised to it.' Or, as Oquist puts it, think tanks are most successful when they 'make the radical seem reasonable'.

'

Think tanks are at their best when they dramatically shift stale policy thinking.

,

14

WHAT DO WINE TASTING NOTES ACTUALLY MEAN?

Did people wax lyrical about booze
in Tutankhamun's day? How can a
shiraz taste like venison? Is 'minerality'
good or bad – and what is it?

Max Allen

'**S**weaty saddle.' 'Hints of ambergris.' 'Oodles of pippy hedgerow fruits.' The way wine people waffle on about what they're tasting can seem fanciful at best – and downright off-putting to anyone who's not obsessed by the subject.

Every specialised area of life, from sport to science, has its own peculiar lexicon that can seem baffling to anyone not intimately involved in that field. But seemingly made-up and often ludicrous tasting descriptors – from 'heady nose of exotic spices' to 'firm, sinewy palate' – can make wine talk particularly intimidating. 'It's just fermented grape juice, for God's sake! Why do you wine geeks need to wrap it up in all these off-putting layers of flowery language?'

The answer is, it's worth making an effort to understand the thinking behind wine words, to learn some of the jargon – even to embrace the odd silly tasting note – because it can truly enhance your enjoyment of this most fascinating subject.

So what are the rules of wine talk? How much is scientific and how much is poetry? And when should you describe your wine as 'funky' – or 'smashable'?

Where did 'wine talk' come from?

People have been talking and writing about wine for as long as they've been making it. Language is particularly important in the wine world because it's pretty much the only way of sharing our impressions of taste and flavour with another person (interpretive dance is another option, of course, but is not commonly practised). When we listen to music or look at a painting we don't need to verbalise our shared experience because we can all hear it or see it out there in the world. But to let someone else know what you think of the wine you're drinking – that's in your nostrils and on your tongue – and to compare your impressions with theirs, you have to talk about it.

Wine talk in the ancient world was mostly limited to distinguishing between the merits of one wine over another. Some of the amphorae of wine buried with Tutankhamun over 3000 years ago are inscribed with the simple phrase 'very good quality'. No indication what it actually tasted like.

In the first century, Pliny the Elder and others wrote about Roman wine in detail. While Pliny's writing is big on technical aspects of winegrowing and is very concerned with the reputation of wines from specific regions, it's short on tasting notes: he described one very old wine as having 'the consistency of honey with a rough flavour'. That's it.

By the nineteenth century, wine was being written about in slightly more evocative but still vague terms, usually by well-educated and well-travelled gentlemen with enough time on their hands to study wine, and money to spend on the best bottles. Wines were described as 'harmonious' and 'health-giving', 'ferruginous' and 'vigorous', all rather grand and Victorian.

This gentlemanly tradition continued into the twentieth century with writers such as the Australian doctor W. S. Benwell who, in the early 1960s, described the colour of a rosé as 'brickish autumn russet, like the faded sail of a Venetian fishing-boat' – presupposing his equally gentlemanly readers would be thoroughly familiar with the references.

The burgeoning middle-class interest in wine in the 1970s and '80s gave rise to a new breed of wine writer: the popular critic. To attract readers, the language became less poetic, more prosaic – and yet more effusive. Influential US critic Robert Parker epitomised this new way of talking about wine, with meandering descriptions of wines that were 'dark, dense and rich, with powerful flavours of cinnamon, leather and blackcurrants, big, tough and fat with exceptional concentration' – and so on.

Are there rules for describing wine today?

In the mid-1980s, in an effort to bring some scientific rigour to the field, Dr Ann Noble at the University of California, Davis, developed the wine aroma wheel. This useful tool grouped wine flavours into general categories (such as 'fruity', 'woody', 'earthy') in an attempt to help tasters take a more analytical approach to wine appreciation.

There are things to be said for both the analytical and evocative approaches to talking about wine. In each case, the trick is to balance effective communication of the qualities of the wine you're tasting with meaningful description of the experience of tasting it.

The analytical approach – finding a word to describe each aspect of the wine-tasting process in order, from looking at the appearance of the wine in the glass to thinking about how long the aftertaste stays with you – is a helpful way to create a memory of what you're tasting. So, to describe a shiraz, say, as having 'medium-full colour, typically varietal aromatic nose, some high-toast oak, moderate concentration of fruit, savoury complexity, noticeable tannins and good length on the palate' is correct and, to a certain extent, objective. But it's a bit dull, isn't it? Much better, I think, to say 'bold purple in the glass, bursting with the perfume of pepper and toasty vanilla, grippy and gamey on the tongue, like well-hung venison and freshly dug truffle, deliciously satisfying'.

But some people might say, at this point, a wine taster is just making stuff up. How can something produced from grapes smell like pepper or vanilla – not to mention well-hung venison and truffle? I'm not making it up, honest. Well, not the pepper bit. Or the toasty vanilla. (We'll come back to the dead deer and fungi in a minute.)

Many grape varieties – and, therefore, the wines produced from them – contain flavour compounds that are found in other foods and plants and elsewhere in nature. The shiraz grape variety, for example, contains an aromatic compound called rotundone, which is also found in peppercorns. So, when I describe a young shiraz as tasting 'peppery', I don't mean it has aromas that remind me of pepper, I mean it has aromas that are the same as pepper. Similarly, describing a glass of riesling as 'smelling like spring blossom' isn't just waffle. Riesling grapes contain aromatic chemical compounds called monoterpenes – geraniol, nerol, linalool – which are also present in the scent of flowers.

> 'How can something produced from grapes smell like pepper or vanilla – not to mention well-hung venison and truffle?'

And the toasty vanilla comes from the barrels that the wine was matured in: barrels are made by bending oak staves around open flames, which chars the wood, creating heaps of complex aromatic compounds – vanillin from the wood itself, smoky flavours from the charring process – that are imparted to the wine as it sits inside the barrel.

Okay, I get all that. But what about the 'well-hung venison'?

Ah, yes, well this is where we wine people do stray into the realm of figurative language – metaphor, analogy, and even, dare I say, poetry. The English language doesn't have a lot of words to directly describe the sensation of having an aromatic alcoholic liquid in our mouths, or words that help us distinguish one aromatic alcoholic liquid from another. So, we are forced to use comparisons. The wine doesn't taste precisely of venison and truffles but it does elicit feelings in me when I drink that are similar to the feelings I get when I eat those foods (which would, by the way, taste great washed down with the shiraz).

Take my description, too, of the tannins in the shiraz. Tannins are the astringent-tasting phenolic compounds found in grapes. They don't literally grip your tongue as you drink the wine – but using the word 'grippy' is a good way of conveying the drying sensation of the astringency in the liquid.

When we describe how the wine makes us feel when we drink it, we also resort to emotional qualifications such as satisfying or disappointing or bold, and tend to attach them to the wine rather than ourselves, making it appear to the casual reader that the wine possesses these attributes, not the taster. That's why it's so easy to make fun of the figurative, emotive aspect of wine talk – as many people have. The enduring example of this comes from Evelyn Waugh's 1945 novel *Brideshead Revisited*. As Sebastian and Charles drink their way through the cellars, the language becomes increasingly farcical: 'It is a little, shy wine, like a gazelle ... Like a leprechaun ... Dappled, in a tapestry meadow ... And this is a necklace of pearls on a white neck ... Like a swan ... Like a unicorn.'

One of the reasons why evocative wine talk is so easily lampooned – even when it's sincere – is that it's specific to the person speaking and to their cultural assumptions, and those specifics may mean nothing to the listener or reader. Back to the venison and truffle again: to me, with my Anglo-Australian upbringing, and my middle-aged love of game and European-influenced culinary traditions, these words perfectly convey the pleasure I get from the deeply savoury, very earthy characters I taste in the wine (shiraz, especially older shiraz, actually can have a marked fungal, sanguine quality, like tasting blood on the tongue). But modern wine communicators are becoming more conscious of how this may be meaningless to someone else from a different cultural background. Simon Tam, educator and former head of wine at Christie's Hong Kong, argues that Western descriptors such as blackberry and forest floor are 'so uncommon [in Asia] as to be meaningless'. Better, he says, to use descriptors such as Chinese dried plums or aged golden hair tea, known for its earthy scents.

Wine talk tends to reflect winemaking trends; how wines are made now are quite different to how they were made a generation ago. Take Australian chardonnay. In the 1980s and '90s, most examples of this grape were golden-coloured and rich-tasting because the grapes were picked ripe, and the wine was aged in new oak barrels (toasty vanilla, remember?). They were described positively using words such as tropical and peachy and buttery. But twenty years later, the language has changed: citrus and lean and mineral are instead being used as desirable descriptors because chardonnay is being made differently – grapes are picked earlier, less new oak – and is lighter in colour and body.

Wines with 'minerality' are all the rage, in fact, and you come across this word a lot. It's controversial, though: soil scientists grumpily point out that there is no direct relationship between the minerals in the ground and the flavour of wine grown in that ground. The vine's roots do not take up granite and deposit it as trace elements in the grape, so wine cannot feasibly taste of granite – despite the fact that wines grown in soils derived from those rocks do indeed often taste distinctly minerally, like sucking on river pebbles. Some canny researcher will, no doubt, solve this mystery one day.

'Funky' has become particularly popular in recent years with the advent of natural wines – wines made with as little as possible added or taken away, wild fermented, unfiltered, no preservatives. It's a catch-all word for aromas and tastes that aren't pristine and fruity: a hint of barnyard, perhaps, some of Pliny's 'roughness'. It's a handy word to have up your sleeve when your friend/ sommelier pours a glass of murky, still-fermenting, orange-coloured liquid and raves about it – but it makes you gag. A touch of funk can be a lovely thing, bringing complexity and deliciousness to the wine. But if the funk becomes the dominant flavour then it can be a rather unlovely thing. 'Mmm,' you can say through a clenched smile, not wanting to offend. 'Funky.'

'**'Funky' has become particularly popular in recent years with the advent of natural wines.**'

Another wine word that's emerged from the natural wine scene is 'smashable'. It's not so much a tasting note as a way of describing how the wine is drunk – or 'smashed', thirstily, with great pleasure (the French term for such wines is *vins de soif* – thirst-quenching wines). Smashable wines are made from grapes that are picked a little earlier, lower in alcohol, higher in acidity, often fermented with whole bunches to increase the juicy, sappy flavours, bottled without preservatives, intended to be drunk immediately. So: 'Here, try this, it's really smashable booze.'

And texture – the way a wine feels on your tongue – is big in wine-tasting circles these days, especially now so many producers are making white wines more like red wines, fermenting and macerating the grape skins with the juice, looking for more richness and grippiness in the mouth. Talking about texture indicates you're more than just a newbie wine taster – but have fun with it. It may well be correct to describe a riesling, for example, as 'very dry, with a high level of acidity' but isn't 'zesty and refreshing, like crunching into a tart, green Granny Smith apple' just a bit more evocative – enticing, even?

15

HOW DOES SCOTT PENDLEBURY STOP TIME?

This AFL champion seems to
shift games into slow motion,
outfoxing opponents and wowing
spectators with moves that baffle.
How does he do it? Is he the only one?

Jake Niall

Roger Federer has always had that extra fraction of a second. In cricket, the majestic Mark Waugh seemed utterly unhurried when a red missile was hurled at him at 150 kilometres per hour. And, in the hectic chaos of Australian football – a game in which thirty-six players run in different directions and crash into one another – there is one man who appears to have considerably more time than any of his 800 AFL peers. Scott Pendlebury, the captain of Collingwood, doesn't merely have more time than other footballers. On the field, when he gets the ball, he creates an impression that the game itself has slowed – sometimes, even stopped. Pendlebury has been likened to the character of Neo played by Keanu Reeves in *The Matrix*, who can swerve around oncoming bullets as if in slow motion while others are stuck, and struck, in normal speed.

Pendlebury, an understated guy with obsessive tendencies (he used to weigh his food), isn't a mysterious, semi-reclusive personality in the mould of, say, Gary Ablett Senior or Dustin Martin; nor is he an irreverent larrikin such as his old teammate Dane Swan. But if Pendlebury isn't mysterious, there is a mystery at the heart of his game – namely, what is it that he does on the field to create the impression that this most frenetic of sports has slowed down, or hit the pause button, for him?

> '*Pendlebury has been likened to the character of Neo played by Keanu Reeves in* The Matrix, *who can swerve around oncoming bullets as if in slow motion while others are stuck, and struck, in normal speed.*'

Just as cameras from various angles capture Reeves in *The Matrix* in scenes of thrilling variable-speed action, so is the on-field phenomenon of Pendlebury best understood from several vantages:

his own perspective; forensic analysis by boffins; the perception of a teammate; and what we, the madding crowd, see when we watch him waft around the field, tacklers clutching at him vainly or avoiding rushing at him for fear of what he might do.

So what is it about Pendlebury that makes time stop for him? What does this phenomenon tell us about how modern footy is played? Do sportspeople in other codes share this gift? And what does the champion say himself?

What does Pendlebury perceive on the field?

The Collingwood captain doesn't feel like he's slowing the game when he has the footy. 'It's normal for me. It's how I play,' he says. 'It's not a conscious thing that I've added to my game. I don't feel like I'm doing it. I'm sort of just trying to find the right decision.' Yet Pendlebury is aware that he isn't hurried. 'I don't feel like I ever have to rush. But I put that down to doing a lot of work at training.'

Many great sportspeople can't explain their artistry. 'You can't explain what it's like to score a goal to someone who's never done it,' said the late George Best, the notorious Northern Irish soccer genius. While Pendlebury can't fully describe the 'time-warp effect', he offers this explanation of what he tries to do with the footy: 'More often than not, I'm trying to release someone into time and space to make a really good decision. There's no point me selling candy [see below] and baulking people and giving it to somebody who's hot.' In short, he describes his intentions thus: 'Try and make guys around me better.'

Surprisingly, Pendlebury says he doesn't try major time-and-space creative manoeuvres early in games either. Like a batsman, he waits until he's confident and has seen enough balls to play more enterprising shots. 'Early in the games, I will do the first things that come to mind … usually by the third or fourth quarter, I feel like I've built a fair bit of confidence. Then I might take that extra second or I might see something and say, "If I fake that way, he might bite on that and then I can open up that kick behind him," which is a bit more damaging. I never go out there at the start and try and just go whack and do something pretty special or something cool.'

How do experts explain the time-warp effect?

The AFL's Damian Farrow, manager of umpiring innovation and coaching, has an academic background in studying decision-making by athletes. He describes Pendlebury as 'a master of deception' with the ball in his hands. 'He's expert at selling false information,' says Farrow. 'When he knows he's got them hooked, that's when he'll move in another direction.'

Pendlebury is versed in what Farrow calls 'pattern recognition'. 'Selling candy', the euphemism for faking a disposal (mainly a handball) but then holding on to the ball, is one of Pendlebury's deceptions. 'He usually puts it out there, like he's going to handball it,' says his Collingwood teammate Steele Sidebottom.

Just under six minutes remained in the final-round Collingwood–Essendon game in 2019 when Pendlebury roved the loose ball from a marking contest. As he moved, three Essendon players – Kyle Langford, Paddy Ambrose and Mason Redman – hung back rather than rushing at him, in order to anticipate where Pendlebury would go next. Pendlebury at first faked a handball. Then he changed direction, gliding towards the centre corridor before faking again and standing still. Many in the 85,000-strong crowd gasped as Pendlebury – and the game – went into *Matrix* mode. The three Bombers were by then no longer a tackling threat. Pendlebury subsequently found a teammate with a handball that set up a shot on goal (to Jamie Elliott, who missed). Once the ball left Pendlebury's hands, the slow-motion seconds ceased and normal time resumed, as if Neo had walked off the set.

Great AFL midfielders are notoriously hard to tackle. But whereas Geelong's Paddy Dangerfield and Fremantle's Nat

Fyfe burst through with power, and Richmond's Dusty Martin deploys the stiff-arm fend, Pendlebury uses smaller, almost innocuous moves.

'He gives off subtle cues,' says David Rath, the AFL's former head of game analysis, a trained biomechanist and now senior assistant coach at St Kilda. Rath likens Pendlebury's evasive talents to former Hawthorn wizard Cyril Rioli, except they involve less extravagance. 'There's an economy to his moves.'

The opposition does not want Pendlebury to 'draw' players to him and then release a disposal to a teammate in dangerous space. Thus, as with the Essendon trio, players are sometimes reluctant to rush and tackle him. But, in turn, this holding off affords him more time to find a teammate. So, Pendlebury's reputation and the opposition's wariness of his talents arguably give him additional time.

A further quirk of Pendlebury's evasive game: he kicks with his left foot but favours his right hand when handballing. Left-footers routinely wrong-foot would-be tacklers. Pendlebury, as he acknowledges, differs from many left-footers in that he's more willing to kick on his right boot: 'I can use my opposite foot.' As with Hawthorn's ex-skipper Sam Mitchell, the ability to 'go both ways' affords him more time and space and compensates for moderate leg speed.

And then there is the legacy of years spent playing another sport. The calibre of Pendlebury's basketball skills was such that he was offered a scholarship to the Australian Institute of Sport (AIS). He spurned that opportunity in favour of footy but his spot in the AIS was serendipitously grabbed by Patty Mills, who has had a celebrated career in the National Basketball Association and as an Australian Boomer.

In the early 2000s, an AFL research project posed the question of how footballers fare when they've played other 'invasion' sports in childhood – games such as soccer, the rugby codes, basketball and hockey, which involve invading the opposition's territory. It found that a background in those sports assisted the development of footballers and that, as Farrow puts it, 'basketball was number one on the list'. Farrow says basketball has been found to help footballers' 'composure in traffic and awareness in contests' – traits that almost define Pendlebury's timeless style. Interestingly, Federer also played basketball and various other sports as a kid.

Why does it look to us as if the game has switched to slow motion?

When Pendlebury has the ball and the game visibly slows, what the viewers – live or on television – are really seeing is a hesitation in his opponents. 'The illusion of time slowing down is best explained as the hesitation Pendlebury induces in his opponent, as the defender battles the tendency to react automatically to the subtle cues or "tells",' Rath explains. 'It's a pause in the game created by hesitation.'

Rath says that, as spectators, we're seeing an almost subconscious 'battle' between Pendlebury and the opponents seeking to defend him – 'the defenders who want him to commit and Pendlebury who wants them to commit'.

Sidebottom puts it bluntly: 'I guess he puts them in two minds, and yet he just holds it [the football] … Everything does slow down.'

As with soccer's Lionel Messi, Sharne Warne in his leg-spinning pomp and fellow AFL midfield architects such as Marcus Bontempelli, Pendlebury's mastery of the basic skills – one-touch ball-handling, kicking (both feet) and handball – allows him to direct his focus to strategic objectives. As the AFL's Farrow explains, whereas less skilful players have to concentrate on executing their skills, Pendlebury can spend 'the spare attention' on making the best decisions with the ball, or on reading the play.

'In football, the person with more time evades his opponents,' says Dr Machar Reid, Tennis Australia's head of innovation. Federer, conversely, uses the extra time at his disposal to *reduce* the time of his opponent to play shots. Whereas Rafael Nadal will stand well behind the baseline, Federer uses time to take the ball early and play with more aggression. 'Individuals [in tennis] who have more time take it away from their opponents,' Reid says.

Lindsay Gaze, the godfather of Australian basketball and coach of the Australian Boomers in four Olympic Games, uses the analogy of a chess master such as Bobby Fischer for elite players – of different sports – who have the capacity to read what will happen early. 'He [Fischer] saw the game three or four moves ahead,' says Gaze, who theorises that Pendlebury, like Gaze's own basketball champion son, Andrew, has that chess-master's knack for seeing what might unfold.

There is another sense in which Pendlebury has defied time: he has been close to the peak of his freaky powers for longer than comparable footballers. Time's winged chariot was hurrying near him back in 2018 – or so we thought – when a back injury saw him struggle (by his Olympian standards) in the finals series, as the Magpies fell one straight kick shy of a flag. Yet in 2019, his fourteenth season in the AFL, the meticulous man from Sale in country Victoria who wears an activity tracker to bed, made the AFL's All Australian team for the sixth time, and continued to thrive in 2020.

'I don't know if it's from basketball or it's how I see the game,' says Pendlebury on the source of his gift. For a footballer with acute awareness of those around him on the field, what he eats, drinks and how he sleeps, there are still parts of Scott Pendlebury that remain inexplicable, even to him.

16

ARE WE ALONE IN THE UNIVERSE?

Is there anybody out there – or at least, anything? Scientists are training telescopes and listening devices into space. What do they hope to find? And how do UFOs fit in?

Sherryn Groch

You are here in the universe: on a rock with clouds and oceans and fire in its gut, orbiting a star in the outer suburbs of the Milky Way galaxy. As far as we know, nothing else beyond this rock is alive and chances are you haven't left it. But our radio waves have.

Since humanity's very first broadcasts hit the air one hundred-odd years ago, they have travelled more than one hundred light years (or roughly 900 trillion kilometres). They've reached other planets and other stars. Those within sixty light years of Earth would already know we have a space program. That is, if anything is out there listening.

It's no longer such an outlandish idea, says Australian astrophysicist Alan Duffy. About a decade ago, a telescope shot into space dramatically changed the odds of finding life beyond Earth. NASA's Kepler scope, free-floating among the stars, revealed there were more planets than suns – an estimated 100 billion. One in five of these 'exoplanets' is thought to be Earth-sized. What's more, astrophysicists believe they are orbiting within their sun's so-called Goldilocks or habitable zone where the conditions are neither too hot nor too cold for life. And that's just in our own galaxy – the Milky Way is one of billions, likely even trillions.

Astronomers have been rubbing their hands together at those odds ever since. 'It's become a numbers game,' Duffy says. 'The bet is now billions to one there's life out there. It's turned the question around from "Do you believe in aliens?" to "Why don't you?"'

NASA, which once had its funding for such research gutted, is preparing to launch another planet-finder into space, the James Webb telescope, in 2021. Search missions closer to home on Mars and the icy moons of Jupiter and Saturn are also in the pipeline.

And there are other signs we may not be alone, too. Strange radio signals without a clear source. Even stranger sightings on Earth, some of which have been captured on film by the US military. And stars that flicker or vanish entirely – are they shielded by cosmic debris, or some artificial 'alien megastructure' far out in space?

But if the universe is so mind-bendingly vast, how can we ever hope to find ET? What new technology is improving our chances? And could a rock star and a former spy already have found proof of alien intelligence?

'The bet is now billions to one there's life out there. It's turned the question around from "Do you believe in aliens?" to "Why don't you?"'

How likely are we to find life outside Earth?

Imagine creatures that breathe methane instead of oxygen and live at temperatures hotter than the surface of Venus – but locked away from the sun's light. This isn't a theoretical scene on some far-flung planet. This is Earth. Scientists keep finding life where it is least expected – from boiling hydrothermal vents on the seafloor to inside nuclear reactors. So why not the rest of the galaxy?

While astronomers sometimes joke that 'like art, I'll know life when I see it', Duffy says, 'Now it's not clear we will … And we still don't know how life gets started. We only have one example – our own planet. But we're now living in a time when, at any moment, the most profound discovery in history could be made. Aliens would change everything, revolutionise our understanding of life here. The next generation could be going into entirely new fields of science.'

Perhaps Earth's 'extremophiles' – the uranium-loving bacteria or huge red tube worms of the deep sea – first came into being back on the surface, where there was sunlight, and then evolved to survive in harsher conditions without it. 'Or perhaps we're just too limited in imagining what life needs,' Duffy says.

169

Yet, with so many planets on which life could take root, the question remains: where are all the aliens? If all that's needed are the right conditions – on Earth that usually means water, atmosphere and heat – wouldn't at least one species have evolved to interstellar capability by now and come calling?

This question, famously posed by the physicist Enrico Fermi, has one possible answer: the hurdles on the journey from primordial soup to astronaut could be too high for widespread success. Suppose life is more miracle than recipe, a chance alignment of molecules unlikely to be repeated, even with all the right ingredients. Or perhaps life evolving beyond just single-celled organisms is the fluke. The Earth itself was a slime world ruled by microbes for its first two billion years before cells began to join together and complex life exploded into the plants and animals we see today.

'Or the barrier could be yet ahead of us,' Duffy says. 'Some people [suggest] once civilisations get to a certain technology level, they collapse, AI takes over, you nuke yourself … Or perhaps interstellar travel is just too hard [or resource] intensive.'

Others say aliens are keeping their distance on purpose – deeming humans too stupid or insignificant or underevolved to visit. But philosopher Anders Sandberg at Oxford University says that, when the odds of life are so high, any explanation the silence in our skies has to make sense for every possible scenario. 'Wouldn't there be at least one rascal alien teenager or Jehovah's Witness alien butting in anyway? And since it's unlikely we're the first planet with life, we're advanced enough that it seems [interstellar] travel alone wouldn't be the barrier, if other species had millions of years on us.'

In 1961, astronomer Frank Drake set down into mathematics seven factors from which to estimate the number of intelligent civilisations within our galaxy. Those factors start out in the realm of the knowable, Sandberg says, such as the number of new stars forming each year, but then steer into the wildly speculative such as the fraction of intelligent life forms likely to develop technology.

'We've all had a go at the Drake equation, especially at the pub after an astrophysics conference,' Duffy says. 'I only got two.'

Astrophysicist Professor Sara Seager (who also got two) notes that searching for advanced technology assumes a certain, human kind of intelligence: 'Dolphins are intelligent but they live in the ocean, they're not going to invent a radio.'

But what if aliens are sending us messages?

In 1977, a strange signal from the constellation Sagittarius was picked up by the Big Ear radio telescope in Ohio. On the computer print-out, astronomer Jerry Ehman spotted the anomaly right away, thirty times more intense than the usual background noise of the universe and lasting more than seventy seconds. He circled it and wrote 'Wow!'. To this day, the Wow! signal, as it is known, has not been explained – but it has also never been heard again, says astronomer Danny Price. He mans Australia's famous Parkes telescope for the Search for Extraterrestrial Intelligence Institute (SETI), a former offshoot of NASA now in the middle of the world's largest interstellar eavesdropping exercise to date. The $100-million project Breakthrough Listen, funded by the Russian tech billionaire Yuri Milner, is scanning millions of nearby stars for 'techno-signatures' – radio waves or light that bear the hallmarks of artificial design. But if the Wow! signal had come through our machines today, Price says, it probably wouldn't have set off many alarm bells. 'We're very conservative now, we look to see if something is repeating.'

After all, the universe is a noisy place. Once you get past the radio interference from satellites and frequencies near Earth, you have faraway stars colliding and shooting out huge amounts of electromagnetic radiation – that's light and radio waves. Mysterious 'fast radio bursts' first recognised in 2007 are now thought to be part of this natural cosmic cacophony, as is the famous 'Little Green Men' radio signal picked up in 1967 which kept time better than an atomic clock but was later revealed to be a pulsar – a previously unknown, highly magnetised type of star.

'Sometimes you'll be about to pick up the phone and then you'll find out it's another satellite,' Price says. That phone isn't connected to the White House – SETI is not bound by any government secrecy or reporting provisions, although Price notes 'we do have a duty of care to get it right and not cause unnecessary alarm.' But suppose a signal did come, and it was verified as 'alien' – unnatural and unknown. ('We have a bottle of champagne set aside for that moment,' Price admits.)

> *'The saying goes it's like searching the ocean for a whale by looking in just one glass of seawater.'*

Any resulting conversation with our neighbours might be drawn out over hundreds, even thousands of years. The closest 'habitable' exoplanet to Earth, Proxima Centauri, is still four light years away, meaning we'd have to wait eight for a reply to any message we sent back 'assuming aliens don't take too long to think of a witty retort,' Duffy says.

Price is not put off by the radio silence thus far. Perhaps aliens are using a different medium to communicate across the galaxy – from gravitational waves to the ghost particles known as neutrinos. More likely, if they are broadcasting something, it just hasn't reached us yet. 'The saying goes it's like searching the ocean for a whale by looking in just one glass of seawater,' he says. 'Today we've searched more like a hot-tub-full, and soon it'll be an Olympic-sized swimming pool or even a lake.'

While SETI operates on a slim and almost entirely philanthropic budget, advances in computing have allowed it to rapidly scale up its cosmic search – piggybacking its systems onto existing telescopes scanning the skies including Parkes. SETI's Breakthrough Starshot project, meanwhile, plans to use lasers to push tiny spaceships out of our solar system and over to Proxima Centauri at roughly one-fifth the speed of light. That would cut the physical journey from 6000 years to twenty or thirty.

Still, if alien life is revealed to humanity, Seager hopes it will be over the airwaves. 'That would be so clear-cut.' At the Massachusetts Institute of Technology (MIT), in collaboration with NASA, she is taking a more difficult route – searching distant exoplanets for signs of life. 'We can't see as far as SETI ... but we're not just looking for intelligence. We're looking for the slime in your fridge ... I think in my lifetime we might even find it.'

Could we see life faraway using telescopes?

Almost a decade after Kepler ushered in a new renaissance in space exploration, its successor, James Webb, is due to take to the skies. Through it, scientists hope to find the telltale chemical signature of alien atmospheres encoded in starlight. Seager had the idea twenty years ago as a 'newly minted PhD' – every chemical absorbs colours differently, so what if you could analyse the starlight passing by a planet for signs of familiar gases?

Of course, getting a good glimpse of a planet as it travels in front of its sun is akin to picking out the detail of a fruit fly buzzing in front of a spotlight. 'You'd go blind before you saw it,' Price says. It requires forensic investigation, Seager explains. That's why, although her idea of examining the colour 'barcodes' of starlight is now routine among astronomers, only big gas planets have been analysed so far out of the 4000-odd confirmed exoplanets in our galaxy. 'But Webb will change that,' she says. 'I'm hoping to look at some of these habitable planets we've found.'

Finding oxygen will be a 'smoking gun', Price says, particularly if it is discovered alongside methane. 'Those gases cancel each other out so we'll know something is replenishing them.'

They may even find artificial gases – pollutants such as the ozone-eating CFCs produced on Earth. 'Then we'll really know something's out there,' Duffy says. 'Aliens that didn't get onto their Montreal Protocol.'

What if aliens have already visited as UFOs?

Some people say aliens have already made contact – and even come to Earth – but our governments are keeping it a secret. For years, the US military base Area 51 in the Nevada desert has been a lightning rod for such conspiracy theories, even after strange craft sighted in the area were revealed to be a secret program testing spy plane prototypes rather than aliens.

While UFOs are widely dismissed as fantasy, 'sightings' have been reported all over the world, from the coastal city of Sochi, Russia, to the Nullarbor Plain of Outback Australia. Usually, they turn out to be more familiar objects such as satellites and comets, but questions linger over some recorded 'encounters'. In 2017, *The New York Times* revealed that the Pentagon had funded a shadowy UFO investigation unit into sightings even its own military couldn't explain, which the agency claimed had wound up in 2012. Another plot twist came soon after: the three videos published by the paper were confirmed as genuine, taken by US pilots and still classified as 'unexplained aerial phenomena' or UAPs. And one of the people instrumental in their public release was the musician Tom DeLonge, the former frontman of Blink-182. Earlier that year, DeLonge had turned his lifelong fascination with UFOs into a research and entertainment company called To the Stars alongside a number of ex-defence spooks. One of them was the man who had been running the Pentagon program, Luis Elizondo, a long-serving US secret service and counterterrorism agent who left the military in 2017 over concerns its UFO investigations were being buried under excessive secrecy.

These sightings are not your blurry picture in a cornfield but strange readings consistently picked up under the close eye of military equipment, Elizondo says, and there are more like them in defence force vaults. 'Back in 2017, no one knew about them. I think it will become clear just how seriously the US is taking UAPs now. The phenomenon is real and we need to find out what it is.'

Among the military sightings that couldn't be explained, Elizondo says patterns emerge – objects without obvious engines that accelerate at impossible velocities, clocking speeds that would rip apart any craft made by human hands, that don't leave the usual telltale signs of their passage in the air, or appear to defy gravity. 'Other nations have their own UAPs, it's not just the US,' he says. 'But there are some hotspots, we know there's a link between nuclear tech, like power stations and defence capabilities – they pop up there.'

> *'If they can travel between the stars, why do they keep winding up in blurred photos in Kansas? Our iPhone cameras have gotten better but the UFO pictures haven't.'*

The Australian Department of Defence did not answer questions on whether its personnel had picked up the same phenomena on their instruments but said it doesn't have a 'protocol covering UFO sightings', after officially ending an old program investigating civilian UFO reports in 1993.

Unlike a natural phenomenon such as lightning, Elizondo stresses, genuine UAPs show signs of intelligent control.

'When we lock onto them with our radar, they respond, they move away. Either this is super-secret tech the US is testing on its own unsuspecting personnel, who are armed, or a foreign nation has leapfrogged ahead of us and rendered all our tech obsolete, or it belongs to something else entirely. But for either [of the first] two scenarios I find it hard to believe we wouldn't have some idea this kind of tech exists. And why would you fly these things over cities if you want to stay secret? That's why we have Area 51.'

But the majority of scientists remain unconvinced aliens are the most likely culprit – earthly explanations may still come to light. 'Aliens would've had to set off for Earth long before there were any signs of intelligent life here,' Duffy says. 'And if they can travel between the stars, why do they keep winding up in blurred photos in Kansas? Our iPhone cameras have gotten better but the UFO pictures haven't.'

Elizondo says low visibility is a common feature of sightings, even by the military, and some have theorised the objects could be distorting the light or space around them. 'We see it with other phenomena like black holes or desert mirages,' he says. 'Nothing we've made can do that.'

To the Stars is now looking to harness artificial intelligence to analyse public UFO sightings via an upcoming app called SCOUT. 'That'll check them against everything from comets, balloons, migrating birds,' he says. 'We think the tech could eventually identify [digitally altered] videos and deep fakes.'

While DeLonge has made some grand claims about his relationship with the US Government, in 2019 To the Stars did secure a partnership with the army to research 'novel materials' the company claims to possess, as well as camouflage tech.

But what about alien encounters? Those persistent stories of late-night abductions, shadowy figures, white lights and, yes, probing. Some experts say many can be explained by conditions such as sleep paralysis or lucid dreaming, where the sleeper experiences real pain and makes decisions as if awake. It's likely these conditions have plagued humanity for centuries, Sandberg says – what was once explained away as demons, angels or vampires has now become flying saucers in our modern scientific era, and aliens our new monsters.

Where are we looking for life in our own solar system?

This doesn't mean there isn't life close to home. Duffy and Price say they are 'tremendously excited' by the new generation of NASA missions gearing up to search Mars and beyond, and Sandberg says finding life in our own galactic backyard is a strong possibility given the chance of 'cross-contamination' from asteroids and other cosmic debris.

'We're in a golden age for exploration just in our own galaxy,' Duffy says. 'It's very possible that in my lifetime we'll find something.'

Mars might be called the dead planet, its surface scorched by solar radiation, but scars remain from ancient oceans, and scans have found a salty lake more than a kilometre below the surface. If there is life on Mars, scientists expect we will find it underground. Seager and her colleagues have even discovered a strange gas, phosphine, in the boiling clouds of Venus that their analysis suggests could only be caused by life, although the verdict is far from settled.

Duffy thinks exciting prospects also await us on the icy moons of Saturn and Jupiter, where water vapour has been captured shooting into the sky through cracks in the surface – containing salt and nutrients. 'Everything that life needs appears to be in these worlds,' he says. 'Some [moons in our solar system] even have an atmosphere.'

If organisms can thrive in the hydrothermal vents of Earth's seafloor, without sunlight, then perhaps there is something living in the dark 'world-spanning' oceans of Europa and Enceladus. The pull of gravity from the gas giants heats up the core of their moons, allowing liquid to form about a kilometre or two below the surface, while thick ice on top acts as a shield against the freezing touch of space. 'The biochemistry might be completely different,' Sandberg says. 'But if an alien squid swims up and tries to eat us, we're not going to care. That's life.'

If we instead determine that we are alone in the universe, this in itself will be a profound development, experts say, underlining the preciousness of our planet and its biodiversity. Or perhaps what we'll ultimately discover is the universe is just too big to ever be sure. Our galaxy alone is more than 100,000 light years wide and we are more than 25,000 light years from its centre. Our first old-timey radio waves haven't even made it halfway through since we started broadcasting.

'If you had a photo of the galaxy filling your screen, that little bubble of 100 light years in every direction, where we can be heard, that would just be one pixel,' Duffy says. 'The entire galaxy is dark to our presence.' Perhaps, then, civilisations on different worlds are like ships in the night. 'Those signals could be echoing in the darkness, and forever missing each other.'

'

We're in a golden age for exploration just in our own galaxy.

'

17

WHAT HAPPENS AS WE DIE?

As with birth, dying is a process. How does it unfold? Can you prepare for it? And why should you keep talking to a dying person even if they don't talk back?

Sophie Aubrey

We're born, we live, we die. Few things are so concrete. And yet, while we swap countless stories about the start of life, the end is a subject we're less inclined to talk about. Conversations about death – what it is, what it looks like – are scarce until we suddenly face it head-on, often for the first time with the loss of a loved one.

'We hold a lot of anxiety about what death means and I think that's just part of the human experience,' says Associate Professor Mark Boughey, director of palliative medicine at Melbourne's St Vincent's Hospital. 'Some people just really push it away and don't think about it until it's immediately in front of them.' But it doesn't need to be this way, he says. 'The more people engage and understand death and know where it's heading … the better prepared the person is to be able to let go to the process, and the better prepared the family is to reconcile with it, for a more peaceful death.'

Of course, not everyone ends up in palliative care or even in a hospital. For some people, death can be shockingly sudden, as in an accident or from a cardiac arrest or massive stroke. Death can follow a brief decline, as with some illnesses; or a prolonged one, as with the frailty that can come with old age; or it can come after a series of serious episodes, such as heart failure. And different illnesses, such as dementia and cancer, can also cause particular symptoms prior to death. But there are key physical processes that are commonly experienced by many people as they die – whether from 'old age', or indeed from cancer, or even following a major physical trauma.

What is the process of dying? How can you prepare for it? And how should you be with someone who is nearing the end of their life?

What are the earliest signs a person is going to die?

The point of no return, when a person begins deteriorating towards their final breath, can start weeks or months before someone dies. Boughey says refractory symptoms – stubborn and irreversible despite medical treatment – offer the earliest signs that the dying process is beginning: breathlessness, severe loss of weight and appetite, fluid retention, fatigue, drowsiness, delirium, jaundice and nausea, and an overall drop in physical function. Simple actions, such as going from a bed to a chair, can become exhausting. A dying person often starts to withdraw from the news, some activities and other people, to talk less or have trouble with conversation, and to sleep more. This all ties in with a drop in energy levels caused by a deterioration in the body's brain function and metabolic processes.

Predicting exactly when a person will die is, of course, nearly impossible and depends on factors ranging from the health issues they have to whether they are choosing to accept more medical interventions. 'The journey for everyone towards dying is so variable,' Boughey says.

What happens in someone's final days?

As the body continues to wind down, various other reflexes and functions will also slow. A dying person will become progressively more fatigued, their sleep–wake patterns more random, their coughing and swallowing reflexes slower. They will start to respond less to verbal commands and gentle touch. Reduced blood flow to the brain or chemical imbalances can also cause a dying person to become disoriented, confused or detached from reality and time. Visions or hallucinations often come into play.

> 'Hallucinations often help a person die more peacefully, so it's best not to "correct" them. "Visions, especially of long-gone loved ones, can be comforting."'

'A lot of people have hallucinations or dreams where they see loved ones,' Boughey says. 'It's a real signal that, even if we can't see they're dying, they might be.' But Boughey says the hallucinations often help a person die more peacefully, so it's best not to 'correct' them. 'Visions, especially of long-gone loved ones, can be comforting.'

Instead of simply sleeping more, the person's consciousness may begin to fluctuate, making them nearly impossible to wake at times, even when there is a lot of stimulation around them. With the slowing in blood circulation, body temperature can begin to seesaw, so a person can be cool to the touch at one point and then hot later on. Their senses of taste and smell diminish. 'People become no longer interested in eating ... they physically don't want to,' Boughey says. This means urine and bowel movements become less frequent, and urine will be much darker than usual due to lower fluid intake. Some people might start to experience incontinence as muscles deteriorate, but absorbent pads and sheets can help minimise discomfort.

What happens when death is just hours or minutes away?

As death nears, it's very common for a person's breathing to change, sometimes slowing, other times speeding up or becoming noisy and shallow. The changes are triggered by reduction in blood flow, and they're not painful. Some people will experience a gurgle-like 'death rattle'. 'It's really some secretions sitting in the back of the throat, and the body can no longer shift them,' Boughey says.

An irregular breathing pattern known as Cheyne-Stokes respiration is also often seen in people approaching death: taking one or several breaths followed by a long pause with no breathing at all, then another breath. 'It doesn't happen to everybody, but it happens in the last hours of life and indicates dying is really front and centre. It usually happens when someone is profoundly unconscious,' Boughey says.

Restlessness affects nearly half of all people who are dying. 'The confusion [experienced earlier] can cause restlessness right at the end of life,' Boughey says. 'It's just the natural physiology, the brain is trying to keep functioning.'

Circulation changes also mean a person's heartbeat becomes fainter, while their skin can become mottled or pale grey-blue, particularly on the knees, feet and hands.

Boughey says more perspiration or clamminess may be present, and a person's eyes can begin to tear or appear glazed over. Gradually, the person drifts in and out or slips into complete unconsciousness.

How long does dying take? Is it painful?

Ken Hillman, University of New South Wales professor of intensive care, says when he is treating someone who is going to die, one of the first questions he is inevitably asked is how long the person has to live. 'That is such a difficult question to answer with accuracy. I always put a rider at the end saying it's unpredictable,' he says. 'Even when we stop treatment, the body can draw on reserves we didn't know it had. They might live another day, or two days, or two weeks. All we know is, in long-term speaking, they certainly are going to die very soon.' But he stresses that most expected deaths, especially in the elderly, are not painful. 'You gradually become confused, you lose your level of consciousness, and you fade away.'

Should there be any pain, shortness of breath or distress, Hillman says it can be relieved with medications such as morphine, which, in appropriate doses, does not interfere with the dying process. 'If there is any sign of pain or discomfort, we would always reassure relatives and carers that they will die with dignity, that we don't stop caring, that we know how to treat it and we continue treatment.'

'For a dying person there can be a real sense of readiness, like they're in this safe cocoon, in the last day or two of life.'

Boughey agrees, saying the pain instead tends to sit with the loved ones. 'For a dying person there can be a real sense of readiness, like they're in this safe cocoon, in the last day or two of life.' Boughey believes there is an element of 'letting go' to death. 'We see situations where people seem to hang on for certain things to occur, or to see somebody significant, which then allows them to let go,' he says. 'I've seen someone talk to a sibling overseas and then they put the phone down and die.'

How can you prepare for death?

Firstly, there is your frame of mind. In thinking about death, it helps to compare it to birth, Boughey says. 'The time of dying is like birth, it can happen over a day or two, but it's actually the time leading up to it that is the most critical part of the equation,' he says. With birth, what happens in the nine months leading to the day a baby is born – from the doctor's appointments to the birth classes – can make a huge difference. And Boughey says it's 'absolutely similar' when someone is facing the end of life.

To Hillman, better understanding the dying process can help us stop treating death as a medical problem to be fixed, and instead as an inevitability that should be as comfortable and peaceful as possible. Then there are the practicalities to discuss. Seventy per cent of Australians would prefer to die at home but, according to a 2018 Productivity Commission report, fewer than 10 per cent do. Instead, about half die in hospitals, ending up there because of an illness triggered by disease or age-related frailty (a small percentage die in accident and emergency departments). Another third die in residential aged care, according to data from the Australian Institute of Health and Welfare.

Hillman believes death is over-medicalised, particularly in old age, and he urges families to acknowledge when a loved one is dying and to discuss their wishes: where they want to die, whether they want medical interventions, what they don't want to happen.

'[Discussing this] can empower people to make their own decisions about how they die,' he says.

Someone's end-of-life preferences should be understood early, says Palliative Care Nurses Australia president Professor Jane Phillips, but also revisited throughout the dying process as things can change. 'People are not being asked enough where they want to be cared for and where they want to die,' Phillips says. 'One of the most important things for families and patients is to have conversations about what their care preferences are.' While it will not always be possible to die at home, sometimes it is. Phillips' role with a dying patient, she explains, is to 'help you adapt and get meaning out of every day and enjoy your days within the constraints of what you're dealing with'.

How can you help a loved one in their final hours?

Studies show that hearing is the last sense to fade so people are urged to keep talking calmly and reassuringly to a dying person as it can bring great comfort even if they do not appear to be responding. 'Many people will be unconscious, not able to be roused – but be mindful they can still hear,' says Phillips. 'As a nurse caring for the person, I let them know when I'm there, when I'm about to touch them, I keep talking to them. And I would advise the same to the family as well.'

On his ICU ward, Hillman encourages relatives to 'not be afraid of the person on all these machines. Sit next to them, hold their hands, stroke their forehead, talk to them about their garden and pets and assume they are listening,' he says. Remember that while the physical or mental changes can be distressing to observe, they can be controlled with medication and they're not generally troubling for the person dying, says Hillman. Once families accept this, they can focus on being with their dying loved one.

Boughey says people should think about how the person would habitually like them to act. 'What would you normally do when you're caring for your loved one? If you like to hold and touch and communicate, do what you would normally do,' he says.

Other things that can comfort a dying person are playing their favourite music, sharing memories, moistening their mouth if it becomes dry, covering them with light blankets if they get cold or damp cloths if they feel hot, keeping the room air fresh, repositioning pillows if they get uncomfortable and gently massaging them. These gestures are simple but their significance should not be underestimated.

What is the moment of death?

In Australia, the moment of death is defined as when either blood circulation or brain function irreversibly cease in a person. Both will eventually happen when someone dies, it's just a matter of what happens first.

Brain death is less common, and occurs after the brain has been so badly damaged that it swells, cutting off blood flow, and permanently stops, for example following a head injury or a stroke. The more widespread type of death is circulatory death, where the heart comes to a standstill. After circulation ceases, the brain then becomes deprived of oxygenated blood and stops functioning. The precise time it takes for this to happen depends on an individual's prior condition, says intensive care specialist Dr Matthew Anstey, a clinical senior lecturer at the University of Western Australia. 'Let's say you start slowly getting worse and worse, where your blood pressure is gradually falling before it stops. In that situation your brain is vulnerable already [from reduced blood flow], so it won't take much to stop the brain,' he says.

The brain remains momentarily active after a circulatory death. 'But if it's a sudden cardiac arrest, the brain could go on a bit longer. It can take a minute or two minutes for brain cells to die when they have no blood flow.' While research in this area is ongoing, Anstey does not believe people would be conscious at this point. 'There is a difference between consciousness and some degree of cellular function,' he says. 'I think consciousness is a very complicated higher-order function.' Cells in other organs – such as the liver and kidneys – are comparatively more resilient and can survive longer without oxygen, Anstey says. This is essential for organ donation, as the organs can remain viable hours after death.

In a palliative care setting, Boughey says the brain usually becomes inactive around the same time as the heart. But he says that, ultimately, it is the brain's gradual switching off of various processes – including breathing and circulation – that leads to most deaths. 'Your whole metabolic system is run out of the brain … [It is] directing everything.' He says it's why sometimes, just before death, a person can snap into a moment of clarity where they say something to their family. 'It can be very profound … it's like the brain trying one more time.'

What does a dead person look like?

'There is a perceptible change between the living and dying,' Boughey says. 'Often people are watching the breathing and don't see it. But there is this change where the body no longer is in the presence of the living. It's still, its colour changes. Things just stop. And it's usually very, very gentle. It's not dramatic. I reassure families of that beforehand.'

A typical sign that death has just happened, apart from an absence of breathing and heartbeat, is fixed pupils, which indicate no brain activity. A person's eyelids may also be half-open, their skin may be pale and waxy-looking, and their mouth may fall open as the jaw relaxes. Boughey says that only very occasionally will there be an unpleasant occurrence, such as a person vomiting or releasing their bowels. In most cases, death is peaceful.

And while most loved ones want to be present when death occurs, Boughey says it's important not to feel guilty if you're

There is a perceptible change between the living and dying; it's usually very, very gentle. It's not dramatic.

not, because it can sometimes happen very suddenly. What's more important is being present during the lead-up.

What happens next?

Once a person dies, an authorised healthcare professional verifies the death and a doctor must sign a certificate confirming it. 'It's absolutely critical for the family to see … because it signals very clearly the person has died,' says Boughey. 'The family may not have started grieving until that point.'

In some cases, organ and tissue donation occurs, but only if the person is eligible and wished to do so. The complexity of the process means it usually only happens out of an intensive care ward. Boughey stresses that an expected death is not an emergency – police and paramedics don't need to be called. After the doctor's certificate is issued, a funeral company takes the dead person into their care and collects the information needed to register the death. They can also help with newspaper notices or flowers. But all of this does not need to happen right away, Boughey says. Do what feels right. The moments after death can be tranquil, and you may just want to sit with the person. Or you might want to call others to come, or fulfil cultural wishes. 'There is no reason to take the body away suddenly,' Boughey says.

You might feel despair, you might feel numb, you might feel relief. There is no right or wrong way to feel. As loved ones move through the grieving process, they are reminded support is available – be it from friends, family or health professionals.

*

If you are dealing with grief and loss and want support, you can call Beyond Blue on 1300 224 636.

18

WHAT'S IT LIKE TO BE CHASED BY A CASSOWARY?

Most animals will hurt humans only in self-defence. What happens if you startle a snake, step on a stingray or brush against a box jellyfish? And why should you never, ever corner a cassowary?

Simone Fox Koob and Emma Young

Rare and beautiful, the southern cassowary is considered shy by nature, despite its hefty body, muscular legs and capacity to kill. Nowadays, the flightless bird is forced to navigate menacing cars, marauding dogs, picnicking tourists and other perils of civilisation as it struts and fossicks for fruit, usually alone, in just a few areas of Far North Queensland forest.

The southern cassowary, scientific name *Casuarius casuarius*, is no shrinking violet, though. Corner one of them, get close enough to ruffle its glossy black feathers or venture near its nest of emerald-green eggs and its response will be swift. It will fight you – if not to the death then until you have retreated a long, long way away.

So what happens when a cassowary takes umbrage with you? And how much damage can they do? Veterinarian and cassowary expert Graham Lauridsen, who works to protect and conserve the endangered species in North Queensland, has had a number of memorable encounters with cassowaries. While working with sick and orphaned animals for the Queensland Government at Mission Beach one day, he noticed a wild male cassowary with a bad limp watching over three chicks. 'Eventually, he only had two chicks, then one – he was simply not getting around the bush enough to feed them,' says Lauridsen. 'So we decided we probably needed to take the chick off him because it would get skinny and starve, and that way we could treat him too.

'They make bloodcurdling noises.'

'The bird was hobbling really badly. It was on a retaining wall and we had put some food to get it to come in,' Lauridsen says. 'I said to the guys, "I'll grab the chick when I get the opportunity. It all should be good, the male is so sore and in pain, he won't move."' As he grabbed the chick and started to run, the cassowary jumped off the wall. Then came the sound. 'They make bloodcurdling noises,' says Lauridsen. 'It's hard to imagine until you hear them. They really fluff up, their feathers come out and they make this deep, deep, deep booming sound. They do it as an aggressive sound but also during mating season. When they make the sound, it's actually subsonic, part of it. You hear this noise but feel the vibration of the noise going through you.' The low-frequency, thunderous call is used to let others know of its presence, or to respond to danger. A 2003 study that recorded and analysed these sounds found the southern cassowary call can get down to 32 hertz, at the very bottom of the human hearing range.

The sight of an angry cassowary is alarming, too. Adults can grow to 2 metres tall. Females are bulkier than males, weighing up to 76 kilograms, while males reach around 55 kilograms. They also have a kind of helmet, called a casque, that 'looks quite like a weapon, although it's actually not,' says Lauridsen.

The bird's weapon is at the other end of its body. 'They have three toes on each foot and the inside toe has a claw that is super sharp at the end. That's the weapon they do damage with. They attack each other, karate kicking out – and they can do that to people as well if you mess with them,' explains Lauridsen. At up to 12 centimetres long, the middle toe functions as a dagger that can puncture and gash. So when Lauridsen saw the cassowary jump off the retaining wall, he bolted. 'I did an Indiana Jones slide to the four-wheel drive and jumped in, shut the door and looked out – and saw it looking right at me,' he says.

Cassowaries are now found in just three small populations in rainforest in Far North Queensland: one in the wet tropics and two in Cape York. The last reported fatality in Australia was in 1926 when Phillip McClean, sixteen, was kicked in the throat by a cassowary on his Queensland ranch. In 2019, a seventy-five-year-old Florida man who kept exotic birds on a farm was attacked by his cassowary and died in hospital from his injuries.

Queensland's Department of Environment and Heritage Protection urges people to never approach, feed or get out of a car to look at cassowaries. Feeding them is illegal and dangerous, and has caused the deaths of some birds. If a cassowary is coming your way, back away slowly and put something, such as a tree, between yourself and the bird – then let it go on its way.

For Lauridsen, the rules of the rainforest are clear: 'If you do happen to get on your own in a fight with a cassowary, unless you can run or climb, you will lose. Literally, you know that this bird has the weapons to do you damage and you want to get as far away as possible. They will bluff and do some fake noises but once they come at you, you can't scare them away, yell at them and make them turn. They will come at you to hurt you.'

Of course, many animals will offer you no sign of impending trouble. Just the slightest brush with some can have the most severe effects. Consider delicate box jellyfish, for example. They jet silently through our warm seas, toothless and clawless and trailing an arsenal of 60 billion toxic stinging cells. They are found between the tropics of Capricorn and Cancer so are a concern for humans not only from Rockhampton in Queensland to Exmouth in Western Australia, but also in favoured holiday destinations, including the Thai island of Koh Mak, where Andrew Jones and his family holidayed one Christmas. Jones, his wife and two young sons had all been swimming when he left the water to rest. The next thing he heard was the sound of four-year-old Lewis screaming. 'Even now, to remember that scream gives me chills,' he says. 'His mother swam towards him and I darted in … he had these things hanging off him, almost like cooked vermicelli, transparent. I ran with him back onto the beach.'

It takes about 2 metres of tentacle contact from a box jellyfish to kill a person. The venom can stop a heart in one to three minutes. (In such a situation, knowing how to perform CPR can save someone's life.) Authorities advise first rinsing with vinegar, to disable the tentacles; ripping them off willy-nilly is like setting off a booby trap, triggering the stinging cells that fire off venom-coated barbs.

But all Jones knew was he had to get them off his son. So he grabbed one, and pulled. 'The drag was like pulling velcro. It left a big gash on his left thigh,' Jones says. 'But as soon as I did that, he stopped screaming and fell immediately unconscious and within seconds he was turning blue. I checked his pulse and there was nothing.' The venom had flown into Lewis's bloodstream, hitting him like a bomb.

In Australia, there have been about seventy deaths from box jellyfish stings in the past fifty years, none for nearly a decade, but in South-East Asia there are one hundred per year.

The family ran back to their bungalow, yelling for help. The resort manager knew immediately what had happened and began pouring vinegar over Lewis's legs. 'Maybe two minutes later, he drew in a big breath and his eyes opened extraordinarily wide and he let out an almighty scream and started to cry,' Jones says. 'It was almost like a rebirth, some kind of miracle. Every expert we have spoken to has said he should have been dead after that amount of venom.'

The island's single taxi just happened to be outside. They bundled Lewis in, moaning and delirious, eyes rolling, and headed towards a medical clinic, only to find it closed. So they returned to their resort and kept talking to Lewis, to keep him conscious, while the resort manager made calls, and forty-five minutes later help arrived. Lewis's wounds were cleaned, the remaining tentacles removed and he was given pain relief. His parents were told he would be okay.

'You go far off the beaten track looking for paradise; but we were stuck there,' Jones says. 'And it could have turned out much worse.'

Another type of marine animal that it's best not to get on the wrong side of is the stingray. As with jellyfish, rays ripple through our oceans gracefully, a low-key presence often half-buried in sand. But make no mistake, they carry protection wherever they go – on top of their tails are serrated barbs smeared in venom. While the stingray is not looking for trouble, an unsuspecting beachgoer can still put a foot wrong with them.

Steph Gould was wading at a beach one day when she stood on something 'rubbery'. 'I felt this pain in the back of my ankle and my first reaction was, "I think something bit me."' Back on the beach, in suburban Brighton on Port Phillip Bay, Gould realised there were cuts on either side of her heel. 'Whatever it was had gone in on the outside, come out on the other side of my Achilles tendon, and pulled back out again.' As blood dripped down her foot, Gould struggled to walk. Her Achilles tendon was severed. She had been stabbed by a stingray.

'I was wondering, how do I control my body in this situation?' Worse than that, she could feel pain creeping up her leg, which she now knows was venom. 'It was a burning pain that felt like it was paralysing me – definitely the most excruciating pain I've ever felt.'

At a nearby medical clinic, a doctor asked how much pain she was in on a scale of one to ten. 'Ten,' she told him. 'Eventually, they gave me one of those [emergency pain-relief] green whistles and that helped a lot. They actually put my foot in a bucket full of hot water, which is apparently the thing to flush it out.' Gould was moved to a local hospital where an ultrasound found three small pieces of stingray-tail barb in her tendon. She would need surgery to remove them.

When threatened or stepped on, a stingray will thrust up its tail, causing a 'stab' wound. The barbs, some of which face backwards, get stuck in the skin and can create a bigger gash on the way out.

The scar left behind was 'horrific', says Gould. 'I couldn't believe it. I didn't know it was going to be that big.'

The biggest danger, though, is the risk of secondary infection or the slow necrosis, or tissue death, caused by the venom. 'The most important complication is secondary infection,' says toxicology emergency medicine and clinical expert Professor Geoffrey Isbister. 'Especially in wounds that penetrate into a joint space, or wounds that are not cleaned or debrided [the removal of damaged tissue] when appropriate.'

There are nearly 500 species of stingrays in Australia but fatalities caused by the animal are rare. Conservationist Steve Irwin died in 2006 after a stingray barb pierced his heart while he was filming on the Great Barrier Reef.

Gould spent five weeks on crutches – but she thinks the scars will be with her forever. Some time later, she was walking along the water's edge at Black Rock, not far from the beach where the ray had lashed her. 'I saw a stingray right near the shore. I thought, it's come back to finish me off.'

Another beast that it's best to avoid stepping on is a snake, particularly the species named after a tiger. Tiger snakes are one of the most venomous snakes in the country, named for their 'tiger' bands and found mainly in southern and temperate areas. The snake's venom affects the ability of blood to clot, causes muscle damage, can spread to the kidneys and can attack the nervous system and cause paralysis.

Five-year-old Poppy Carson felt some of these effects one warm October day when she trod on a snake, believed to be a tiger snake, while on a kindergarten bushwalk in bayside Mount Martha in Victoria. 'It reared up and bit her on the right ankle,' recalls her mother, Erin. 'It wasn't until she felt the bite that she even knew the snake was there. It got one fang in and thankfully – still to this day, I'm thankful – it didn't get both fangs in or we wouldn't have her.'

The bite looked like a 'minuscule' pinprick, noticeable only due to the redness around it. But within a minute, Poppy was on the ground, vomiting. 'The venom took hold that fast. Thankfully, the kindy teachers, they saw a snake – they weren't sure what type – but they knew to [apply a pressure bandage] and call the ambulance. She was taken to Frankston Hospital and within twenty minutes she had lost her eyesight, was unable to move her legs, and had lymph nodes the size of golf balls.

'She was highly, highly distressed, in extreme pain,' Carson recalls. 'She was still vomiting so when I arrived, I looked at her and she looked like she was going to die. As any parent can imagine, it was absolutely terrifying. Seeing my daughter lying lifeless in a hospital bed is something I'll remember for the rest of my life.'

Poppy was given antivenom for both a brown snake and tiger snake as they couldn't be sure which species had bitten her. But already the venom was breaking down her muscles – and she couldn't move her legs. She was rushed to the Royal Children's Hospital. 'She was stable at this point, unconscious but stable – and given another lot of antivenom, so altogether four lots. She had two blood transfusions; they thought they were going to have to replace her kidneys,' Carson says.

Poppy was in hospital for four days but 'waltzed out of there like she owned the shop,' says her mum. 'There are no other lasting effects other than memories. Now it's like a badge of honour.'

If you are bitten by any Australian snake, lie very still, apple a pressure bandage and call triple zero.

*

The information contained in this chapter is not intended as a substitute for professional medical advice. You should phone 000 for potentially life-threatening bites and stings. For specialist advice on stings, bites and other poisonings, call the Poisons Information Centre 24-hour emergency hotline on 13 11 26.

19

WHO RUNS ANTARCTICA?

It's cold, wet, windy and hard to get to – so why do so many nations want to be in Antarctica? And what are the rules when they get there?

Felicity Lewis

By 1959, the Cold War and the first space race were well under way. In September of that year, a Soviet spacecraft became the first to touch down on the moon and Washington was jolted again in October when the Russians took the first photographs of the moon's dark side. The superpowers were jockeying for supremacy in places near and far.

At the southern end of the world, Antarctica had been the subject of various claims for years, with even the question of who saw it first, in 1820, up for debate – was it the Russians, the British or an American? With the race to the South Pole 'won' in 1911, by Norway's Roald Amundsen, explorers from various countries scoped parts of the region, and by the 1950s, seven nations had staked formal (in some cases, overlapping) territorial claims.

As well as politics, there was another post-war force at work: science. In a thawing of divisions, the governments of more than sixty nations had allowed their scientists to work together on a massive study of the Earth and its planetary surrounds for International Geophysical Year in 1957–58. The polar regions were a focus for study – especially the mysterious Antarctica. Scientists from countries including Australia, New Zealand, the United States and Russia led the way in putting everything from cosmic rays to glaciology, penguins to the aurora australis under the microscope. The US military support operation for its scientists was codenamed Operation Deep Freeze.

'But what do nations want in Antarctica? What does the treaty say? What are the rules?'

As groundbreaking discoveries ensued, US president Dwight Eisenhower proposed a means by which 'this same kind of co-operation for the benefit of all mankind shall be perpetuated'.

Just two months after Russia snapped those pictures of the moon, the Antarctic Treaty was signed by a dozen countries in Washington. It would become a storied model of international cooperation with more than fifty signatories today, from Argentina to Uruguay, Austria to Mongolia.

But what do nations want in Antarctica? What does the treaty say? What are the rules? And what are the points of tensions in the coldest, windiest and driest place on Earth?

Who owns Antarctica?

The world's fifth-largest continent is one of those realms, as with outer space and the deep sea, that is owned by no nation and where ambiguity is the order of the day. Contrary to the idea that it has been carved up like an icy pie, slices of it had been the subject of territorial claims by seven countries – Australia, New Zealand, Chile, Argentina, Britain, Norway and France – before the Antarctic Treaty was signed. Some claims, such as those of Argentina, Chile and Britain, overlap. All claims, including those of Australia, New Zealand, France and Norway, were effectively frozen when the treaty entered into force in 1961. Russia and the United States, both present at the treaty negotiations, each said they had the basis of a claim which they had not asserted – but they reserved the right to do so in the future. Countries coming in later, such as China, which joined in 1983, are subject to an article in the treaty that says activities conducted in Antarctica cannot constitute the basis of a claim.

There are now more than thirty nations operating across the claims, as well as in an unclaimed segment. The largest territory, Australia's, which accounts for 42 per cent of the continent, is the site of the three main permanent Australian stations – Mawson, Casey and Davis – plus year-round stations of the United States (one), Russia (three), China (one), France and Italy (one shared) and India (one), as well as seasonal stations, including for Belarus and Poland. Australian laws apply in this territory but only to Australian nationals.

'Australia's Antarctica estate, including the land claim and the 200-mile nautical zone [a product of having the land claim], is about 8 million square kilometres,' says Dr Julia Jabour from the Institute for Marine and Antarctic Studies at the University of Tasmania. 'They are not going to give it up – because in the future, some time, they may want to inhabit it or to exclude others who use resources there. Each claimant would have a similar reason for wanting to maintain their claim.'

In not recognising any claims, the United States and Russia's position, she says, would be that 'they want to claim the lot – maybe or maybe not – at some point in the future.'

The 5,896,500km² of Australian Antarctic Territory claimed in 1933.

Graphic: Matthew Absalom-Wong

How do nations actually operate in Antarctica then?

The Antarctic Treaty not only headed off conflict over territorial claims but 'poured cold water on any militarisation that might have occurred,' says former Australian Antarctic Division head Dr Tony Press. 'Its simplicity is one of its strengths,' says Press, an adjunct professor in the Institute for Marine and Antarctic Studies at the University of Tasmania. 'It sets aside the whole of the area below 60 degrees south as a place of peace and cooperation.'

As well as prohibiting 'nuclear explosions', the treaty says scientific personnel and their discoveries should be shared among nations in Antarctica. That spirit of cooperation has largely endured, says Press, who describes the atmosphere down south as 'very international, very open, very warm. Most countries, particularly in a wide, open area like East Antarctica, actually rely on the logistics of others.'

Engineers, mechanics, chefs, meteorologists, doctors and others live at the stations, which all have 'research laboratories, medical facilities, powerhouses, stores and workshops,' says the current Antarctic Division director, Kim Ellis. There were seventy people living on Australia's bases during winter 2020 (nineteen more at a station on subantarctic Macquarie Island), he says, with the usual intake of more than 500 summer expeditioners due to be scaled back, along with science projects, because of the coronavirus pandemic.

The treatment of other occupants of the area, from corpulent seals to minuscule krill, and the ice and waters themselves are dealt with in other agreements, including the Madrid Protocol. The sum total of these and the treaty are called the Antarctic Treaty System.

So, no military activity?

'It is a demilitarised area,' says Press, 'in so far as military manoeuvres are banned, military conflict is banned, the testing of weapons is banned,' as are military bases and fortifications and any 'measures of a military nature.' What is not banned is the use of military personnel or equipment 'for scientific research or for any other peaceful purposes.'

This has become complicated since 1959. 'Satellite technology is now central to Antarctic operations and research,' notes Anthony Bergin, a senior fellow at the Australian Strategic Policy Institute, in a report commissioned by the Australian and French governments. 'The inland environment of Antarctica is optically very clear and ideally suited for astronomic and space research. It is also remarkably quiet, with little human radio interference. With technological developments in information processing, nanotechnologies and astrophysics, research is now possible in Antarctica that was inconceivable in past years. Much of that research also has military applications.'

How does anyone know what goes on behind closed doors? Under the treaty, each of the twenty-nine consultative members – those whose presence in Antarctica has qualified them to be involved in active decision-making – have an unfettered right to inspect one another's facilities, which now amount to more than seventy (about half are seasonal). 'Now, whether that's been done well enough, often enough and comprehensively enough – that's a question many could ask,' says Press. 'Inspections are expensive, logistically difficult – those sort of things play into why every facility in Antarctica isn't inspected every two years.'

Australia has carried out ten inspections since 1963, its most recent, in January and February 2020, being its most extensive to date with a team led by Ellis flying 10,000 kilometres to six stations. 'We were the first team to inspect four of the stations,' he says, '[South Korea's] Jang Bogo, [China's] Inexpressible Island, [China's] Taishan and [Belarus's] Mountain Evening – these are all relatively new. [Russia's] Molodezhnaya has not been inspected on the ground since 1983.'

Ellis says in addition to 'confirming peaceful use', the team – which also looked at Germany's Gondwana Station – made environmental checks. 'Our activity was well researched and planned so we didn't encounter any surprises,' he says. The team was impressed by some 'innovative' station designs, 'renewable energy installations, ambitious scientific and operational achievements in difficult environments, clean-up of past wastes and adaptive re-use of older buildings – and the commitment to high environmental standards.'

Nations must also report what equipment and personnel they are using in Antarctica. 'Most countries do report,' says Press, 'but how good that reporting is, how transparent and comprehensive, is something that's up for discussion.'

But what do nations want in Antarctica?

That Antarctica is cold and windy and hard to get to and around may well be, at least partly, why membership of the polar club is such an aspirational goal – being there has long been seen as an achievement. In a rare criticism of the treaty system in the 1980s, Malaysian leader Mahathir Mohamad argued on behalf of the G77 coalition of developing nations that instead of the continent being run by a 'select group' of states, all territorial claims should be surrendered and the United Nations given control under a new treaty.

'Mahathir accused the treaty of being an old boys' club and being secretive – and he was absolutely right,' says Jabour. She says Malaysia was subsequently invited to treaty meetings and its scientists were sponsored by Australia, New Zealand and the United States on expeditions. Malaysia finally joined the treaty in 2011. Other relatively recent joiners include Kazakhstan, Pakistan, Portugal and Iceland, who are non-consultative members like Malaysia – they go to meetings but are not formally involved in making decisions.

Among the consultative members, who do make decisions, building stations is another fillip for a nation's polar profile. The effect of China's fifth station, at Inexpressible Island, may be to strengthen the nation's position in Antarctica for the future, says Jabour, but 'whenever China builds another base it's reported as "staking a claim" in Antarctica and, legally, that's simply not the case.' Under the treaty, any activities that a nation undertakes in Antarctica won't change an existing claim to sovereignty – nor will it create one.

What else is coveted in Antarctica?

Mining may be big in the Arctic but in Antarctica it has been banned indefinitely since the Madrid Protocol came into effect in 1998, designating the continent a 'natural reserve, devoted to peace and science'. The protocol, which is part of the treaty system, also covers issues such as waste management, marine pollution and the conservation of fauna and flora. Still, the presence of minerals may be a scintillating prospect for some nations, especially as melting ice leaves more land exposed. ('If you want to find out what minerals there are in Antarctica, just look at Australia,' says Press, who points out that the two continents were once joined.) Bergin describes the ban as 'a long-term investment that will require assertive diplomacy to maintain.'

More of a current going concern is bioprospecting – leveraging the often-remarkable qualities of specially adapted Antarctic species and microorganisms to make drugs. Once a microorganism is found, synthetic versions can be produced in laboratories. In the 1960s, antifreeze proteins, for example, were discovered in a family of fish called notothenioids, which thrive in sub-zero waters.

Tourism had been steadily on the rise, too, with visitors from the United States, China, Australia and beyond attracted by the majestic scenery, exotic creatures and frontier frisson. Most of the 56,000 or so visitors a year had arrived on ships, according to the International Association of Antarctica Tour Operators. China, which sub-charters tourist vessels, had placed orders for its own tourist expedition ships, says Bergin. Tourism was put on hold, of course, when the coronavirus pandemic took hold – although not before port closures left some returning vessels stranded.

Fish are a perennial lure – and catching them has the potential to be a source of tension in Antarctica as it is in so many waters around the world. 'Antarctic krill is a resource that will most likely become the centre of increased exploitation well before any push to overturn the prohibition on mining,' says Bergin. Whales, seals, penguins, seabirds and fish all rely on the tiny krill for food – but krill are also sought after by fleets from Norway as well as South Korea, China and a handful of other countries. China is among nations boosting its ability to haul in the omega-3-rich crustaceans, with one firm having launched what it says is the world's biggest purpose-built krill-fishing vessel, with state-of-the-art freezing technology.

Marine life, from fin fish to molluscs, has been protected under the Convention on the Conservation of Antarctic Marine Living Resources (CCAMLR) since 1982, which is part of the treaty system. The convention doesn't rule out fishing but says it must be done sustainably. Krill catch limits are regulated under the convention, and so is the creation of 'marine protected areas' – China and Russia have consistently opposed bids to create new ones, blocking moves at meetings that require consensus for proposals to pass.

Future challenges will include keeping tabs on illegal and unregulated fishing, says Bergin. While the illegal targeting of Patagonian toothfish has dropped off, the potential remains for new players to enter the scene. Warming oceans may also cause some types of fish to migrate further south, attracting vessels that have run out of fish in their own waters.

What's next?

With the world in huge flux, 'one of the fears of the existing consultative parties is that the new kids on the block will come

'The biggest physical threat facing Antarctica is, of course, climate change.'

in with completely different norms, completely different ideas about the intent and the value of the treaty ... and that will shake up everything,' says Jabour. Press cites Beijing and Moscow's objections to the proposals for marine-protected areas as a case in point. If what he characterises as the current 'stalling' over these plans becomes entrenched, 'that poses a problem for the overwhelming majority of Antarctic Treaty partners because it means one or two thwart the good intentions of the collective.'

The biggest physical threat facing Antarctica is, of course, climate change, something the architects of the Antarctic Treaty could not have foreseen. And its melting ice affects sea levels all over the globe. 'At the moment, we are learning every day more and more about the impacts,' says Jabour. 'We've identified the sea temperature rise and air temperature rise, ocean acidification, the reduction of sea ice and land ice. That science is really valuable and it legitimises scientists being in Antarctica.'

Bergin, meanwhile, warns of the dangers of complacency and benign neglect. 'States participating in the Antarctic Treaty System are operating under global conditions of uncertainty,' he says. 'That puts a premium on establishing systems that can adapt to changing circumstances ... in an area of the world that is of critical importance to understanding the wider global environmental system.'

20

HOW MUCH DOES IT COST TO HAVE CANCER?

Out-of-pocket costs are brutal sucker punches for cancer patients. Where do the costs come from? And which cancers cost more to treat than others?

Kate Aubusson

An estimated 145,000 Australians will have been diagnosed with new cancers in 2020. Grappling with the physical and emotional anguish of their diagnosis, each of them will have to navigate a complex tangle of public and private providers across sectors. They will be propelled along a nebulous trajectory of appointments, tests and treatments – from diagnostic scans, specialist consultations, drugs, radiation therapy and surgery to rehabilitation. At some stage, they will be asked to pay out-of-pocket costs.

Australian cancer patients pay a relatively small proportion of the total costs of their care, although more than patients in the United Kingdom and Canada, where out-of-pocket costs are minimal under almost fully funded systems. But out-of-pocket costs here can still range from a few hundred to tens of thousands of dollars. The 'bill shock' of these hidden payments can be eye-watering for some patients, financially crippling for others, particularly when the primary income earner is off work getting cancer treatment or caring for their loved one. In many ways, the heftier end of out-of-pocket costs are a brutal sucker punch for patients already reeling.

So what are these costs? How are they decided? And what can you do about them?

What are out-of-pocket costs?

Out-of-pocket costs are all the additional payments that patients and families fork out for all the healthcare services inside and outside of hospitals that are not covered by Medicare or private health insurance. You might need to pay in full, or pay the gap for services that attract Medicare or private health insurance rebates. On average, Medicare covers 63 per cent of the total costs of cancer care, ranging from 51 per cent for prostate cancer to 89 per cent for lung cancer patients, a 2018 analysis found. Then there's the private health insurance excess.

How much patients pay varies dramatically, even between people with the same cancer diagnosis. Half of Australians with cancer have out-of-pocket costs in excess of $5000, a 2018 report from the Consumers Health Forum of Australia found. More than one in four cancer patients paid more than $10,000 out of their own pockets over two years, and one in three paid between $2000 to $4999. We don't have a complete picture of how much each individual pays – what we do know is that out-of-pocket costs can affect anyone.

Breast and prostate cancer are known to attract exorbitant out-of-pocket costs for some patients. A federal ministerial advisory committee's report into out-of-pocket costs found that patients were charged up to $5000 for breast cancer surgery, $3000 for pathology and $5000 for radiation treatment, all out of pocket.

A 2018 Queensland study of more than 452 patients with one of the five most common cancers (melanoma, breast, prostate, lung and colorectal) found the median out-of-pocket costs were highest for breast cancer patients, who paid anything from $1165 to $7459, and prostate cancer patients, who paid from $971 to $8431. A separate study found the average out-of-pocket expenditure for prostate cancer patients was $9205 – with some patients paying in excess of $17,000.

Meanwhile, people with rare or less common cancers can be hit with crushing costs as they bounce between specialists, collecting tests and scans in search of a definitive diagnosis and racking up bills at every juncture. Their treatments are less likely to be covered by the pharmaceutical benefits scheme (PBS) than medicines for more common cancers, and crowd-funding sites are populated by pleas from desperate families trying to raise the cash needed for unsubsidised or experimental treatments, which can cost hundreds of thousands of dollars.

What, exactly, determines a patient's out-of-pocket costs?

Let us count the ways. Surgeons, oncologists and anaesthetists set their own fees, and often charge what the market can bear. The Queensland study found that a quarter of cancer patients paid upfront doctors' fees of more than $20,000 over two years. One notorious example involves surgeons' fees for robotic prostatectomy to treat prostate cancer. Some surgeons are known to charge patients up to $30,000 to perform the procedure, while other patients pay no gap for the same surgery in a public facility. Current evidence-based research shows robotic surgery is no better than traditional prostatectomy performed by a skilled surgeon.

In some cases, patients might agree to pay a known gap for surgery only to get a shock when they later learn that the price didn't cover their anaesthetists' and surgical assistants' fees. It's up to the patient to 'shop around' for better prices – but when the spectre of cancer hangs over your head, and the cost of a consultation is in the hundreds of dollars, shopping around can be a big ask. There is also an imbalance of power between a patient and the specialist sitting across the desk. If a specialist charging high fees has a reputation for being 'the best' or explicitly claims to have superior skills to their colleagues that would offer a better chance of survival, what is a patient to do?

In December 2019, the federal government launched a specialist fees transparency website in response to growing public concerns over 'bill shock' and to crack down on doctors charging egregious out-of-pocket sums. The Medical Costs Finder site enables people to look up the typical out-of-pocket costs incurred by private patients in their local area for sixty-two common in-hospital procedures and treatments for cancer and other conditions. But the database does not include health-fund rebate information nor the Medicare gap payment information. And it doesn't tell us which specialist charges what fees. Health Minister Greg Hunt says it soon will but it will be an opt-in system and will not compel specialists to publish their fees.

Of course, treatments also determine costs. Almost one in five cancer patients reported out-of-pocket costs for medication. The excess cost a patient is charged largely depends on whether their treatment is subsidised by the Medicare Benefits Schedule (MBS), PBS or private health policies. Intravenous chemotherapy is free in public hospitals but patients prescribed oral chemotherapy need to shoulder some of the cost, especially from community pharmacies.

Chemo patients, in public as well as private systems, also have to pay for any medication they need to relieve the side effects of their treatments, such as anti-nausea drugs – just one example of where Australia's public health system doesn't equal free care.

Radiotherapy is generally free in public facilities. The problem is that roughly 50 per cent of public radiotherapy is now provided by the private sector, which increases the chances of patients incurring out-of-pocket fees. Radiotherapy is commonly provided as an out-patient service and, as private health insurers aren't able to cover out-patient services, this is at the expense of the patient.

Then there are new therapies for cancer, which are rapidly emerging and can be prohibitively expensive. They can cost patients tens of thousands – even hundreds of thousands – of dollars a month if they are not covered on the PBS. For instance, the immunotherapy drug Keytruda is subsidised for people with advanced lung cancer, Hodgkin's lymphoma, non-small cell lung cancer, early-stage acute lymphoblastic leukaemia and inoperable stage III or stage IV malignant melanoma. For patients who don't meet these PBS criteria, Keytruda can cost between $4500 and $11,000 per script – or over $150,000 a year. The drug is approved by the Therapeutic Goods Administration to treat squamous cell carcinomas in the head and neck, for example, but it is not subsidised on the PBS, meaning patients would pay full price. But other immunotherapies are PBS-listed for this type of cancer.

Cancer patients might get free access to these types of promising and experimental treatments on clinical trials but their numbers are limited and access is often confined to large metropolitan centres. Those who can afford it travel overseas to access astronomically expensive treatments with no guarantees they will work. In some cases, expensive cancer drugs are available through compassionate access schemes offered by drug manufacturers, but these schemes aren't transparent.

Meanwhile, more than a quarter of cancer patients report paying out-of-pocket for diagnostic imaging. Many public facilities have privatised their radiology and pathology services; and patients access these services closer to home, which often incurs costs. This isn't always clear to patients who may believe they are being treated as a public patient. More than 300,000 Australians skip radiology each year because of cost, according to the Australian Bureau of Statistics. If a diagnostic imaging service isn't covered on the MBS, patients can pay up to $1000 for a single scan.

Before the federal government introduced new Medicare items for breast cancer imaging scans, women would pay $1500 for MRI and $1000 for PET scans. Patients with rarer cancers still report paying in excess of $3000 for imaging scans just to establish a diagnosis.

What difference does private health insurance make?

People with private health insurance have reported double the out-of-pocket costs of cancer than those without insurance, regardless of the time since diagnosis. This might be due to higher gap payments, or paying for treatments that would have been free or subsidised if accessed under the public system.

The average out-of-pocket costs reported by privately insured women with breast cancer was double that of uninsured women ($7000 compared to $3600), according to the Breast Cancer Network Australia's financial impact report. One quarter of privately insured women reported out-of-pocket costs greater than $2000. Prostate cancer patients with private health insurance reported double the out-of-pocket costs (an average $10,052) of patients without private health insurance ($5103 on average), regardless of time since diagnosis. Out-of-pocket costs are also significantly higher for melanoma patients who choose to use their private health insurance.

Many patients often have their first consultation in a specialist's private rooms, setting them on a private patient 'pathway' and incurring higher expenses for treatments with higher gap payments over the course of their care, which can be many months or years. They often don't realise – or aren't told – that they are not locked into private treatment and could choose to be treated as a public patient. It can also be hard for patients to talk about any impact out-of-pocket costs may be having on their ability to pay for treatment or everyday living expenses.

To confuse matters, private health insurance benefits for the same service are paid at different amounts depending on which insurer you're with, where the service is done, and what the arrangement is between the doctor or hospital and the private health insurer.

What else factors in?

Distance matters. Cancer patients living outside the major cities have seventeen times the odds of reporting geographical or financial barriers to care. It's often about supply and demand, with some specialists charging what the market can handle. For instance, if their private rooms are located in affluent areas, or they face little competition, they could charge much more than the national average.

The further away you live from your treating hospital, the higher the out-of-pocket costs. A study of regional cancer patients found travel expenses accounted for the biggest share of out-of-pocket costs (71 per cent) followed by medical appointments

(10 per cent) and co-payments for medications (9 per cent). Cancer patients in regional areas paid an average $2263 in out-of-pocket costs over six months, another Queensland study found.

'Distance matters.
Cancer patients living outside the major cities
have seventeen times the odds of reporting
geographical or financial barriers to care.'

A litany of other costs is easily overlooked but add up, from parking fees at hospitals and clinics, which can be up to $70 per day; to wound dressings and over-the-counter medication; to organising childcare while undergoing treatment.

What can you do?

The best defence against exorbitant out-of-pocket fees and bill shock is understanding the system and making sure you can give informed financial consent. Know that you can shop around. You are not 'locked into' a financial relationship with a specialist or service simply because your GP referred you to them.

Ask for an itemised estimate of the costs and who else will be involved in your care. Once you've been given a fee estimate, there's no harm in asking if they can offer you a better price. Specialists will often adjust their fees for patients who would struggle to cover the cost.

Here are some questions to ask specialists:

- Do I need this treatment? What are the risks if I do not have this treatment?
- What are your fees? Is this an estimate?
- Are there any other costs, or fees for medications or other doctors (for example, anaesthetists or assistant surgeons)?
- Will I have any out-of-pocket costs?
- What are the MBS item numbers for the services you are going to perform? (You can look up the MBS schedule fee for these later.)
- Do you have a no-gap or known-gap arrangement with my health fund?
- If the cost changes, when will you let me know?
- How will you bill me?
- When will I need to pay?
- Can I get this in writing?

Here are some questions to ask your health fund:

- Am I covered for this treatment and MBS item?
- How much will my policy cover?
- How much am I likely to have to pay myself (including excess)?
- Can you confirm this in writing (if there is time)?
- Does my insurer have a no-gap or known-gap arrangement with my doctor and hospital?

21

HOW DOES SPYING WORK IN AUSTRALIA TODAY?

Spies do not always know how their work fits in the big picture. But we can tell you this: our government is on a mission to shake up our intelligence community, and the changes are not over yet.

Anthony Galloway

Theresa May was less than two months into the British prime ministership when she met her Australian counterpart in September 2016, on the sidelines of the G20 summit in China. The encounter with her old friend from Oxford, Malcolm Turnbull, in the city of Hangzhou, would lead to one of the biggest shake-ups of Australia's security and intelligence agencies in history. While Brexit dominated the discussion, Turnbull wanted to raise another matter with May: whether to create a 'super department' modelled on the United Kingdom's Home Office.

While the idea had been floated before, including by Scott Morrison when he was immigration minister after the 2013 election, there was a growing push within senior ranks of the government to make Immigration, Border Force, the Australian Security Intelligence Organisation (ASIO) and the Australian Federal Police (AFP) work together more closely under one portfolio. Under the plan, Australia's domestic security agencies would maintain their statutory independence but answer to one minister.

With Australia facing escalating threats of foreign interference, cyber attacks and serious and organised crime, along with the persistent threats of terrorism and violent extremism – all against the backdrop of a rising China – it was thought a more unified policy approach was needed. There was also growing anxiety about Chinese corporations gaining a foothold in Australia's critical infrastructure, including power and telecommunications.

How did the government unify our approach to national security? Who do our intelligence operatives now work for? And what makes a good spy today?

How is a security mega-portfolio created?

In Hangzhou, May, who had just served as home secretary for six years, told Turnbull that reorganising domestic security under one umbrella was an idea worth pursuing. May made officials from the Home Office available to Turnbull's department to talk them through how the British mega-portfolio operated.

In early 2017, Martin Parkinson, who was at the time secretary of the Department of Prime Minister and Cabinet, gave Turnbull a concept paper setting out how a proposed Department of Home Affairs should operate. Work on the super portfolio had been tightly guarded within Turnbull's own department, but Parkinson said it was time to start consulting other agencies.

The then immigration minister Peter Dutton was naturally supportive of the idea – he would likely be in charge of the new portfolio. Other Cabinet ministers, particularly Attorney-General George Brandis, told Turnbull he was apprehensive about giving Dutton more power.

It was soon decided that the person to be given the mammoth task of putting it all together should be Michael Pezzullo, the then secretary of the Department of Immigration and Border Protection, who had been pitching the concept of a home affairs department for more than a decade. Pezullo, a tough-minded former Defence bureaucrat known within senior ranks of the government for 'getting things done', would be appointed secretary of the new department.

There was another important decision that needed to be made, and it would forever change the makeup of Australian spies. While the Turnbull government was putting the finishing touches on the structure of its super department, ex-Department of Foreign Affairs and Trade (DFAT) secretary Michael L'Estrange and former senior intelligence officer Stephen Merchant were nearing completion of their review into Australia's intelligence services. The review recommended that the Office of National Assessments (ONA) be turned into the Office of National Intelligence (ONI), with an augmented ability to supervise the nation's other spy agencies. The nation's premier foreign cyber intelligence agency, the Australian Signals Directorate (ASD), would also become its own statutory agency, reporting directly to the Defence Minister, giving it more independence – and highlighting the escalating threat of cyber attacks by state-based actors and sophisticated cyber criminals.

On 18 July 2017, Turnbull announced the creation of Home Affairs, giving Dutton control of the new department and revealing that the government was accepting all the recommendations in L'Estrange and Merchant's report. Nick Warner, the then head of ONA, would lead the newly created ONI, essentially becoming Australia's top spy.

Was everyone on board?

Partly because of the personalities involved and partly because the two major changes were revealed on the same day, this announcement has led to a number of misconceptions. Firstly, the creation of Home Affairs immediately sparked accusations that Turnbull was placating Dutton, his eventual challenger for the prime ministership. In fact, Turnbull's own department, as well as Morrison and Pezzullo, had been urging him to explore the model for years.

> *'Spies tell you what the problem is while senior bureaucrats and politicians work on the policy response.'*

Secondly, some insiders argue the creation of Home Affairs has undermined the rationale for the establishment of the ONI as the main coordinating agency for our spies. In truth, Home Affairs is no different to any other department – just a lot bigger. Its coordination role is centred on policy and action; in other words, working out how to best manage a risk or respond to a threat. Intelligence coordination – the role of the ONI – is primarily concerned with discovering things and making sense of them. Spies tell you what the problem is while senior bureaucrats and politicians work on the policy response. So if everyone stays in their lane, there is no contradiction between the two major changes.

Other gripes centre on the sheer size and power of Home Affairs. Some senior officers in the AFP were never happy with moving, along with ASIO, from the Attorney-General's Department. Others say having the Attorney-General as the person who signed off on warrants for the AFP and ASIO, while also being the minister responsible for their day-to-day operations, was never appropriate.

How did the running of spies change?

The ONI, like its predecessor the ONA, is Australia's peak intelligence assessment agency. It draws on information collected by Australian agencies and other countries, as well as unclassified and 'open source' material, to assess potential threats. The key difference between the ONA and the ONI is that the latter now plays a major coordination role for the entire Australian intelligence community. Whereas before, the ONA primarily assessed foreign intelligence, its successor deals with intelligence relating to foreign as well as domestic threats.

Former ONA head Allan Gyngell says the ONI is much better resourced and the 2017 overhaul recognises it is no longer possible to sustain a clear distinction between foreign and domestic intelligence. After all, international terrorists operate both within and outside Australia. Gyngell, national president of the Australian Institute of International Affairs, says the creation of the ONI helped fulfil the vision of Australian intelligence originally put in place by the Hope Royal Commissions in the 1970s and '80s. 'It places the national intelligence assessment and analytical capability – clearly independent from the direction of policymakers – at the centre of the Australian intelligence community, elevates the position of the director-general within the public service and gives him or her the necessary resources to coordinate and evaluate the work of the other intelligence agencies,' Gyngell says.

The ONI is headed by one of Australia's most experienced diplomats and top spies in Warner, the former head of both the Australian Secret Intelligence Service (ASIS) and the Department of Defence. With the creation of the ONI, Warner also became Australia's first director-general of national intelligence. When Warner's term as the ONI boss expires, he is expected to retire. One replacement could be current Cabinet secretary Andrew Shearer, a former deputy director of the ONI, according to senior government sources.

What do modern spies do?

Australian spy agencies require a mix of different talents. The computer whizz who sits in an office in the ASD trying to detect the next cyber attack is a world away from the ASIO agent installing a listening device on the car of a potential terrorist or agent of foreign influence. Some operatives – especially within espionage and counterespionage agencies such as ASIO and ASIS – need to have considerable interpersonal skills to cultivate sources and get the information they need. For spies engaged in signals intelligence – the interception of electronic transmissions – these kinds of skills may be less important.

> 'The computer whizz who sits in an office in the ASD trying to detect the next cyber attack is a world away from the ASIO agent installing a listening device on the car of a potential terrorist or agent of foreign influence.'

ASIO is the nation's domestic spy agency. It counters threats of terrorism, violent extremism, espionage and foreign interference. The agency is headed by Mike Burgess, part of a new breed of national security leaders appointed by the Morrison government. Security chiefs would once have been drawn mostly from the ranks of DFAT or from Defence, but Burgess, who also holds the title of director-general for national security, has spent most of his career working in the cybersecurity space – an area that poses an ever-increasing threat to Australia's national security.

Sometimes spies themselves are not aware of where their jobs fit into the big picture. John Blaxland, one of the principal authors of a three-volume official history of ASIO, says the role of the agency and its spies has changed significantly since its inception in 1949. Blaxland, professor of international security and intelligence studies at the Australian National University, says one of the most gratifying experiences of writing the history was giving former ASIO operatives a broader understanding of what they'd been doing all those years. 'Insiders, by and large, operate according to the "need to know" principle. So you get your own little very narrow laneway of information and responsibility with very strict blinkers on what you are and are not allowed to see and delve into,' Blaxland says. 'They were given certain responsibilities but the broader context was never given to them and in reading the books they were able to put their life experience into [that] broader context, and they said that was very rewarding, very satisfying, because they said it made things make more sense.'

Blaxland, who was given 'unparalleled access' to the secret organisation when investigating its history, says the modus operandi of spies is drastically different today. Technology makes it almost impossible to hide identities, meaning traditional espionage and statecraft are a lot more difficult.

Cyber attacks, foreign interference and espionage are now front of mind for an agency such as ASIO. 'Twenty years ago, espionage was arguably seen as a quaint little Cold War anachronism, a holdover from the Cold War,' Blaxland says. 'But nowadays, there is a broader recognition that it's actually pretty darn serious and the game is back on. If it was ever off, it's certainly not off now – it's well and truly life and death stuff.'

What is the Australian Secret Intelligence Service?

ASIS, which sits within DFAT, is Australia's principal overseas intelligence collection agency – it's the equivalent of MI6 in Britain, made famous by James Bond. Sometimes referred to within the government as 'the other DFAT', the agency's mission statement is 'to protect and promote Australia's vital interests through the provision of unique foreign intelligence services as directed by the Australian Government'.

ASIS agents are embedded in Australian embassies around the world – in some cases they are registered with the host nation and in other cases they are under deep cover – to report intelligence to Canberra. It's one of the most secretive organisations – it was formed in 1952 but its existence remained hidden until 1972 – and the work of its agents rarely sees the light of day.

ASIS officers were involved in the bugging of Timor-Leste's Cabinet building to listen in to discussions about the nation's claim to oil in the Timor Sea, the revealing of which has led to the prosecution of former senior ASIS intelligence officer Witness K and lawyer Bernard Collaery.

Are there spies in the military?

The Department of Defence includes a number of military intelligence units with a mix of uniformed officers from the navy, air force and army, as well as civilian intelligence officers.

There are three main Defence intelligence agencies. The Defence Intelligence Organisation (DIO) is the principal intelligence assessment agency for Defence. The Australian

Geospatial Intelligence Organisation (AGO) is responsible for the collection of satellite and aerial imagery as well other geospatial intelligence. The Australian Signals Directorate (ASD) is responsible for cybersecurity and the collection of foreign signals intelligence while it assists security agencies in preventing and disrupting offshore cyber-enabled crime – its mission statement is 'Reveal Their Secrets – Protect Our Own'.

As insiders put it, the ASD is both a defensive and offensive agency: it protects against cyber attacks, but it also eavesdrops on electronic transmissions abroad and disrupts the activities of would-be hackers. ASIO and the AFP require a warrant to enlist the ASD for technical help to pinpoint servers on domestic soil. The ASD was subject to some controversy after reports that the government was considering a proposal to give the agency the power to track down online paedophiles, terrorists and other serious criminals within Australia. In June 2019, the AFP raided the house of senior News Corp journalist Annika Smethurst after she wrote an exposé of the proposal.

While ASIO still sits within the Defence portfolio, it became a statutory agency in 2018. The nation's cyber resilience agency, the Australian Cyber Security Centre (ACSC), which supports government agencies and businesses, also sits within Defence. The ACSC has a significant policy function in advising the government, and Dutton is the minister responsible for cybersecurity, so there is a need to work with Home Affairs on a regular basis. In the coming years, there may be a growing rationale to move some of the signals directorate's functions, including the ACSC, into Home Affairs.

Who are the new kids on the block?

The 2017 intelligence review recommended the expansion of the Australian intelligence community from six to ten agencies. This resulted in the addition of the AFP, the Department of Home Affairs, the Australian Criminal Intelligence Commission (ACIC) and the

Australian Transaction Reports and Analysis Centre (AUSTRAC) into what is now known as the 'national intelligence community'. The change in technology, crime and other threats have meant these organisations have steadily grown their intelligence functions.

The new entrants joined the ONI, ASIO, ASD, AGO, DIU and ASIS – see breakout box – as the original members of the intelligence community. There are about 7000 staff spread across the ten agencies with an annual budget of about $2 billion.

Who watches the watchers?

There's another agency charged with keeping tabs on spies – and yet another acronym to go with it. The Inspector-General of Intelligence and Security (IGIS) has the enduring powers of a royal commission. Established in 1987 in the wake of the Hope Royal Commissions, the IGIS has the power to require the attendance of witnesses, take sworn evidence and enter the premises of intelligence agencies.

Blaxland says the oversight of spy agencies today is a 'different world' from the past. The former Defence intelligence officer devoted his biggest criticisms of ASIO in the organisation's official history to 'the Protest Years', from 1963 to 1975, when he says the agency spent too much of its time monitoring private citizens whose views and actions were better described as dissent rather than subversion. Blaxland says the IGIS's powers are now a 'sobering restraint on the abuse of power' and forces intelligence agencies to behave. 'On any day, a member of [the IGIS] team can come into their office and demand to see the files they're working on, the emails they've been sending and the correspondence they've been having,' Blaxland says. 'The critics of the Cold War days, particularly the sixties and early seventies, who haven't kind of moved on, they tend to overlook the reforms that have been instigated since then and they see the world through the prism of 1968 and 1969 when ASIO was chasing the Communist Party of

Australia and perhaps missing the wood for the trees. It is a long way from where it was in the dark old days – a very different beast.'

Apart from IGIS, there is also the Independent National Security Legislation Monitor (INSLM), the Parliamentary Joint Committee on Security and Intelligence (PJCIS) and the security division of the Administrative Appeals Tribunal (AAT), which all have key oversight roles.

Blaxland says the expansion of the national security community into ten agencies means the two main oversight bodies – IGIS and INSLM – need to be better resourced.

Where to now for Australian spies?

Since two of the biggest shake-ups of Australia's intelligence and security agencies were unveiled on the same day in 2017, the changes have all been bedded down. While it is not difficult to find disaffected people within some agencies under the Home Affairs portfolio, the complaints tend to lack a specific gripe. The changes put in place are no doubt here to stay. But in the world of Australian spies, there are always new developments around the corner.

Justice Robert Hope delivered two landmark royal commissions into Australia's national security and intelligence services, in 1974–77 and 1984. These led to major changes, including the establishment of the ONA, greater accountability for ASIO, the establishment of a parliamentary watchdog and the IGIS.

Meanwhile, former ASIO boss Dennis Richardson's review of national security laws could lead to their biggest overhaul in four decades.

Know your acronyms:
a bluffer's guide to national intelligence

AAT (security division): Part of the Administrative Appeals Tribunal, the tribunal reviews administrative decisions by the government and its agencies that relate to national security.

ACIC: The Australian Criminal Intelligence Commission is the conduit for sharing criminal information and intelligence among state, territory and Commonwealth law enforcement agencies.

ACSC: The nation's cyber resilience agency, the Australian Cyber Security Centre, supports government agencies and businesses – it's part of the ASD (see below).

AFP: Australia's Federal Police force, which has steadily grown its intelligence functions in recent years, works closely with ASIO when the intelligence agency has found evidence of criminal wrongdoing.

AGO: It's amazing what you can see from space these days, but how to make sense of it? The Australian Geospatial Intelligence Organisation collects and interprets satellite and aerial imagery and other location, or geospatial, data.

ASD: 'Reveal Their Secrets – Protect Our Own' is the motto of the Australian Signals Directorate, which handles cybersecurity and the collection of foreign signals intelligence while helping other agencies tackle offshore cyber-enabled crime.

ASIO: The Australian Security Intelligence Organisation is the domestic spy agency, countering threats of terrorism, violent extremism, espionage and foreign interference.

ASIS: Australia's answer to MI6, the Australian Secret Intelligence Service is the main overseas intelligence collection agency, part of the Department of Foreign Affairs and Trade (DFAT) – and it's top secret.

AUSTRAC: The Australian Transaction Reports and Analysis Centre combs through financial reports to collect financial intelligence that might expose serious and organised crime.

Department of Home Affairs: This mega-department housing ASIO, the AFP, AUSTRAC, ACIC and Australian Border Force helps coordinate a policy approach to domestic security threats.

DFAT: The Department of Foreign Affairs and Trade is responsible for Australia's diplomatic network around the world. ASIS is part of DFAT.

DIO: The Defence Intelligence Organisation is the principal intelligence assessment agency within the Department of Defence.

IGIS: The Inspector-General of Intelligence and Security keeps an eye on the spies, deploying the powers of a royal commission to ensure that intelligence agencies are behaving.

INSLM: The Independent National Security Legislation Monitor is actually one person in a part-time role who reviews national security and counterterrorism laws and checks that they uphold the rights of individuals.

ONA: The Office of National Assessments is the superseded version of the ONI (see below).

ONI: The Office of National Intelligence orchestrates all the agencies, as well as being the peak assessment body.

PJCIS: Made up of federal politicians from both major parties, the Parliamentary Joint Committee on Security and Intelligence reviews the running and expenditure of security agencies and the performance of the AFP, as well as any new national security laws that go before parliament to ensure they are needed, will work and are not an overreach of power.

22

WHAT CAN WE LEARN FROM THE KILLER PLAGUES OF HISTORY?

The diseases have changed over the centuries but the human responses have been similar. What happened during past pandemics? And are we getting better at handling them?

Sherryn Groch

They must have felt like nightmares, those plagues of the past. When sickness came, it seemed to come from nowhere, carving off huge swathes of the population as if at random. Was it divine intervention, an internal imbalance, ill-humoured vapours rising from the Earth?

By the late nineteenth century, scientists had found and named the culprit. Invisible though they are to the naked eye, microbes have killed more people throughout history than war. They are the tiny invaders (germs such as viruses and bacteria) that unleash disease. They've led us to riot and murder but also to art and innovation. Much of modern medicine, from vaccinations to germ theory itself, took root in the panic of a pandemic. In cities such as Venice, where the quarantine measures we now know so well were born under the medieval waves of the Black Death, plague paintings still soar overhead in churches built by its survivors.

Some illnesses, such as influenza, malaria and HIV, now linger in our lives; others, notably smallpox, have been beaten into extinction or somewhere near it. This time, the disease on the loose is less deadly than the first dangerous coronavirus to emerge in the modern era, SARS, but it's also more infectious. While SARS made it into less than thirty countries before it was stamped out (over nine anxious months) in 2003, it took COVID-19 less than twelve weeks to morph into the first major pandemic to hit the world since Spanish flu a century ago.

What can we learn from the outbreaks of the past? How did they end? And is humanity really getting better at handling infectious disease?

When did pandemics start happening?
Disease has always stalked humanity, but pandemics – the significant worldwide spread of a pathogen – are a modern phenomenon, says Professor Frank Ruhli, who heads the Institute of Evolutionary Medicine at the University of Zurich in Switzerland.

He'd know – a lot of his work days are spent poring over ancient mummies to crack the cold cases of diseases past. The molecular proof of a germ tends to break down fast in fossils, Ruhli says, but, even in prehistory, there were outbreaks. The difference was that because we lived spread out in small groups of hunter-gatherers, the new pathogen of the day tended to fade just as quickly as it emerged, having run out of people to infect. Then, as the world opened up to large-scale trade and travel roughly 6000 years ago, Ruhli says, viruses suddenly had an easier way to cross borders, countries, even continents. 'Now, today, a virus can get on a plane and go global within twenty-four hours.'

Sir Richard Evans, provost of Gresham College in London, is a leading authority on the great plagues of our past. He says you don't need a magic number of people before a pandemic can take hold; rather, you need a way for a disease to reach unfamiliar populations, perhaps marched in by an invading army, hitching a ride on a railway or docking with a ship from another land. 'In 1492, Christopher Columbus took smallpox to the Americas and returned to Europe with syphilis,' Evans says. Columbus, it turned out, came off better – the pox had long ravaged European populations but left survivors immune, giving them an advantage over the Indigenous peoples of the Americas and even Australia, where 'the speckled monster' wrought a devastating toll.

> *'You don't need a magic number of people*
> *before a pandemic can take hold;*
> *rather, you need a way for a disease to*
> *reach unfamiliar populations.'*

Even today, well-established diseases can 'break out' again when long-isolated communities in remote corners of the world at last collide with modern civilisation. During the 1950s and '60s, a group of Yanomami people living in Brazil were nearly decimated by measles after making contact with the outside world; COVID-19 has reached them too.

Much about how a pandemic unfolds is up to the germ. Does it jump from person to person only after close contact, travel through the air or thrive in contaminated food or water? But the lifestyles and responses of those afflicted – even the accidental kind – play a role, too.

One of the world's earliest plagues, likely of typhoid, bred in the cramped, squalid conditions of a city under siege as Sparta attacked Athens around 430 BC. Seeing the smoke from funeral pyres rising over the walls, those invading troops very smartly went home (possibly to self-isolate). While the contagion did return again, and again, it did not spread far beyond Greece.

Then, in the fifth century, the Roman Emperor Justinian's conquest of the Mediterranean brought a tiny bacteria all the way out of Egypt and into the heart of Europe, igniting what is often considered the world's earliest pandemic, the first wave of the bubonic plague. Its toll was so devastating some even credit it with bringing down the Roman Empire. Having wound its way out of Asia along the Silk Road, it would return for at least two more pandemic hits, including the Black Death that wiped out more than a third of Europe's population over just four years in the fourteenth century.

Overall, the bubonic plague remains history's biggest killer – between 75 million and 200 million people were felled by it before the twentieth century – and even today it rears its head from time to time. But we know its secret now: the disease is spread by bacteria that live on the backs of rats, and we have both antibiotics and a vaccine (of limited availability) to treat it.

How have societies reacted to past pandemics?

Down the pandemic records, much of humanity's responses have been guided by instinct if not science, Ruhli says, a memory gene deep. Just as our body tells us to run when we see a tiger stalking through the jungle, we also know to keep away from the sick as much as we can. In some parts of medieval Europe, whole cities were built around the idea of isolation.

'It was recognised by the Renaissance period that diseases did travel,' Evans says. To stop it, ships arriving in Venice during a wave of plague in the fifteenth century were forced to sit at anchor under the first quarantines – a period of forty days or *quaranta giorni* in Italian, hence the word quarantine.

'It's why we've seen people [panic] buying toilet paper, there's a selfish evolutionary imperative to protect yourself,' Ruhli says. 'But humans also live together in groups so there's altruism built in too. In COVID-19, we've [seen] the whole range of behaviour from the idiot who steals masks and hand sanitiser to the healthcare worker risking their life to care for the sick.'

Often pandemics were blamed on outsiders or on poverty, the 'great unwashed'. Bad hygiene, a common concern in slums where people are packed together without access to proper sanitation, does play a role in most infectious disease transmission. Contaminated food and water carried the great cholera outbreaks throughout history, Evans notes. But disease does not discriminate by class or race. Even the pharaohs of ancient Egypt, revered as gods, were not immune. Ruhli has found that the same infectious bugs that struck down commoners took out their kings, too.

Evans notes authorities have never coped particularly well with pandemics, even when authoritarian states already had extensive powers to control people's movement. 'There's always been a tension in government between fear of economic disaster and fear of epidemics,' he says. 'In almost every pandemic, authorities initially refused to report the outbreak, in case it led to panic on the exchange, or the crippling of trade.' In Hamburg in 1892, he says, the refusal of the Senate to report deaths on the waterfront from cholera saw 10,000 people die in just six weeks.

In the early days of COVID-19, China tried to cover up and downplay the outbreak – as it did, to a much greater extent, during the SARS epidemic twenty years earlier. This time, as the new coronavirus exploded, China did something without precedent in our modern era – it locked down more than 10 million people in an effort to starve the virus of new hosts. That move drastically slowed down the outbreak but proved challenging to replicate in democratic societies. Italy hesitated long enough to give the virus a foothold; within weeks, its hospitals were overrun.

Still, even when governments have tried to follow the medical dogma – with case isolation and social restrictions – it hasn't always been well received. Russia sealed off its slums when cholera hit during its second great pandemic of 1829. That slowed the spread but the sick (and sometimes even those who weren't) were largely left to fend for themselves. In 1831, as rumours swirled that the lockdowns were a Tsarist plot to kill off the poor, violent riots broke out, with doctors the main targets.

London authorities also struggled with rioters – grave-robbing scandals involving scientists (and revelations that two serial killers had sold bodies to a local anatomy school) fuelled stories that cholera victims were being taken away to be murdered for experiments. By contrast, in Hamburg, where respected medical scientist Robert Koch helped deliver the message on the need for containment, the streets were quiet. Riots have also broken out alongside more recent outbreaks – such as in 2010 when UN peacekeeping troops brought cholera to Haiti.

How did past pandemics end?

Most diseases, once loose, tend to linger in some form in humans. But there are two main ways a pandemic wave comes to an end, says Nobel prize-winning immunologist Professor Peter Doherty. The old road of early history saw infections burn out once enough people had either died or recovered with natural immunity then encoded into their cells. The other way is intervention – quarantine and, today, medicine.

Back in the Middle Ages, when the plague kept returning, there wasn't a choice. Without a treatment or an inoculation, survivors could avoid the sick only via quarantines and hope they would be spared next time the Black Death came to call. Their DNA helped shape the evolution of the human immune system. COVID-19 is a 'virgin soil' pandemic, Doherty notes, brand new to humanity. So scientists knew 'letting the virus rip' in order to build up a faster 'herd immunity' against it could have been catastrophic, especially given it is much deadlier than flu.

In the case of the other main killer in history, smallpox, the turning point came in 1796. The virus is from the same family as the less severe cowpox and monkeypox and is thought to have first emerged around the time humans began domesticating animals; it was found in the tombs of ancient pharaohs, Ruhli says. Last century, it became the first human disease to be wiped off the face of the Earth. How?

English doctor Edward Jenner had observed that milkmaids with cowpox tended not to be stricken by smallpox. He took fluid from a cowpox lesion and injected it into the arm of a nine-year-old boy before exposing him to various viruses. The boy didn't catch smallpox and so the modern method of engineering immunity against disease began. But it would take almost another 200 years to drive out the pox altogether as some countries held out against mandatory inoculations.

The 1918 Spanish flu – to which 2020's pandemic is routinely compared – killed more people than World War I, which was just drawing to a close when it emerged. Both Doherty and Professor Marc Pellegrini, an infectious diseases clinician at the Walter and Eliza Hall Institute in Melbourne, say parallels to that H1N1 influenza strain are fair, but both hope this new pandemic will prove less deadly now medicine has advanced. 'Still, global travel has really changed how pandemics operate; this isn't going away yet,' Pellegrini says.

The Spanish flu didn't burn out for at least two years, having come not from Spain but likely China, France or even the United States. Perplexingly, the people struck down were often in their prime rather than the very young or old typically hit by influenza. And, as the disease arrived before the age of antibiotics, secondary bacterial infections likely killed more people than the virus itself. Evans notes it was also malnourishment and poor hygiene in overcrowded medical camps that pushed the death toll to an estimated 50 million worldwide.

As with COVID-19, the mutant flu strain was very infectious, jumping from person to person in close quarters, and so society largely shut down to contain it. 'It was really the birthplace of [modern] public health,' Ruhli says. The US city of Philadelphia took a now-notorious fourteen days to react after its first case, even pressing ahead with a big public march to celebrate the war effort. St Louis, meanwhile, cracked down on people's movement and gatherings within just two days of the influenza strain entering its borders. By the end of the crisis, its death toll was less than half of Philadelphia's, even though a second wave of infections hit it a little harder.

Australia held out longer than most of the world under strict land and marine quarantines. But by 1919 the virus had found a way in, including in the lungs of soldiers returning from war, and went on to infect millions. People were often outraged by the new social restrictions – some priests weren't allowed to give the last rites in quarantine zones; forgetting your mask was a fineable offence; and, in some states, pubs could let in only three people at a time for five minutes each.

Are we getting better at handling pandemics?

Three years before COVID-19, US infectious diseases expert Michael Osterholm said there had never been a more daunting time to control an outbreak than the modern era. Why?

While medicine might be more up to the task, the likelihood of a spillover – in which a new virus jumps from animals into humans – is more likely than ever. Humans are in more places than ever before and, as we churn through the last pockets of the wild, clearing forests and poaching wildlife, we collide with more species.

Ruhli muses that because of our ancestry as hunter-gatherers, living from one day to the next, much of our brain is wired to deal with immediate dangers. We're not the type of species to stockpile for a rainy day. 'At least not ordinarily,' he laughs. This helps explain why the world responded so quickly to this crisis, he says, with the extraordinary lockdown measures experts called for, but has struggled to avert the likely more serious but less immediate threat of climate change.

Likewise, others have pointed out that in the face of repeated warnings from scientists that another pandemic was coming – as more SARS-like viruses were discovered in the wild and the wildlife trade boomed – the world did very little to prevent it. 'In certain ways, [as a species] we're still in the Stone Age,' Ruhli says. 'We can't deal with the spread of [disease] like this.'

Doherty says the world was starting to head in the right direction when COVID-19 arrived, having launched a rapid pandemic response vaccine program – the Coalition for Epidemic Preparedness Innovations (CEPI) – in 2017, with coronaviruses even earmarked as a priority. But in hindsight, he says, there should have been a similar accelerator set up for reactive drug therapies, too. Such drugs have helped bring the other pandemic of the modern era, HIV/AIDS, into line, even if it is still with us. Against the HIV virus, which writes itself permanently into a patient's

DNA, vaccines have so far failed. But scientists have developed ever more efficient drugs to stop HIV killing once inside the body.

As Ruhli puts it, 'We are in a constant arms race against pathogens.' A lot of the world's preparation for COVID-19 is based on a more familiar foe: pandemic influenza, which often sees a second wave of infections hit six months after an outbreak. This virus is different – it is the first coronavirus to ever go truly global and is already full of strange contradictions. 'It's less predictable, it's something new,' Pellegrini says. 'And [it's] writing its own history.'

'

We are in a constant arms race against pathogens.

'

23

HOW ARE BUSHFIRES AND CLIMATE CHANGE CONNECTED?

More extreme weather means increasingly severe wild fires in Australia. How has climate change escalated fire risk? What other bizarre phenomena are on the rise?

Peter Hannam with Laura Chung

In the eight months leading up to the summer bushfires of 2019–20, Australia's Bureau of Meteorology gave more than one hundred bushfire-risk presentations – to agencies ranging from emergency services to the electricity grid operator – to warn of looming risks.

The complex drivers of climate in the oceans surrounding Australia thankfully don't often align so punishingly to generate the record-obliterating heatwaves and the deeper drought that contributed to that summer's catastrophic fires. But even though back-to-back record fire seasons are unlikely, the bureau has been taking no chances, readying for another active season for 2020–21, just in case. Its alerts ahead of the 2019–20 season were actually not so novel. Ross Garnaut's Climate Change Review in 2008 presciently predicted that, without adequate action to curb greenhouse gas emissions, Australia would face more frequent and intense fire seasons by 2020. Others made similar warnings even earlier. And yet, curiously, some sections of the media attributed the ferocity of the Queensland-to-Victoria blazes to arson or insufficient prescribed burning – anything, in fact, other than climate change. Some conservative politicians blithely echoed the sentiments.

> 'Human-forced climate change caused
> by rising greenhouse gas levels is already
> increasing the frequency, severity and duration
> of a range of extreme weather phenomena.'

For years, Australian researchers at the bureau, the Commonwealth Scientific and Industrial Research Organisation (CSIRO) and universities have been observing long-term trends linked to global heating that made extreme fire seasons more likely. Partner agencies in Europe, the United States and elsewhere have plotted similarly rising threats in regions from Spain to California. Their common assessment is pretty clear-cut: human-forced climate change caused by rising greenhouse gas levels is already increasing the frequency, severity and duration of a range of extreme weather phenomena, from intensifying cyclones and storms to heatwaves. These more extreme events also happen to include severe bushfire seasons in southern Australia. And should those carbon dioxide, methane and other heat-trapping emissions continue to alter the chemical mix of the atmosphere, those trends will likely worsen.

So how are climate change and bushfires connected? How do changing rainfall patterns factor in? And what do dry lighting and pyrocumulonimbus clouds have to do with them?

How do we measure fire danger?

One standard measure of fire weather in Australia is the McArthur Forest Fire Danger Index. Developed in the 1960s by CSIRO scientist A. G. McArthur, the fire danger index examines the risks to forests from fire, based on four components: temperatures, rainfall or drought conditions, predicted wind speeds and humidity.

In its presentation to the Royal Commission into National Natural Disaster Arrangements in mid-2020, the bureau said there had been 'a long-term increase in dangerous fire weather, and in the length of the fire season, across large parts of Australia related to the changes in temperature and rainfall'. Not only had there been an increase in the frequency and severity of those seasons since 1950, but those changes were projected to worsen, it said. The CSIRO echoed those findings.

'Across the country, at a number of high-quality, long-term weather stations, there had either been an increase, or no change [in the fire danger index],' says Hamish Clarke, a former New South Wales government scientist now with the University of Wollongong. 'We didn't find a significant decrease anywhere.'

The temperature shift is perhaps the most marked sign of increased risk among the fire index components. Take 2019, easily Australia's hottest year with maximum temperatures beating the previous record set six years earlier by half a degree Celsius. Australia has warmed about 1.4 degrees since 1910, roughly tracking the global warming rate. But it is the 'spikiness' of exceptionally hot days that exacerbates fire risks. In 2019, average temperatures across the nation reached the top 1 per cent of historical records on forty-two days – or about one in every nine days. A hot year before 2000 would barely have counted ten such days. But if spikiness elevates the risks, these peaks ride on top of increased threats from overall warming. Since 2001, heat records have exceeded cool records at a three-to-one pace for maximum temperatures, and five-to-one for minimum readings. In a stable climate, hot and cold records would be expected to occur at roughly the same rate, the bureau says.

CSIRO told the royal commission that, during the 2020–39 period, Australia could warm between 0.6 and 1.3 degrees – in addition to the 1.4 degrees warming seen already – compared with the climate of 1986–2005. Should greenhouse gas emissions 'continue to accelerate', the jump could reach as high as 5.1 degrees by the final two decades of the twenty-first century.

How do rainfall – and drought – affect bushfire risk?

Australians can intuit that warming temperatures would contribute to busier fire seasons, but what of drought trends? Rainfall can be more nuanced because it's not just the total rain that matters but what time of the year it falls and its intensity when it does.

Physicists have long known that for every degree of warming, the atmosphere can hold about 7 per cent more moisture. In many parts of the world, heavy downpours are becoming more common but also – perhaps counterintuitively – dry spells are getting longer.

For southern Australia, the unhelpful rainfall trend is happening during cool months. There is less rain between April and September for both the south-west and south-east, areas that happen to host much of the human population, the nation's foodbowl and those famously fire-prone eucalyptus forests. For the south-west, annual cool-season rainfall has dropped about 20 per cent since the 1970s. The region stretching from south-east Queensland, near and west of the Great Dividing Range southwards, has posted a rainfall decline of about 10 per cent since the 1990s, the bureau says.

In combination, the warmer and drier winter days mean vegetation can cure sooner, becoming fire fuel. That's one reason why the bushfire season is getting longer, particularly in the spring. More intense spring heatwaves have added to those risks.

The bureau highlights the New South Wales South Coast and Eastern Victoria as among the areas enduring the starkest changes. These regions are recording 'high' fire danger weather – as measured by the first day of a fire index reading of 25 or above after July 1 – coming about three months earlier than it did in the middle of the twentieth century.

An index reading of between 12 and 25 is considered a 'high' degree of danger, while above 100 is 'catastrophic' or, in Victoria, Code Red. The Victorian Black Saturday fires of 2009 registered well above 100 – perhaps hitting 150, by some accounts – while the Sydney Basin had its first 'catastrophic' forecast in November 2019. Many sites across southern Australia reached 100 on 20 and 30 December 2019.

With the autumn fire weather period lengthening, too, that means the bushfire season for those regions is now about four months longer, which pushes it out to eight or nine months of the year, the bureau says. Both areas happened to be hit hard by fires during the 2019–20 summer. Just as February rains had doused most of NSW's fires, heavy falls in July finally brought the forested parts of the South Coast, the parts that hadn't burnt in 2019–20, out of drought, easing concerns about the 2020–21 fire season.

Incidentally, the longer bushfire season means the window of opportunity for authorities to safely conduct so-called hazard reduction is shifting into winter, if not shrinking. So those traditional spring or autumn controlled burns may become less of a tradition.

Declining rainfall is one thing but fire dangers are particularly elevated when drought takes hold, as it did well before the run-up to the 2019–20 season. Much of Australia entered 2020 in the grip of a severe dry spell, including the Murray-Darling Basin, which was marking its worst drought since at least the Federation Drought of the early 1900s. By December 2019, the accumulated fire risks, based on fire index readings, had reached record levels for more than two-thirds of Australia, the bureau found.

If those trends aren't bad enough, the nation's droughts themselves are becoming both more likely and also hotter when they do roll out across the landscape.

What's dry lightning?

Some might take comfort in the fact that fires typically don't start spontaneously. Even here, though, climate scientists have identified an increase in the occurrence of so-called dry lightning from thunderstorms in parts of south-eastern Australia in recent decades. Dry thunderstorms produce lightning and thunder but any rain typically evaporates before it hits the ground. As a result, fires sparked by those lightning strikes don't get doused by a rain dump from the same storm.

Those trends were also why Dr Karl Braganza, head of climate monitoring at the bureau, told the very first day of the commission's public hearings in June 2020 that the background warming climate was 'loading the dice' for weather extremes. 'Really, since the Canberra 2003 fires every jurisdiction in Australia has seen this,' Braganza said. '[We] have seen some really significant fire events that have challenged what we do to respond to them, and have really challenged what we thought fire weather looked like preceding this period.'

What role do natural weather trends play?

Australia's climate, of course, varies from year to year, based on the interplay of influences from the Indian, Pacific and Southern oceans. Researchers Chris Lucas and Sarah Harris from Victoria's Country Fire Authority examined the role of natural climate variability and the nudging brought about by rising greenhouse gas emissions, in work they published in September 2019. Rainfall changes from one year to the next, with phenomena such as El Niño events in the Pacific and shifting Indian Ocean conditions playing a role. Still, a signal is emerging from the natural noise. '[Anthropogenic] climate change is the primary driver of the [upward trend in the fire danger index], through both higher mean temperatures and, potentially, through associated shifts in large-scale rainfall patterns,' they found.

The latest generation of climate models show that variability will likely increase further. Australia is one of the global 'hotspots', along with the Amazon and the Mediterranean, that can expect longer, more frequent and more intense droughts, researchers at the University of New South Wales and the Australian National University found when they ran the new models out to 2100.

What do these trends mean for the future?

For veteran fire researchers such as Professor Ross Bradstock, head of the University of Wollongong's Centre for Environmental Risk Management of Bushfires, the future is coming in a rush. In 2009, he published forecasts for how the fire danger index would track to 2030 and 2050 only to see the levels reached or exceeded as the season ramped up by November 2019.

The warming world has many implications for how we manage fire, including the effectiveness of hazard-reduction burning,

Bradstock told the royal commission. Think of controlled burning and climate as two dials, he said. 'You can try and turn down the fuel dial and that's what we're intending to do through fuel reduction,' Bradstock said. 'But as the weather dial is being turned up through climate change, that's counteracting the effect of turning down the fuel dial.'

'The future is coming in a rush.'

Former fire chiefs such as Greg Mullins tried to warn the federal government of the bushfire risks ahead of the disastrous 2019–20 season, and others in active leadership roles have spoken out since. Their efforts to alert politicians were prompted, in large part, because they knew it would be largely volunteer crews out on the fire grounds battling these increasingly wild fires and the sometimes bizarre phenomena that go with them.

Pyrocumulonimbus clouds, for example, were once considered rare and unique weather events generated by major bushfires. Such clouds form when the intense heat from the fire causes air and smoke to rise in the fire's plume, drawing in cooler air. If the air rises high enough into the atmosphere, a cumulonimbus cloud is formed that would not otherwise have happened. While they create a monstrous, towering presence over a fire, it's on the ground that they wreak the most havoc, causing winds to behave erratically, pushing the flames in directions that are alarming, unpredictable and perilous.

In the twenty years to 2018, a global consortium of researchers, including Jason Sharples, a professor of bushfire dynamics at the University of New South Wales, identified around sixty of these dramatic cloud events in Australia. In the 2019–20 season alone, around thirty more events were confirmed, while about another fifteen remain under investigation.

University of Tasmania fire ecologist David Bowman told the royal commission that it was very difficult to pinpoint when pyrocumulonimbus clouds would form. 'Fire behaviour models break down when they're confronted by these events because the systems start generating their own weather systems,' he said. 'So something happened this last summer, which is truly extraordinary because what we would call statistically a "black swan event" – we saw a flock of black swans. That just shouldn't have happened.' Black swan events, those unpredicted, semmingly impossible occurrences, are notable for both their severe consequences and yet for how obvious they were in hindsight. Australia's lurch towards more extreme weather, including fire weather, shares some of those characteristics writ large – we can see the drivers and we can anticipate where these challenges are heading. What's missing so far, it seems, is the political will to do anything about it.

24

HOW DID PERIMENOPAUSE GO FROM HUSH-HUSH TO HOT TOPIC?

It affects half of the world's population, and now women are comparing notes. What happens before and after menopause? And what have we made it mean?

Melissa Cunningham

You have to surrender to it, British comedian Dawn French has proclaimed of menopause. 'I promise that, afterwards, there's life.' Despite being a fundamental biological transition affecting half the world's population, the symptoms of menopause – from disturbed sleep to memory loss – have not been the stuff of dinner party banter, generally, nor a popular subject for chit-chat at the pub. Now, however, they are starting to become part of the public conversation.

In Britain, women are gathering at pop-up 'menopause cafes' and going online to swap notes on their 'change of life' experiences. Workplace policies to cater for menopausal employees are up for discussion, too.

What is menopause – and what is it with a 'peri' in front? What happens afterwards? And is there a male equivalent?

What's menopause?

A woman in Australia will have an average 400 to 500 periods in her lifetime. Menopause is when the periods stop. The word itself stems from the Greek *pausis* ('pause') and *men* ('month'), meaning the end of monthly cycles.

Women are on a path to menopause from birth. A baby girl has more than a million eggs in her ovaries. Steadily, as she ages, they deplete. By puberty, only about 300,000 remain, and so it goes through her adult life.

'[Menopause] represents the end of a woman's reproductive life,' says Martha Hickey, professor of obstetrics and gynaecology at the University of Melbourne. 'Specifically, menopause is the final menstrual period a woman experiences – it is a one-off event. All women will go through menopause. It is inevitable.' (In a reproductive life spanning decades, the average Australian woman will have two or fewer babies.)

Menopause is considered a normal part of ageing when it happens after the age of forty – the average age is fifty-one – but some women can go through menopause early, either as a result of surgery such as hysterectomy or damage to the ovaries such as from chemotherapy. When menopause happens before forty, regardless of the cause, it is called premature menopause.

What's perimenopause then?

The symptoms women experience in the lead-up to menopause are actually perimenopausal. *Peri*, Greek for 'around' or 'near', refers to this transitional state near menopause when a woman's ovaries begin to make less oestrogen and the body responds. It's a phase that begins when a woman is forty-seven, on average, although it can last from a year to a decade. As the body makes less oestrogen, the pituitary gland produces higher levels of signalling hormones – follicle-stimulating and luteinising hormones – in an effort to keep the ovaries producing eggs and to make oestrogen and progesterone levels 'normal'. This can lead to ovulation occurring twice in a cycle, the second time during a period, which can lead to high hormone levels. In other cycles, ovulation might not occur at all.

Some women describe perimenopause as a time of hormonal chaos akin to a second wave of puberty. Symptoms include hot flushes, changes in libido, mood swings, memory problems, vaginal dryness and a higher risk of osteoporosis. Periods can be less regular, lighter or heavier, last longer or be briefer. Women's experiences vary greatly – some barely register anything.

Genetic factors play some role in timing. If your mother and other close female relatives had an early or late perimenopause, it's likely you will, too. But various studies also point to lifestyle factors, such as smoking, being linked to early onset, while other studies have pointed to alcohol consumption delaying perimenopause.

Although eggs succumb to menopause, pregnancy is still possible using a donor egg. During perimenopause, ovulation can occur, meaning a woman can conceive naturally, even if she is using hormone therapy.

What happens after menopause?

After a woman has had twelve consecutive months of amenorrhea (lack of menstruation), she is said to be postmenopausal. Perimenopausal symptoms ease but health risks related to the loss of oestrogen rise.

> *'Women are advised to keep active, which also releases endorphins that improve mood.'*

This includes a decrease in bone density, which can lead to osteoporosis, where bones become thin and fragile. It also includes weight gain, which can increase the risk of obesity, diabetes and cardiovascular disease. Women are advised to keep active, which also releases endorphins that improve mood, and to do strength training to increase blood flow and strengthen the heart.

How effective is hormone replacement therapy?

More than 300,000 Australian women and about 12 million women in Western countries are using hormone replacement therapy (HRT), or menopausal hormone therapy (MHT) as it's now known. It's currently the most effective type of treatment available for perimenopause symptoms, but it has been linked with breast and ovarian cancers.

'All medications carry risk and benefits,' Hickey says. 'A benefit of HRT is that it's really good for symptoms. A risk is that it does increase the risk of cancer – I don't think we should beat around the bush about that. But it varies by the type of hormone therapy you take and it might vary depending on how long you take it for.'

The risks are greater, for example, for users of oestrogen-progestogen hormone therapy than for oestrogen-only therapy.

A large study by the Institute of Cancer Research in London found that women who took hormone therapy for five years were 2.7 times more likely to develop breast cancer than those who did not. Recent research also suggests that, in some cases, the danger can persist for more than a decade after treatment stops.

Another study found that women using hormone therapy for between one and four years had a 60 per cent higher chance of developing breast cancer compared with those who have never used it. The report's authors, who examined fifty-eight studies across the world, found that of 108,647 women who developed breast cancer at an average age of sixty-five, almost half had used hormone therapy.

When asked if women should avoid hormone therapy due to the increased risk of cancer, Professor Kelly-Anne Phillips, the founder of the Peter MacCallum Breast and Ovarian Cancer Risk Management Clinic, says the decision should be made on a case-by-case basis. 'Some women will find, short term, it can help relieve their symptoms,' she says. Phillips warns, however, that women who have been on hormone therapy for a year should have their treatment reviewed, adding there are alternatives for treating symptoms including weight loss, moisturisers for vaginal dryness and avoiding caffeine or alcohol.

Why does menopause happen at all?

Apart from humans, most mammals stay fertile until the end of their lives. There are a few exceptions: killer whales, short-finned pilot whales, belugas and narwhals can live for decades beyond their reproductive years. Guppies also appear to go through a fish version of menopause. But long postmenopausal lifespans are an aspect of biology that appears to be at odds with natural selection. Why do women suddenly stop having periods when they still have at least a third of their lives to live, during which they could be producing offspring?

Some experts, including Hickey, believe high death rates of mothers during childbirth throughout history emphasised the importance of grandmothers in rearing future generations, unhindered by more children of their own. This is known as the grandmother theory.

Do men experience menopause?

Not really – but andropause can affect men older than forty. Andropause is the gradual reduction of the male sex hormone (testosterone) with increasing age. Its symptoms include sexual dysfunction, weakness, fatigue, insomnia, loss of motivation, mood disorders and reduction of bone density. Though the symptoms aren't as severe as those of menopause, they can last for as long as fifteen to twenty years.

What have we made menopause mean?

When UK-based former magazine editor Lynnette Peck and her friend Paula Fry first began to experience symptoms of perimenopause, they found they had no safe space to share their feelings on the matter. In a bid to open up dialogue, they started a secret Facebook page in 2017. Word got around quickly. Soon they had more than 700 members and then Feeling Flush was born, a public online community for women across the world to connect. 'We wanted women, including ourselves, to have places to share information and educate each other – and have a moan,' Peck says. 'Women mostly ask us about hormone replacement therapy and the pros and cons. We are not medical experts so we point them to people who are. There is now a conversation. It was hidden before. Here in the UK, even political parties and huge brands are getting involved.'

Hickey notes that women make up almost half of the workforce in Australia and two-thirds of the voluntary sector. They continue to look after children across generations and are often the primary carer for parents. 'Our society has a big focus on youth, and the preservation of youth, and menopause is a marker of age in women – and ageing in women is not a topic we still have very much discussion about,' she says. 'It's quite likely that women who experience menopause may not have been informed fully about what to expect. It's quite possible a lot of men don't know very much about menopause at all.'

> *'Our society has a big focus on youth and the preservation of youth, and menopause is a marker of age in women – and ageing in women is not a topic we still have very much discussion about.'*

British free-to-air television station Channel 4 now has a menopause policy to support women experiencing perimenopausal symptoms such as hot flushes, anxiety and fatigue by giving them access to flexible working arrangements and paid leave if they feel unwell. It's a shift Hickey wants in Australia. She would like to see menopause treated as a 'diversity issue' with workplaces actively supporting women experiencing it. 'Pregnancy would be a similar example: only women get pregnant, and we've learnt to adapt, and I think we need to take a similar perspective to menopause,' she argues.

*

For information and support, you can contact the Australasian Menopause Society on (03) 9428 8738 or menopause.org.au; not-for-profit women's health organisation Jean Hailes is at jeanhailes. org.au; or contact the Royal Women's Hospital Menopause Symptoms After Cancer clinic on (03) 8345 2000.

25

HOW DO POLICE AND CRIMINALS GET ALONG?

It's a complicated relationship that has changed over time. What makes a good cop and a 'good crook'? And what happens when a line is crossed?

John Silvester

The world is not always black and white and that is certainly the case when it comes to police and criminals. We see it as a battle between good and evil but, behind the scenes, there is often dialogue between the two sides. In the old days, underworld informers were called snitches, fizzes or gigs. Now they are called human sources.

The best detectives are always the ones who can talk to people and make them feel at ease – that includes victims, witnesses and suspects. The bad detective relies on intimidation and doesn't relate to the different strands in society.

By its nature, law enforcement involves police and criminals having to relate to one another. But what forms can these relationships take? And how have they changed over time?

> '*The best detectives are always the ones who can talk to people and make them feel at ease – that includes victims, witnesses and suspects.*'

How did cops and robbers traditionally relate?

Let's talk about crime before drugs changed the landscape. Crooks' and coppers' careers often mirrored each other. They grew up in similar suburbs and moved up the ranks together: one side committing and the other investigating petty crime, then moving to more serious offences. It was not unusual for a serious career criminal to say he would speak only to a senior ranked officer he had known for more than twenty years.

Christopher 'Badness' Binse is one of Australia's most notorious armed robbers and escapees. In the early 1990s, armed robbery squad detective Ken Ashworth began investigating him over a series of bank raids and Binse's response was to post teasing messages in a newspaper public notice section. When he was finally caught, he expected to be bashed in the police interview room. Ashworth told him that wasn't going to happen and that he would be charged purely on the evidence. A visibly shocked Binse was even more surprised when he was offered a beer after the formal interview.

For decades Binse kept in contact with Ashworth, sometimes when he was in prison and when he was on the run. About twenty-five years after they first met, Binse contacted the now senior policeman and said he wanted to confess to a series of unsolved armed robberies saying, 'I'm a leopard whose spots are fading.' In Barwon Prison the crook greeted the cop as if they were old friends. The young detectives in the room were somewhat surprised when the career criminal related an anecdote about 'when Ashy and I were working together.' Ashworth interjected, 'No Chris, we didn't work together. I wore the white hat and you had the black hat.' The devil is in the detail.

Binse confessed to seven armed robberies between 1988 and 1991, escaping with a total of $390,000. He later pleaded guilty, and a judge assessed his prospects of rehabilitation as 'reasonable'.

What makes a 'good crook' – and a good cop?

Police would refer to some offenders as 'good crooks'. This meant they were professional, remained calm and didn't use unnecessary violence while committing crimes. Graham Kinniburgh was considered a good crook. He was the leader of the Magnetic Drill Gang that set off the alarms in the days before their raids, so that if they were tripped during the robbery, security would assume it was a false alarm. They would use electromagnets to precisely hold a diamond-tipped drill to access lock tumblers. Then, using a doctor's cystoscope, they could look into a safe to manipulate the combination.

Kinniburgh's team grabbed $1.7 million from a Murwillumbah bank, a huge jewellery haul from a Lonsdale Street office, valuables from safety deposit boxes in Melbourne and gold bullion in Queensland. One of the key investigators, Detective Inspector Bernie Rankin, reflects, 'Kinniburgh was one of the smartest crims I ever dealt with. He kept his own counsel and had a tight circle of friends.' But he did have enemies. He was shot dead outside his home in the Melbourne suburb of Kew in 2003.

One detective, who looked more like a middle-aged dad than some crime buster, was reputed to have the best criminal contacts on the east coast. I asked him why and he said there was no secret – just treat people decently. Once, when checking a house for stolen property, he asked the occupant, who was a career crim, what was behind a closed door. The man said it was his young son, asleep in his cot. 'I asked him, "Should I go in there?" and he said there was nothing that would interest me.' He took him at his word, which was a calculated risk. Years later, the crook rang the policeman to tip him off about a pending armed robbery, to square the ledger.

During a raid, one police officer more interested in humiliation than resolution said to a frightened young boy, 'Do you know your daddy is nothing but a crook?' He made no friends among his colleagues and an enemy for life.

Consider a typical homicide squad interview. The suspect may have committed the worst possible crime but the detectives remain non-judgemental, quietly asking questions and refusing to allow their faces to betray any sense of horror or disgust. This is because they don't want the offender to go back into their shell. The aim is not to win the argument in the interview room but to win it at the Supreme Court trial.

Well away from the headlines, police who have good relationships with criminals are able to broker deals, negotiate surrenders and stop underworld wars.

In 1997, the Bandidos National Run, an annual road trip for the bikie club, was to take them through Wangaratta on Year 12 muck-up day. Local police were horrified at the thought of hundreds of bikies and an equal number of drunken teenagers crossing paths. Instead of marshalling hundreds of police to confront the bikies, an experienced detective reached out to the then Bandidos national president, Michael 'Chaos' Kulakowski, who gave assurances there would be no trouble. There was none. Two days later, they were involved in a huge brawl and a shooting in Geelong. Chaos was later murdered in Sydney.

Anti-bikie police don't just work on confrontations. As well as sometimes negotiating rules for bikie runs, the police broker peace deals between warring parties. There are no headlines in the murders they have stopped.

Who had the upper hand?

In every major Australian city there were bars, pubs or clubs that were treated as neutral ground. In Melbourne in the early 1980s it was the Galaxy Nightclub where detectives would mingle with serious gangsters. Once a well-connected detective told a notorious gunman he knew there was a contract out on the life of another gangster. The cop said if the gangster was shot, 'I'll be coming after you.' The trouble with these informal meetings is that they were uncontrolled and sometimes the crooks would have the upper hand.

By any definition, Melbourne drug dealer Dennis Bruce Allen was a psychopath, but he remained free to deal drugs and kill with apparent impunity. Allen made between $70,000 and $100,000 a week way back in the 1980s from drugs and was on bail for sixty different offences with sureties of $225,000, then the price of five inner-suburban homes.

To stay on the street, he would inform on other crooks – a win-win for Allen. He was free to deal drugs and had police arrest his competition, growing his own market. He tipped off police about the murder of bikie Anton Kenny, even helpfully pointing out the spot in the Yarra River where the dismembered body had been dumped in a concrete-filled drum. What he omitted was that he shot

Kenny and, with the help of his half-brother Victor Peirce and a chainsaw, shoved him in the barrel and rolled him into the river.

In Sydney, hard-nosed detectives would often drink with some of the most notorious crooks, particularly Arthur Stanley 'Neddy' Smith. Sure, Neddy would occasionally provide tidbits of information to make the relationship look semi-legitimate. The reality was they were corrupt partners and Neddy was given the green light to commit crime, sharing the profits with bent detectives. It was a sweet deal until Neddy proved to be an impulsive idiot. The green light turned red when he beat a tow-truck driver to death in a road rage attack.

In Queensland, in the late 1970s and '80s a corrupt deal was called The Joke, involving regular payments to police all the way to the commissioner Terry Lewis. In Melbourne, prolific drug dealer Tony Mokbel secretly met with police in a park to try to broker a deal with the anti-ganglands Purana taskforce. 'I don't want to see ... anyone else getting f---in' killed,' Mokbel told police in April 2004. Mokbel claimed he could guarantee an end to the underworld war and would organise several key figures, including Carl Williams and a prodigious drug cook, to plead guilty to drug offences. This, he said, would be conditional on an agreement that his people received minimum jail terms. His brother, Kabalan, he added, was off the table, because he expected those charges to be dropped.

In Tony's vision of the world, the murders would stop and the Mokbels could go back to selling drugs, while Purana chased other crooks, just like the good old days. 'Con [his lawyer Con Heliotis] and Paul [the then director of public prosecutions Paul Coghlan] will be able to work out the details,' the super-confident Tony told police. As you would imagine, the police declined the offer. Mokbel was usually polite to the detectives investigating him, realising everyone was just doing their jobs. Now, in prison, his attitude has soured considerably.

While police try to befriend crooks to infiltrate their networks, some crims use the same tactics to cultivate cops. It can be a slip of the tongue during a conversation or something more sinister. Secret police operations in every state have been sabotaged by corrupt leaks. In Victoria, a drug squad document known as the Blue File, which showed underworld figure Terence Hodson was a police informer, ended up in the wrong hands. As a result, Hodson and his wife, Christine, were murdered in their Kew home in May 2004. When, in June 2008, the alleged killer, prolific hitman Rod Collins, was arrested for a 1987 double murder, police found a loaded handgun, a balaclava, burglary kit and surveillance equipment in his Northcote home. They also found a fifty-eight-page confidential police report on a major drug dealer. Collins claimed he found it at a bus stop.

How has the relationship changed over time?

Bikie groups have a track record of recruiting double agents. Young police have been seduced to the dark side, meeting bikies at gyms (and given muscle-building hormones), tattoo parlours and strip clubs. One, who was later sacked for leaking, had applied to join an anti-bikie taskforce.

The growth of drug trafficking shattered the old model where crooks and cops progressed through their respective ranks. Would-be gangsters could become millionaires in months if they found a reliable flow of product.

Carl Williams, previously gainfully employed as a supermarket shelf stacker, had an insignificant criminal record. By the age of twenty-nine he was making up to $100,000 per month from producing a variety of amphetamine products and was charged over drugs with a value of $20 million. By the age of thirty he was employing multiple hitmen and was ordering the murder of his enemies. One of his team was Andrew 'Benji' Veniamin, a pumped-up car thief who became a ruthless hitman. Benji, who was shot dead in Carlton in 2004, was responsible for at least five murders.

Huge money means bribe offers and a need to rotate police through corruption-prone areas, which makes it more difficult for police to establish underworld contacts. The cycle of scandals involving inappropriate and unexplained relationships between crooks and cops has led to tightening the rules. Meetings must be documented, supervisors notified, criminals listed as informers and, on occasions, conversations recorded. Human source protocols mean if a crook wishes to tell tales, specialist 'human source' officers step in, creating a 'sterile corridor' between the cop and the crim.

The use of rogue Melbourne barrister Nicola Gobbo as a police informer has created outrage, the potential for multiple convictions to be reviewed and a royal commission certain to savage police procedures.

The modern era, with CCTV and everyone in public carrying a camera, has led to a drop in face-to-face clandestine meetings. In the new world, the void created by not cultivating underworld sources has been filled electronically. Police use phone records, telephone intercepts, CCTV vision and social media footprints as frontline intelligence sources.

Now the 'good' crooks have vaulted police in technology. Using the dark web and apps designed to thwart monitoring, they are able to communicate in secret. This means detectives around Australia need to be retrained in the old ways. Getting out there and talking to the crooks will be more effective than staring at a computer screen.

> *Police who have good relationships with criminals are able to broker deals, negotiate surrenders and stop underworld wars.*

26

WHY IS JAKARTA SINKING?

Indonesians are running out of
time to save their capital city.
But their president has a plan. What is
it and will he be able to pull it off?

Michael Bachelard and James Massola

It seemed a drastic measure: move the entire administrative centre of Indonesia from crazy, overcrowded Jakarta to a new settlement 180 kilometres away in Borneo. But when he announced the move in August 2019, President Joko Widodo cited a number of reasons for the change. 'First, [Borneo] has fewer earthquakes, floods and forest fires. Second, it is strategically located as it lies right in the centre of the country. Third, it is located near developed cities including Balikpapan and Samarinda. Fourth, it has sufficient infrastructure; and, fifth, some 180,000 hectares of government land is available.'

Joko also said that Jakarta and Java, the island on which it sits, host a disproportionate amount of the country's population and economic activity and he wanted to 'minimise the gap between Java and places outside Java'.

Joko did not mention another key, but slightly embarrassing, truth: Jakarta is sinking.

The northern part of the city is disappearing into Jakarta Bay. Flooding is endemic in the rainy season because thirteen rivers that run through the city are unable to drain uphill into the bay. Sea walls have been constructed to try to prevent inundation but they, too, are subsiding into the mud.

So what's really happening to Jakarta? Why is the best option to relocate the entire capital city? And how does the Indonesian Government propose to go about it?

Why is Jakarta sinking?

In the early 1500s, it was trade that led to Jakarta being built on a swamp. This muddy land had a natural port first that was established by the Hindu kingdom of Sunda. Sultans took it over in 1527 and named it Jayakarta, Javanese for 'victorious city'.

A century later, the Dutch arrived looking for a base from which to send the spoils of colonialism (mainly valuable spices) back to Europe. Having successfully tamed low-lying Holland, they believed they could also tame tropical Jakarta, adding canals, streets and civic squares that, even today, feel something like a grimy Amsterdam.

Unlike Australia, Indonesia does not have a series of dams and pipes to deliver water to all the ten million-plus residents of its biggest city. About 40 per cent of residents rely on bore water, according to the city's tap water company, PAM Jaya, and it is brought up from under their feet by massive pumps running day and night.

It's not just private users either: more than 4000 commercial buildings, such as hotels and office towers, also rely on groundwater. The amount of water a company or individual can remove is supposed to be regulated but, as with many regulations in Indonesia, the rules are poor and enforcement minimal. As the water is pumped out, the ground on which the city is built gradually subsides, like a balloon deflating.

There is also no sewerage system, so most people use septic tanks. As they age and rust, tanks deposit their contents into the same soil from which water is drawn – one of the reasons it's wise not to drink Jakarta bore water.

North Jakarta, which hosts the massive Tanjung Priok port, waterfront apartment developments and 1.7 million people, is particularly under pressure. University of Indonesia geophysicist Syamsu Rosid told the *Jakarta Post* that land subsidence had been aggravated by a lack of green spaces. Concrete and asphalt prevents rainwater absorbing into the soil, and the sediment that makes up the city's soil is prone to erosion. Factories, households and mosques have been abandoned.

Across other parts of the city, the average sinking rate is between 1 and 15 centimetres per year. Together with rising sea levels caused by climate change, it means that almost half the city now sits below sea level.

Pumping out groundwater faster than it can be naturally replenished has combined with other issues to cause 'sinking' in areas of cities around the world, both coastal – such as Bangkok, Calcutta and Houston – and not, such as Mexico City. But Jakarta is giving way faster than any other major city. Researchers at the Bandung Institute of Technology have found that some parts of the city have sunk four metres, or about 25 centimetres per year, since the 1970s. The Institute's Heri Andreas modelled in 2018 that 95 per cent of north Jakarta could be underwater by the 2050s. He's since revised that down to about 90 per cent, as some factories move out of the area to Jakarta's satellite cities such as Bekasi and Tangerang because of higher operating costs in the capital.

'What we have found is that the subsidence has spread in the Jakarta agglomeration (Greater Jakarta). In south and north Tangerang, we have subsidence there. In Bekasi, the subsidence is extraordinary, over 10 centimetres per year in new areas.'

> 'Jakarta is giving way faster than any other major city … some parts of the city have sunk four metres, or about 25 centimetres per year, since the 1970s.'

What are the consequences?

Jakarta is the commercial as well as the administrative capital of Indonesia – more than 30 million people live in Greater Jakarta. Subsidence affects the poor, mainly, as people have moved by their millions from the country's islands in search of work.

They often live in informal settlements (known as *kampungs*) on unclaimed land on the banks of rivers and canals, or in houses built on stilts over the water. They live, fish, cook, eat and wash over the waterways then discard rubbish and defecate into the water. As the city is inundated, many of these people are likely to be displaced.

It's not just the poor areas of the city that are susceptible; the wealthy are affected, too. Commercial buildings, high-rise apartments and government offices are also subject to subsidence, cracking and persistent flooding. A few years ago, a driver was killed when he was trapped by floodwater in the underground carpark of a city building. Even the presidential palace is not immune. It flooded in January 2013, prompting a barefoot examination of the damage by then president Susilo Bambang Yudhoyono and foreign minister Marty Natalegawa.

What solutions are being mooted?

To halt the sinking, the city would need to stop extracting bore water, which would mean the city government would need to build a system of water pipes, dams and river diversions. This would require cleaning the filthy waterways upstream, policing the factories that dump chemicals into them and installing a sewerage system in a mega-city that has never had one. All this in a country renowned for corruption and gouging on any major project. Then they would need to find land to resettle millions of the country's poorest people, who are likely to be unwilling to move.

Or, they could just go somewhere else.

This is the option favoured by the current government, which has proposed moving Indonesia's political centre to another part of the archipelago entirely. They even have a specific spot in mind. Joko has identified land in the two districts of North Penajam Paser and Kutai Kartanegara, in East Kalimantan province on the island of Borneo (known in Indonesia as Kalimantan). The land lies between two major cities, Balikpapan and Samarinda, which are already served by international airports and seaports.

The densely forested location is next to Bukit Soeharto, or Soeharto's Hill, which is named after Indonesia's second president and is near a designated protection area that has, at times, been a timber production forest but that is currently set aside for conservation. The area also hosts small-scale coal mines and a smattering of palm oil plantations and it suffers from illegal deforestation and frequent forest burning, which have further degraded the quality of the land. It's also not far from a sanctuary for rescued orangutans and sun bears.

Map by Ice Cold Publishing

Joko insists the cost will be more than $40 billion, about 19 per cent of which will come from the national budget. The rest will come from selling land and buildings in Jakarta and significant investment from the private sector. There is much speculation about where that investment might come from: the US International Development Finance Corporation and the United Arab Emirates' sovereign wealth fund are among the potential investors, while Japanese engineering expertise has also been discussed. Designs so far include electric cars, monorails and drone taxis.

How do you move a capital?

More than thirty countries or regional states have relocated their seats of power to new cities designed from scratch. A number of cities, but mostly New York, hosted the United States Congress until it landed for good in Washington DC in 1800.

In 1911, King George V decreed that the capital of British India would move from eastern Calcutta to central Delhi, although the new city wasn't inaugurated until 1931. Pakistan switched from Karachi to Islamabad, which was perceived as less vulnerable to attacks, in 1967. Brazil shifted its capital from Rio de Janeiro in 1960 to the purpose-built Brasilia, which is now a UNESCO World Heritage site for its modernist architecture and urban planning but, by some accounts, a very boring place to live.

The moves are not over yet, either. Egypt announced in 2015 that it would move its administrative centre a few kilometres east of Cairo, to ease congestion, and has begun inaugurating various key buildings, including a cathedral and a mosque.

Making such moves usually involves passing a law to designate a new capital then actually building it, and shifting the country's parliament or congress. It helps if the head of state and top executive also live there. Australia did this in 1927 when the prime minister and parliamentary sittings went to Canberra from Melbourne after the first parliament house was built.

On his trip to Australia in February 2020, Joko actually cited Canberra as a potential model for Indonesia's new capital city, saying, 'We are going to take inspiration from the positive elements of [Canberra] to build our new capital city, from its management down to the structural aspects of the city.'

Not everyone is a fan of planned capital cities, of course. In a briefing with journalists in November 2019, Australia's ambassador to Indonesia, Gary Quinlan, delivered a withering assessment of Canberra: the city was 'one of the biggest national mistakes we ever made' and had 'no natural centre', he said.

So, to make a success of a new, planned capital – apart from a natural centre – several elements are crucial. They include government departments, at least one university, religious institutions, support businesses, housing and a critical mass of people and facilities to help the city get up and running.

Though Parliament began to sit in Canberra in 1927, the move to the new capital did not begin in earnest until the 1950s, when then prime minister Robert Menzies championed its growth, including a hefty provision of government housing. Indeed, Australia's High Court didn't move to Canberra from Melbourne until 1980.

One of the most notorious capital-move failures is Naypyidaw, the purpose-built capital of Myanmar, formerly Burma, which allegedly houses a million people. Many doubt this figure but, even if it's true, at five times the geographical size of London – which has a population of nine million – it's sparsely populated at best. The empty, twenty-lane freeways are rumoured to have been built to land aircraft on, in case of anti-government protests. There is a safari park, a zoo, multiple golf courses, electricity, wifi – but there are very few people.

'This city is mainly for government staff, government buildings,' one man told the *South China Morning Post*. 'It's not very interesting here. Most people are not that happy; they are just living here because they can earn money, because they can work here.'

Does everyone like the prospect of a move?

Certainly not, including Kalimantan locals, who are sharply divided over the new city. It's had its critics on social media, too, with some mocking 'Jokowiville' or 'Jokograd'. Land speculators arrived soon after Joko's announcement of the move and prices began to rise sharply.

Husain Suwarno from the environmental group Balikpapan Bay Care Forum fears for the impact on the many rivers that run through the area and out to sea, and potentially on the local forests, too. 'The commitment by the government states they will not be using protected forest. Bukit Soeharto is part of a national park so we expect it [the new city] won't be there. The bottom line is I reject the idea, but what can we civilians do when it is already decided?'

Environmental NGO leader Hafidz Prasetyo told Channel News Asia that, 'as a conservation area, [Bukit Soeharto] should be a home for sun bears, local birds and other kinds of animals as well as teak woods, bengkirai woods – and those should be preserved. The development of hotels and shopping centres will need extensive land clearing. We actually reject the plan.'

> 'Our village used to be prosperous, we were rich, food was abundant. That was before the big [forestry] companies entered our area in 1968.'

The timeline is 'almost impossible' as building a new capital can take decades, says Luca Tacconi, a professor of environmental governance at the Australian National University, who has lived in Indonesia. He has also questioned whether the private sector would invest, even before the pandemic hit. 'My fear is that the plans won't be fully realised and that they'll burn the hell out of parts of the forest.' And then there's the Pasir Balik, the local tribes who lived in the area long before people moved to Kalimantan from Java. Jubaen, who uses just the one name, is an *adat* (an elected cultural leader) of the Balik people in the village of Pemaluan, which is home to about 150 Balik families. Pemaluan sits within the tract of land earmarked for the city and the local man is far from happy that the forests and dusty roads of his village could be replaced by a shiny new capital. 'Our village used to be prosperous, we were rich, food was abundant. That was before the big [forestry] companies entered our area in 1968. Ever since then, we have been poorer, now we have to buy food. If the capital comes here I don't know how poor we will be. Our communities will slowly disappear.'

Will this move actually happen?
Before the pandemic, Joko proposed starting to move public servants to the newly built city in 2024. That timeline was ambitious even before the pandemic hit, but the move-in date is not an accident – 2024 will be the last year of the president's term-limited ten-year rule.

The main problem is money. As the coronavirus pandemic has spread around the world, national budgets have taken a hammering – with Indonesia no exception – and economic growth rates have collapsed. That means getting 80 per cent funding from the private sector is going to be difficult and makes a delay all but inevitable.

Indeed, by July 2020 the chief economists of two of Indonesia's largest banks, Bank Central Asia (BCA) and Bank Mandiri, had cast doubt on the 2024 move-in date for the city's first residents, and about the only work that was being done on the project was writing the legal framework to establish the city. BCA's David Sumual summed it up thus: delay was 'inevitable' and the government's money would be better spent on healthcare as the virus spread around the 17,000-island archipelagic nation.

Although no formal announcement of a delay had been made, even senior advisers to the president were willing to concede some 'rescheduling' would now have to occur. Some sections of the diplomatic community, who will have to actually move to the new capital if or when it ever happens, are deeply sceptical about the project, too. Pre-coronavirus, they argued that, first, the financing of the project relied perhaps too heavily on the private sector and second, the proposed timeline was ambitious, to put it mildly. On top of that, there is concern that moving the administrative capital to a new city won't fix Jakarta's sinking problem – and it could take the pressure off politicians to act.

The prospect of moving the capital has been raised by other Indonesian leaders since the 1950s, when the first president, Soekarno, floated the idea of one day making Central Kalimantan's planned capital, Palangkaraya, into his nation's headquarters. There's little doubt that Joko sees this latest project as the centrepiece of his legacy. Whether you view it as critical investment in a much-needed new city, or a presidential vanity project, it's far from clear what the future holds for Indonesia's ambitious new capital city.

27

WHAT ARE THE ART AND SCIENCE OF REVERSE SWING?

It has perplexed the world's finest batsmen and brought a national team undone. How did a cricket sensation go from secret weapon to dark art? And what's behind the magic?

Greg Baum

I t's a sunny afternoon at Old Trafford in Manchester in August 2005 and the third Test match is at a tense pass. Michael Clarke, future Australian captain but a tyro at this time, leans over his bat, flexing slightly at the knees, watching England's Simon Jones muscle his way towards him. The last four balls have been outswingers – that is, they have curved away from Clarke in flight – and every fibre of his being tells him that this delivery will follow the same trajectory. There is the way Jones grips the ball, with its seam angled towards slips and the polished hemisphere facing the batsman. Then there is Jones's action as he gathers his arms and legs to leap into his delivery stride, the slant of his body, the cock of his wrist. To Clarke, it telegraphs outswinger, outswinger.

A Test batsman needs these cues, to read, to compute, to react. He cannot depend on reflex once the ball has left the bowler's hand; Test-match bowling is too fast for that. It is why you will sometimes see a bowler cover the ball with his free hand as he runs in, to disguise his intentions.

As Jones releases, Clarke presses forward. His brain tells him that the ball is pitched up but not far enough to drive. Since it will also swing away, it cannot hit the stumps but, if he plays at it, there is the risk of a snick to slips. So, as Clarke leans forward, he raises his bat out of harm's way. He leaves it.

But what's this? Instead of veering away, the ball arrows in towards Clarke, contrary to what all the wiring and whirring in his mind tells him. When it bounces, it breaks further towards the batsman. The ball is travelling at around 140 kilometres per hour and it is too late for Clarke to adjust. On the TV footage, you can hear his gasp of astonishment as the ball whistles past his pad and crashes into his off stump. Jones exults, the Old Trafford terraces erupt, commentator Mark Nicholas, after a suitable pause, weighs in with a Benaud-like, 'That is very good.'

As Clarke makes for the pavilion, he looks back and shakes his head slightly. The ball is seventy-five overs old. It should be

'
To the supermen of the Australian batting order, reverse swing was kryptonite.
,

nearly dead. It shouldn't be laying ambushes like this. It shouldn't be defying cricket gravity.

In that 2005 Ashes series, England beat Australia for the first time in nearly twenty years. Their chief weapon was so-called reverse swing, spectacularly exploited. The planning was military, the execution disciplined, the attention to detail meticulous; for instance, the English always selected the darkest available ball so that the seam was harder for the batsman to discern.

To the supermen of the Australian batting order, reverse swing was kryptonite. Jones's defeat of Clarke this day was merely the most graphic of many telling examples. Conventional swing, which most often happens when the ball is relatively new (perhaps for the first twenty overs of the innings), was better understood, though by no means easy to face. Jones's rare skill was that he could reverse swing the old ball in both directions, to produce inswingers and outswingers. Repeatedly, even masterful batsmen such as Ricky Ponting and Adam Gilchrist were left mystified and helpless. Here was a new axis for cricket – or rather, new-old.

So what exactly is swing – and its reverse? How much meddling with the ball is too much? And how did 'ball management' become part of the modern game of cricket?

What makes a ball swing?

The behaviour of balls in flight in all sports has always intrigued. Baseballs, tennis balls, golf balls, footballs and soccer balls, once propelled, don't necessarily fly straight and true, but do the damnedest things. Understanding and harnessing these eccentricities has become a crucial part of all games.

It is well enough accepted that what matters are the irregularities on the surface of any of these spheres: the stitching that holds them together, flaws, insignias, dimples, any indent or anything that stands proud. All are liable to disturb the flow of air around them and affect their trajectory. The cricket ball sits uniquely well in this paradigm. Peculiarly among sports, cricket not only expects deterioration but is predicated on it. The pitch crumbles, the bowling slows, the batting order tapers. Above all, there is the ball, the missile and quarry at the game's heart. Red and gleaming to begin, as it wears, dulls, frays, coarsens and softens, it makes changing demands on the skills of batsmen and bowlers.

Of course, there are statutory rules that stipulate how the ball may and may not be knocked about during its journey to eighty overs (the point at which it is replaced and the game resets). A ball may be polished, though not with an artificial substance, dried with a towel if it is wet, and wiped clean of mud under supervision. Any other action that changes the condition of the ball is against the rules.

There are three basic ways to cause a cricket ball to deviate en route from bowler to batsman. Here, we are concerned with swing bowling as distinct from seam or spin, by which torque and traction combine to cause the ball to deviate as it bounces. Aerodynamics and fluid mechanics explain swing: it's all to do with the asymmetrical flow of air over the ball. 'In simple terms, the aerodynamics of bowling mean that the shiny side travels faster through the air, while the rough side acts as a brake, pushing the ball in that direction,' says the BBC. This is the intuition on which Clarke was acting.

Theory and practice don't necessarily or exactly accord. Not everyone can swing a ball, not everywhere, not every day. Humidity will make a ball swing more, a grassy pitch, too. Scientists say these are cricketing old wives' tales without laboratory validation. Anecdotally, these are incontrovertible. So, too, are the effects on swing of cloud at Headingley, wind at the WACA Ground, high tide at Durban and Southend. At these, physicists tear out their hair. The point is that conventional swing is an art, and reverse swing a more mysterious art still. Trying to explain it, as with trying to play it, is liable to tangle you up in knots.

Where did reverse swing start?

Pakistan fast bowler Sarfraz Nawaz was one progenitor. 'Sarfraz discovered reverse swing by bowling with balls of all conditions, new, semi-new and old,' writes Peter Oborne in his 2014 book *Wounded Tiger*. 'He began on matting wickets, where he could cut the ball. "One day, I shone one side of a very old ball and it swung. It was rough on both sides, but I shone one side and it swung towards the shine. It should not have done this." In that Eureka moment, reverse swing was born.'

Initially, Sarfraz told no one, which means reverse was cloaked in mystery from the start. 'It is fair to say that the cricket world did not really take much notice of reverse swing until its victims started to complain about it,' notes Oborne. Adds Sarfraz: 'When I passed the art on to Imran Khan, and then taught Wasim Akram and Waqar Younis, in those times everyone called it cheating, but when the Englishmen started to reverse swing, it became an art.'

Imran also introduced the concept to English county cricket while playing for Sussex, and in 1984–85 to Australia when he spent a season with the University of Sydney and New South Wales. One of Imran's teammates at New South Wales was Geoff Lawson, the legendary fast bowler, who took 180 wickets in his Test career. He vividly remembers one afternoon at the SCG when South Australian David Hookes was playing a long, stubborn innings. The ball was old, the pitch flat, New South Wales' mood resigned. Suddenly, Imran said to captain Dirk Wellham, 'Give me the ball. I will get him out in three balls.' Teammates thought, 'You're kidding, mate.' Imran set two slips and two gullies, rubbed some perspiration into the ball and delivered two hooping outswingers then a third ball with an identical action that swung in and trapped the startled Hookes as it crashed into his pads. Teammates thought, 'You. Are. Kidding.'

If anything, Australia came late to the reverse-swing party. This might have been due to conditions: grounds are lusher, and the

Australian-made Kookaburra ball does not swing as extravagantly as others. That is not to say reverse engineering passed Australia by. Brett Lee, because he was so fast, could be frightening when he made the ball swing late and counterintuitively. Glenn McGrath was a master of reverse. 'You just held the seam straight with the shiny side facing the way you wanted to swing, and run in and bowl it,' he said in 2015.

Australia's inculturation in the skill had its fullest flowering, or at least its best-known, in the hands of coaches Troy Cooley and David Saker, in the service of the English. Cooley was a modestly performing fast bowler for Tasmania who masterminded England's blueprint in 2005, and later coached Australia's bowlers. He notes three critical ingredients for reverse swing: the condition of the ball, the position of the seam and the speed of the bowler. In 2005, 'all we did was practise it,' he says.

How does reverse swing actually happen?

Reverse swing, as the name suggests, moves in the opposite direction to conventional swing. Instead of the ball drifting towards its rougher side, it veers towards the smooth. Typically, a ball needs to be older, and thoroughly knocked about, before it arrives in 'the zone' to reverse; and it takes a faster bowler to inject enough velocity for the effect to take hold.

In 2005, England possessed two fast bowlers with the speed and skill to exploit reverse swing – Simon Jones and Andrew Flintoff. All the team's bowlers bought into the plan to care for the ball as it aged, polishing one 'slightly rough' side while allowing the other to become, as Cooley puts it, 'super rough' from being hit or bowled into the abrasive pitch. The idea was to create a marked contrast between the rough and super-rough sides of the ball – one that primed the ball for reverse.

While conventional swing involves air hugging the surface for longer on the rough side of the ball, something peculiar happens in reverse. When a reverse-ready ball is delivered at a high enough speed, the layers of air that form on either side transition from what scientists call 'laminar' to 'turbulent' on both sides, but at different times. On the super-rough side, the air layer becomes particularly turbulent and thickens to the point that it separates from the ball much earlier. On the relatively smooth side, the air layer is turbulent to a degree that means it will now stick for longer before separating. The uneven points of separation create an uneven wake behind the ball and a side force, as in conventional swing – only in the opposite direction. Jones confused Clarke by bowling a succession of reverse swing balls that swerved away, then surreptitiously turned the shiny side towards the batsman to produce a reversing inswinger.

Reverse swing, after all these years, is still sometimes spoken of as if it is a secret to all but the initiated. It's not. As Cooley describes it, it is a well-understood tool at the disposal of bowlers whose job, after all, is to make life tough for batsmen. 'Understanding why and how you could get it put the bowler in the drivers' seat when the pitch and the game were flat,' Cooley explains. 'The secret's out. We know what to do now.'

> *'Reverse swing, after all these years,*
> *is still sometimes spoken of as if it is*
> *a secret to all but the initiated.'*

There is a corporatised modern term for the quest for reverse swing now: ball management. To achieve reverse, it was thought that it was necessary to weigh down the so-called shiny side of the ball with whatever moisture was at hand – sweat, saliva – though this is now disputed. It certainly is necessary for one side of the ball, in particular, to become roughed up and kept dry to the point of flaky. Fielding teams see to this by bouncing the ball into the wicketkeeper if the outfield is rough, by keeping it out of sweatier palms and often by commissioning one man, a non-bowler, to supervise the state of the ball as its 'manager'; between every delivery, it passes through his hands.

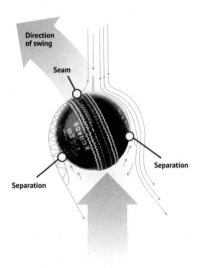

Conventional swing

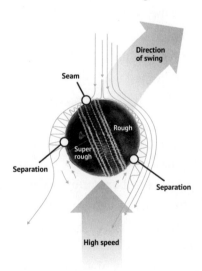

Reverse swing

Graphics: Mark Stehle, Jo Gay

What is the difference between managing and tampering?

Every cricket team works on the ball, either to buff it or scratch it. The inventory of aids used over the years is long. If the pockets of history were turned out, they would show, in no particular order: sweat and saliva, bottle tops, dirt, fingernails, medical tape, lollies, Vaseline, soft drinks, hankies, pen-knives, lip balm, sunscreen and, ahem, sandpaper. Here, ball management crosses the line into ball tampering, and therein lies the darkness of the art. Particularly cute is the pocket zipper, which a fieldsman can use to gouge up the ball while making it look like polishing. (The current South African captain, Faf du Plessis, was fined for rubbing the ball on his zipper during a 2013 game against Pakistan.) Legally, no artificial agent may be used but the grey area is wide and murky: lollies replenish energy but conveniently work sheening wonders. Du Plessis, again, was fined for lolly work in 2016.

Mostly, malfeasance – if that's what it is – is acknowledged only by retired cricketers in autobiographies. Just recently, it was the turn of former English spinner Monty Panesar in his book *The Full Monty*. 'Whether we broke the laws depends on how you interpret them,' writes Panesar, who played for England between 2006 and 2013. 'We found that mints and sun cream had an effect on the saliva, and that helped the ball to reverse. I might also have "accidentally" caught the ball on the zip of my trouser pocket to rough it up a little.'

As often as meddling with the cricket ball has worked, it has not. As Imran Khan said all those years ago, not everyone who he taught reverse swing to could execute it. You can manage the ball all you like but if your bowlers cannot deliver, all you are left with is a prematurely old, defused and useless ball, about as ballistic as a wad of papier-mâché.

Before Cape Town in 2018, cricket was in a permanent state of what might be called a cover-up in plain sight. 'Ball tampering happens all the time,' writes Geoff Lemon in his book on the

Cape Town saga, *Steve Smith's Men: Behind Australian Cricket's Fall*. 'It might be the world's biggest secret society, this bizarre *omerta* of an entire industry, covering thousands of players across international lines with admirable completeness. It is rarely confirmed, but never denied.'

Australia and South Africa, especially, have had mutual blind eyes. When, in 2014, Dave Warner suggested that South African wicketkeeper A. B. de Villiers was using the dimples on his gloves to worry away at the ball, outrage ensued – at Warner, not de Villiers. When, in Hobart in 2016, du Plessis was caught with a trafficable number of mints in his mouth and was brought to book, Australia was noticeably evasive. Then captain Steve Smith said only that every team tried to shine the ball 'the same way' and left it at that.

Back in South Africa at the start of 2018, after a scintillating bowling display from the home team in Port Elizabeth to level the series, then Australian coach Darren Lehmann was phlegmatic: 'Obviously, there are techniques used by both sides to get the ball to reverse, and that's just the way the game goes. I have no problems with it, simple. I don't mind the ball moving. I have no problems with it at all.' Accepted as plain-speaking commentary at the time, it would soon echo sinisterly.

Commentators puzzle over it: was that reverse or not? Sometimes, it 'appears' – stigmata-like – inside twenty overs.

As the Australian bowlers had been on their marauding way during the home Ashes series the previous summer, mutterings could be heard from the English about Australia's, shall we say, cutting-edge approach to ball management. By the time they arrived in South Africa, the alert was out. Australia were in a febrile state of mind. They perhaps became obsessed with reverse swing, even possessed by it; Mark Taylor, for one, thinks so. Typically, it is hard to catch ball tamperers red-handed but, forewarned, South African television ran surveillance for a month, then pounced. Grimly intent on their opponents, and drawn inward by a siege mentality, the Australians did not notice until far too late and had nowhere to hide.

On the third day of the third Test in Cape Town, Cameron Bancroft was caught on camera stuffing a piece of sandpaper down his trousers. Even more startling was Captain Smith's admission that night, that he, Smith, was complicit in a plan contrived at lunch to use a piece of tape (later revealed to be sandpaper) on the ball. Warner, Cricket Australia later alleged in its charge sheet, was the architect of the plan.

Smith and Warner served year-long bans and Bancroft nine months, not for ball-tampering, mind you, but under the Cricket Australia code of conduct for bringing the game into disrepute. Smith's fateful mistake, he later admitted, was to turn a blind eye to the discussion taking place in the Cape Town dressing room. 'I didn't want to know anything about it,' he said. He paid the biggest price, stripped of the Australian captaincy.

Cricket people, on the ground and off, now watch out for when it 'goes', looking for signs like fishermen for salmon to start running. Commentators puzzle over it: was that reverse or not? Sometimes, it 'appears' – stigmata-like – inside twenty overs. Batsmen gesture to one another, registering alarm, and brace to change their ways. Flintoff, England's ultimate hero in the landmark 2005 series, tells of how he would sometimes have to suppress his excitement at the first hint of counterintuitive movement, lest he alert the batsmen.

What's the future of reverse swing?

Post Cape Town, it has to be said, reverse swing's place in the game has receded. It was expected to be a crucial factor in the Ashes series in England in 2019, but was not; orthodox swing was more telling by far. In 2020, there came another twist. When international cricket, like so many other enterprises around the world, was at a standstill because of the coronavirus pandemic, moves were afoot to fortify the game for its eventual resumption. The International Cricket Council outlawed the use of saliva, the most common agent, to shine the ball, one of several measures designed to limit the spread of infection among players. Speculatively, this would make it even harder for bowlers to swing the ball, orthodox or reverse. The always delicate balance between bat and ball would be given yet one more nudge in favour of batsmen.

28

WHY IS THERE A BOOM IN DINOSAUR FOSSILS?

Nearly thirty years after *Jurassic Park* roared on to screens, dinosaurs are still in fashion. What is Australia's dinosaur history, and what more is there to discover?

Sherryn Groch

J ack Horner, the palaeontologist who inspired the movie juggernaut *Jurassic Park*, found his first dinosaur bone when he was eight. His father had seen something sticking out of the earth as he rode across the prairies of Montana, North America, long the heartland of dinosaur discovery, and it was there that he took little Jack fossil hunting. The bone still sits in Horner's office today.

The success of *Jurassic Park* in 1993 would launch a new generation of palaeontologists and unprecedented interest in the field, opening up frontiers from Argentina to Australia and rewriting the story of the scaly monsters on screen. Within three years, on a hillside in China, a farmer stumbled upon the world's first glimpse of a feathered dinosaur.

Today, close to one new dinosaur species is discovered every week. Far from the image of the lumbering lizard doomed to extinction, palaeontologists now know dinosaurs as one of nature's great success stories. In their 185-million-year reign on Earth, they weathered tremendous upheaval. Continents broke apart, volcanoes rained lava, temperatures and levels of toxic gases climbed, monster wildfires scarred the land. Still dinosaurs spread to all the planet's corners, growing to the size of passenger planes or emerging in strange new shapes including, eventually, as birds.

> '*Close to one new dinosaur species is discovered every week. Far from the image of the lumbering lizard doomed to extinction, palaeontologists now know dinosaurs as one of nature's great success stories.*'

In South America and Asia, whole new ecosystems are still being unearthed that include everything from huge spiked herbivores to strange bat-winged 'vampires'. In Outback Australia, a cache of fossils has been found down an opal mine, many species preserved as vibrant gems.

Now, in another era of planetary change, this time of our own making, what can we learn from these creatures? What discoveries have put Australia on the map? And will we ever bring a dinosaur back to life?

Why are scientists still finding so many dinosaurs?

Horner sat next to director Steven Spielberg as a consultant on the set of *Jurassic Park* and remembers well the hordes of students who suddenly signed up for his university classes after the film hit cinemas. But it wasn't a flash in the pan, says palaeontologist and author Steve Brusatte, who has himself helped discover more than a dozen dinosaurs. The students kept coming and today the resulting gold rush of discovery shows no signs of slowing down – even as academic research of all persuasions takes a hit in the economic fallout from the coronavirus pandemic. 'But we're not running out of dinosaurs,' Brusatte says.

Palaeontologist Alfio Alessandro Chiarenza has tracked the rate of new finds since the first bones were unearthed in the 1800s. He, too, belongs to the *Jurassic Park* generation, the scientists 'who never grew up', and says better technology is also speeding up dinosaur hunting as researchers compare finds online.

Out in the field, Horner says the tools are still mostly the picks and fossil brushes he used when he started. Dinosaur bones eventually become rock – and in some places, such as Australia, gem stone – which makes them nearly impossible to pick out from the landscape with scanners. Yet, back in the lab, X-rays, 3D printing, even molecular particle accelerators now come into play.

All of those fresh eyes in the field can sometimes catch what has been missed. In early 2020, the big find to hit headlines was a new species, and likely an entirely new genus, of tyrannosaur. But the bones, originally dug up in Alberta, Canada, had gathered dust in a museum cabinet for almost a decade before PhD student Jared Voris decided to take a closer look. Now dubbed the Reaper of Death, the tyrannosaur is the oldest found in Canada, dated to more than 79 million years ago. In life, it would have been about the length of two cars, and Voris says telltale ridges in its jaw set it apart from other kinds of tyrannosaur.

But sometimes, Horner warns, the hype can get ahead of the science. Many dinosaurs vary wildly in size and shape over their life cycle and baby dinosaurs have on occasion been 'discovered' as their own separate species.

What is Australia's dinosaur history?

On Australia's west coast, some of the world's largest surviving dinosaur footprints are still in the rock, spanning almost 2 metres each. But it is on the east coast that most of Australia's fossil record is being dug up – and it's taken a 'quantum leap forward' in the past few years, according to the Australian Museum.

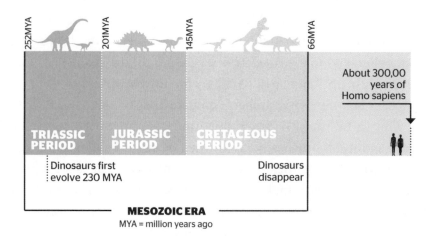

Dinosaurs lived for 165 million years; humans have been around for 300,000.

Graphic: Matthew Absalom-Wong

One hundred million years ago, in the last great age of dinosaurs known as the Cretaceous period, the dry continent was lush and green. Pterosaurs or 'iron dragons' ruled the skies and ancient crocodiles shared hunting grounds with creatures such as Lightning Claw, the largest carnivorous dinosaur ever found in Australia, with its 'grappling hooks' for hands. Much of the east was swamped by a shallow inland sea – creating the perfect conditions for fossils.

While our most complete dinosaur skeletons have come from Queensland, opal miners in remote New South Wales have stumbled upon the most beautiful. Down a mine shaft in Lightning Ridge is one of the richest fossil collections ever discovered from Gondwana, the ancient supercontinent that once accounted for two-thirds of today's land, including Australia. Here, dinosaur remains were buried under reactive minerals – glass or silica ash – from a chain of volcanoes erupting up north near the Great Barrier Reef at the time. Under the 'Martian-like' conditions, the most unique opals in the world took shape in the rock – and in dinosaur bone.

'It seems to be the only place in the world where the dinosaur fossils have turned to opals so it's literally a treasure trove,' says Phil Bell, a palaeontologist at the University of New England. 'Some species have rich veins of colour through them, blues and reds.'

Fossils have been picked out of opal hauls since mining began at the site in the 1900s – Australia's first prehistoric mammals were discovered there as well as some dinosaur species. But it's hard work, climbing metres down rickety ladders into black chasms to dig with pickaxes and jackhammers. Most of what's been found has been unearthed by the miners themselves. Even then, no one had studied the fossils in depth until 2013, when Bell ventured into the dark beneath Lightning Ridge and found a wealth of life, including Lightning Claw and an entire herd of the plant-eater Fostoria.

'Not all of the bones are gem quality, a lot are just the dark or opaque part of the opal, but some of those Fostoria bones do shimmer with the entire spectrum of colours,' Bell says. 'These things are worth tens of thousands of dollars as jewellery but they're priceless as fossils.'

They are so precious that palaeontologists and the Australian Opal Centre are working with the local mining community to save them from commercial trade. When broken up for their gems, the fossils fetch a decent sum. But in a region so often hit hard by drought, they can bring more value, the argument goes, as a tourist attraction.

'Until Lightning Ridge, we'd been dealing with scraps from Victoria's coast and Queensland,' Bell explains. 'We had those beautiful big [sauropod] tracks in Broome but that was our sole image of what dinosaurs in Australia looked like. Suddenly, here was this virtually untapped window into our past.'

Is it finders keepers with bones?

It's not only scientists looking for dinosaurs. While 'bone wars' have been raging since the 1800s as palaeontologists and collectors haggled over finds, the field's technology boom has also made it easier for black market traders to beat researchers to sites. Of course, a lot of dinosaur hunting depends on whose land you're on and regulation varies between countries and states. In Canada, all discoveries are the property of the Crown. In much of Australia and other parts of the world, if the bones are found on private land, they belong to that landowner. If they are held in a private collection, many palaeontologists consider them scientifically worthless as they cannot be studied by others.

Like rare Rembrandts, T-Rex skeletons and other fossils are fast becoming status symbols and stolen bones routinely surface at high-profile auctions with forged paperwork. Bidding wars between Hollywood heavyweights often make the gossip pages;

in 2015, actor Nicolas Cage returned a US$276,000 dinosaur skull he'd secured at an auction when it emerged it had been smuggled illegally out of Mongolia, a mecca for fossils but also a hot spot for dinosaur crime.

Bell is one of a growing number of palaeontologists now using hand-held scanners 'a bit like hairdryers' to trace the chemical fingerprints of bones and so help determine where they might have been poached from. In Australia, our rare opalised fossils cannot be exported without a permit, which are hard to come by. But their rarity makes them highly sought after on the black market.

> *'Like rare Rembrandts, T-Rex skeletons and other fossils are fast becoming status symbols and stolen bones routinely surface at high-profile auctions with forged paperwork.'*

How do we know what dinosaurs looked like?

As palaeontology itself evolves, dig sites are becoming less of a graveyard and more of a crime scene. Researchers hunt for clues that will tell them not just the kind of animal they've found but how it lived. Dinosaurs, like sharks, shed their teeth often, Bell says, and in sites such as Lightning Ridge, palaeontologists can piece together whole ecosystems. X-rays can help them look inside dinosaur brains and see where arteries once carved around the bones. Fossils can be 3D printed, and species run through the same engineering software used to test the structural integrity of dams and bridges, to explore how they would have moved, if they could fly, and the way T-Rex really handled those tiny arms.

Voris's tyrannosaur find in January 2020 also provides clues about the ecology of North America during the Cretaceous period –

further evidence, according to Voris, of an apparent split in the land between 89 million and 74 million years ago. 'In the north – Montana, Alberta – we see really different species to further south, like Utah, alive at the exact same time but there's nothing in the land so far we've found to tell us why,' he says. 'We have to keep digging.'

In parts of the world such as China, whole areas have been preserved under almost Pompeii-like conditions by past volcanic eruptions or sudden floods, allowing scientists to find remarkably well-preserved feathers. Using X-rays, they've even extrapolated the pigments, turning the old drab green and brown dinosaur palette on its head in an explosion of flamboyant blues, reds and yellows. Given feathers appeared on many species too big to fly, Brusatte says it's likely the filaments didn't evolve for the purpose of taking to the skies and might have first been used in mating display.

While feathers on species such as velociraptor were met with a lot of fanfare (some museum collections changed their exhibits overnight), elsewhere scientists such as Bell have made unprecedented finds, too, unearthing the scaly skin of a T-Rex. 'The hype around feathers kind of steamrolled a lot of other evidence,' Bell says. 'There were lots of feathered dinosaurs but we still [think] most had scaly skin.'

Of course, just as it would be difficult to discover from skeletons many of the wonders of the natural world today, such as whale song or lyrebird mimicry, Chiarenza says there are things palaeontology will likely never know. 'Because of the way fossils form [usually near water], we'll probably never find animals that lived in the mountains,' he says. 'There might have been all kinds of strange creatures there, like we have gorillas and [big cats] today.'

What more is there to discover?

The holy grail of palaeontology is still dinosaur DNA. It was Horner's own research on dinosaur babies that helped inspire Michael Crichton to write *Jurassic Park*. Sam Neill would go

'

The key to our future is in the past – and dinosaurs are a huge part of that.

'

on to play the role based on Horner, Dr Alan Grant, in the film adaptation. While Horner didn't meet Crichton until they were both pressed into the back of a limousine en route to the film's premiere, the author's wild idea – that dinosaur DNA could be extracted from ancient preserved mosquitoes – lit the fuse for his next phase of research: could we really build a dinosaur?

DNA breaks down fast, even in the belly of a mosquito, and the amount needed to create a dinosaur would be much more than palaeontologists could ever dream to find, Horner says. Still, there have been flashes of hope over the years, including the breakthrough discovery of soft tissue and intact blood proteins in a T-Rex bone by his student Mary Schweitzer.

But Horner has a plan B: one he's dubbed 'chickenosaurus' for the school kids. Birds are the dinosaurs that escaped extinction. Their genes still carry the building blocks of ancient dinosaurs – but many of their dino traits have been 'turned off' over the course of evolution. Just as there have been rare cases of humans born with a tail or a snake with legs, Horner's plan is to flick back on the dormant lines of genetic code in a chicken.

'We've found the genes we need to turn back on to change the head, the arms, the legs, to grow teeth,' Horner says. 'But we can't figure out how to make the tail. That doesn't seem to be a [dormant or] atavistic gene.' That means the team will now have to turn to high-tech genetic engineering tools, likely the DNA editor CRISPR-Cas9, to finish the job and 'keep the fourth-graders happy'. 'But getting university backing to use a new tool like that, to create a novelty, it's not going to happen soon,' Horner says.

When it comes to solving the mystery of what killed the dinosaurs, meanwhile, scientists have almost closed the case.

The suspect pool has been mostly whittled down from volcanoes, toxic gases and even chronic constipation to a world-shattering asteroid hit one June day 66 million years ago. (They know it was June because fossilised lilies found in North America were in the full bloom of summer at the time, Brusatte says.) The chunk of rock to blame was at least 10 kilometres wide and it hit with the force of more than a billion nuclear bombs, punching a hole in the Earth's crust in what is now the Gulf of Mexico. That was just the right spot, many scientists say, to trigger a chain of unprecedented natural disasters – from firestorms, earthquakes and tsunamis to ocean acidification and soot clouds that choked out the sun.

It also exposed the vulnerability of any biological empire on Earth – including humanity. This time it's not an asteroid radically changing the planet, and while Horner says the importance of studying dinosaurs 'might still be lost on some people', he stresses they can tell us more about the world than ever before, a glimpse into both evolution and extinction. 'The key to our future is in the past – and dinosaurs are a huge part of that.'

29

WHEN IS A STATISTIC NOT WHAT IT SEEMS?

Wealth, health, happiness – it's all in the data these days. But look again: what exactly are the numbers telling you?

Craig Butt

'The average Australian household is worth $1 million.' 'The number of crimes recorded in Australia has reached a record high.' 'Polls predict a comfortable Labor victory.' Sometimes headlines about numbers are not quite what they seem. 'Average' does not necessarily mean typical. The number of crimes may well have risen – in line with population growth, as one would expect. And political polls? Well, their fallibility is well documented.

Most of us weigh up information every day and think about statistics a lot more than we probably give ourselves credit for – being able to interpret data and statistics is a handy skill.

What are some common confusions and pitfalls in the way statistics are expressed? And what should you keep in mind when a headline prompts you to raise an eyebrow?

Mean or median?

'Australians, on average, are now millionaires.' Sounds good, doesn't it? But 'on average' is a phrase ripe for misuse, especially if it's not qualified by one of these two words: mean or median. This headline came from Australian Bureau of Statistics (ABS) research into economic indicators of wealth. There are several different types of indicators and they lead to quite different results. To calculate the mean, the bureau pooled the net worth of Australian households and divided the result by the number of households counted – and came up with $1,022,200. Household net worth includes the total amount of property, assets, shares and savings owned by all the people who live under one roof. It's not correct, though, to describe as typical a household net worth of $1.02 million.

Take, say, five households of varying wealth all living in a cul-de-sac, including one that's worth heaps more than the rest because it's lived in by a multi-billionaire. To calculate the mean household worth in this cul-de-sac, pool the net worths and distribute the total evenly among the total number of households, as the ABS did with its calculation.

NET WORTH

| $200k | $500k | $550k | $750k | $15 billion |

÷ 5
(HOUSEHOLDS)

= $3 BILLION ← MEAN

Now, the average net worth of all five households surges to $3 billion. In other words, one rich person's presence makes a billionaire's row out of an otherwise humble cul-de-sac – on paper. But the typical household in that cul-de-sac is not worth $3 billion bucks. So talking about the mean doesn't help much when there are big differences in what is being compared. Australia isn't a five household cul-de-sac, of course, but incredibly wealthy households inflate the nationwide mean in the same way. But talking about the mean does help if we are referring to, say, mean life expectancy or the mean weight of Australians because the variations are less drastic – you can't be 200 years old or weigh 10 tonnes.

So how would you come up with the typical net worth of an Australian household? Look at the median.* The median is another economic indicator of wealth, which also appears in the bureau's data tables. It's what you get if you take all the things you've counted and put them in a line from smallest to biggest. The one at the exact midpoint is the median value.

So, while the mean household net worth in Australia in 2017–18

---

* A story on data wouldn't be complete without at least one cameo appearance from an asterisked footnote – and, as with anything involving statistics, it's worth reading the fine print. Looking at the median isn't always the best rule of thumb. If you've ever looked through a list of median house prices in each suburb and wondered why some areas are missing, it's because the median figure is not published unless a certain number of properties changed hands. Otherwise, the median figure might not be representative of the area.

(the bureau won't update this figure again until July 2021) was $1,022,200, the median household net worth was $558,900. That means that half of Australian households are worth more than $558,900 and the other half are worth less.

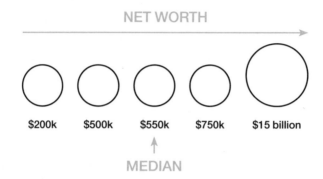

As for that headline? If you dig into the data further, it turns out that about 30 per cent of Australian households have a net worth of more than $1 million – 'roughly a third of Australians are now millionaires' wouldn't have quite the same ring to it.

Bottom line: when we tell stories based on numbers, we can choose our own adventure depending on which measure we look at. Often, taking several measures into account will give a fuller picture. For example, the economic indicators of wealth that the bureau provides also include the gap between rich and poor – indicated by the Gini coefficient, a measure of inequality named after its creator, statistician Corrado Gini. The bureau's figures show that the gap has widened over the past decade. And yet another indicator shows that a higher proportion of households have taken on a large amount of debt.

Cause or correlation?

'Smoking causes lung cancer' – that's an uncontroversial statement, nowadays. But for a long time, while doctors had a hunch that people who smoked cigarettes were more likely to end up with breathing difficulties in later life, proving it was another matter. The most confident statement a doctor could make went like this: people who smoke have also exhibited a higher rate of lung cancer than the rest of the population. In other words, there was a correlation between smoking and lung cancer – they seemed to happen together an awful lot – but until more research was done, it wasn't possible to know whether smoking actually caused lung cancer. This lack of a causal link left plenty of wriggle room to suggest that 'confounding factors' (another term found in statistics and health studies) were really behind cancer in smokers. After all, it might be the chemicals in cigarette lighters that made smokers ill (that theory was actually put forward). Or, as an *Age* editorial suggested, given smog and bad-quality tobacco were both found in other countries, Australia could well be a better place to be a smoker.

It's easy to snicker, with the benefit of hindsight. But it's by testing a theory through experiments (and ruling out other possibilities) that it gains scientific acceptance – and it becomes clear that what was considered a correlation is actually a cause. The type of medical study designed to find causation is a randomised controlled trial, in which people randomly receive one of several interventions, which may include a placebo. Other studies, such as retrospective or observational studies, can only show correlation.

And it goes the other way, too. Sometimes researchers (and humans in general) are too hasty to assert that two things are connected when, in fact, they don't have any bearing on a phenomenon. For example, data scientists were once adamant that real-time Google search data could be used to predict where flu outbreaks were happening. They reasoned that if people started to fall ill, they would search for flu symptoms on the internet. Google engineers published a much-lauded scientific paper on the topic. But when the theory was put to the test, the Google search data didn't match up with the recorded flu cases at all, greatly overestimating infection rates.

Scientists are well aware of this sometimes misguided propensity to make connections. They will often devote sizeable sections of their papers to unpicking evidence of causal links and will tend to include a refrain that more research is needed to say that x causes y.

But questions of correlation and causation are not restricted to science. Every day, countless social media posts and opinion articles argue that there is a direct connection between two disparate things. A popular genre is how millennials are responsible for everything that is wrong with the world.

When is a poll not as precise as it might seem?

All polls and surveys (and a lot of studies) come with a degree of uncertainty baked in. It's just that they often end up sounding so very precise. Consider this population projection for Australia from the ABS: 49,226,089 in 2066. That's very precise, especially when you consider the bureau made this prediction in 2018. But this number is not presented as a crystal clear prediction (it would be madness if it were). It has caveats and qualifiers built in. The figure sits somewhere in a range of values of what the population could be in 2066, based on current trends. The figures are also, by the bureau's own admission, based on assumptions about high rates of fertility and immigration – other projections put estimates considerably lower, at about 38 million.

By their nature, predictions are fraught – in life, in politics and in statistics. So is dealing with uncertainty. Federal political polls typically survey about 1500 people from various backgrounds, age groups and walks of life. The aim is that they mirror the general population – but when about 1500 people are supposed to be a microcosm of Australia's population of about 26 million, it's easy to see how the poll's findings will not be exact.

The uncertainty of a number (such as a poll result) is expressed in its margin of error, which helps set the parameters of how the information should be interpreted. In federal polls, approval ratings have a margin of error of about three percentage points. That's why, if a poll says a prime minister has a 50 per cent approval rating, it means his or her approval rating lies somewhere between 47 and 53 per cent.

There are lots of other reasons why poll results come into question, but that's a whole other story.

Rates or raw numbers?

Every city has its exceptional suburbs. In Melbourne it's Werribee, in Sydney it's Liverpool. Werribee is the most multicultural place in Victoria (as in, it's home to people from more countries than anywhere else), it is home to the most childcare workers, the most Richmond Football Club members and the most online shoppers. It's also home to the most people living on welfare and the most bankrupts. Liverpool is the busiest place in New South Wales for online purchases, the number one spot for first home buyers and among the areas with the most gun owners, people on welfare, disabled-parking cheats and homeowners defaulting on their mortgages.

What makes Werribee and Liverpool stand out so much? Both are among the most populated suburbs in Australia. That means that whenever anybody puts together a list of the top ten suburbs with the 'most' of something, Werribee and Liverpool tend to feature.

We need to put things in perspective by adjusting the figures for the population. There are several ways we can do this. One is by calculating the rate. By expressing what is being counted as a rate, we level the playing field. We can see how many Richmond supporters there are for every 1000 people in Werribee against how many Richmond supporters there are for every 1000 people in a different suburb. Once we adjust for population size we find that there isn't anything unusual about Werribee when it comes to its spread of Richmond supporters – or debtors or welfare recipients. But it still has one of the highest percentages of childcare workers, owing to the area being home to so many young, working families.

At the end of May 2020, the country with the most deaths from COVID-19 was the United States, one of the most populated countries in the world. But the populated country with the highest death rate from the new coronavirus at this time was Belgium, which focused attention on the effectiveness of its public health efforts to slow the spread of infections. Comparing rates among different countries can, however, be fraught because not everyone collects data in the same way. If a country is misrepresenting its death figures, its actual death rate could be much higher than its reported death rate. Belgium's health authorities have argued they have been more assiduous than other countries in counting coronavirus deaths, which they say is reflected in the higher death rate.

Rates are also handy if the population is changing. When we report on crime statistics, we don't tend to focus on whether there has been an increase in the number of crimes reported because these tend to increase each year anyway, in line with population growth. Take Victoria in 2018, for example. There were about 7000 more crimes reported, a 1.8 per cent rise. Crime wave? Not quite. When we account for a 2.2 per cent increase in population over the same period, the actual rate of crime decreased slightly (0.4 per cent).

Rates can be deceptive, too, though, particularly when a population size is really small. For example, in an area that's home to eight people, all it would take is for a few more crimes than usual to be reported and, on a rate per 1000 basis, it could become the crime capital of a state.

Feeling lucky? Risk and percentage rises

Let's say I ran a vegan coffee cart. If I told you that sales had surged by 400 per cent in the past month you might think I'd tapped into the next big thing in refreshments. After seeing this information in a slick-looking graph, you might even consider investing in my burgeoning coffee cart franchise. But you would need these two crucial pieces of information before you stumped up for an investment: how many cups of coffee I sold last month, and how many cups of coffee I sold this month. A 400 per cent surge in sales on its own doesn't tell you anything about the scale of the operation. If it turned out that my coffee cart's turnover was actually one cup last month and five cups in this month, well … pass the full-milk latte.

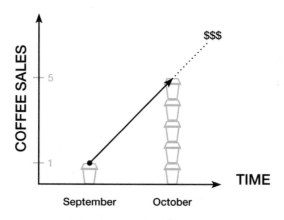

Percentage changes can be even more slippery when it comes to risk. Consider this entirely fictional statement: 'People who drink lots of coffee risk being eight times more likely than a typical person to have their hair turn blue.' 'Eight times more likely' is a relative risk that applies to coffee drinkers: relative to a typical person, the risk is eight times higher. But we're missing a crucial piece of information – what is the risk of hair turning blue for a typical person, whether they drink coffee or not? It might be that the typical risk of this happening is one in 1000. This is known as the absolute risk. That means that for every 1000 people, one person will undergo a dramatic shift in their hair colour at some stage of their lifetime. It follows, then, that a heavy coffee drinker has an eight in 1000 chance of their hair turning blue.

Here's a visual way to think about it. Each blue square is a person whose hair turned blue, while the white squares are people whose hair didn't. If the grid was completely blue that would mean your chances of getting this condition would be certain, while if the grid was blank there would be no chance of it happening. Here's what the blue hair risk looks like for a typical person, and then for a coffee addict side by side, based on one in 1000 and eight in 1000:

THE LIFETIME RISK OF
YOUR HAIR TURNING BLUE

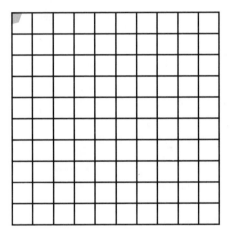

AND IF YOU DRINK LOTS OF COFFEE

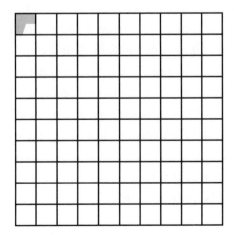

There isn't all that much difference between the two grids is there? Even though, in our faux example, coffee drinkers have an eight times higher risk of their hair changing colour, most of the squares in the grid are blank – irrespective of whether you drink coffee or not, you are far more likely to go your entire life without your hair turning blue.

If an absolute risk is very low, as in our example here, big increases in relative risk don't tend to make that much difference. But if an absolute risk is very high, any increase in relative risk could end up being very serious indeed. For example, the risk of getting sunburnt on a hot summer's day is quite high if someone goes sunbathing, but if they skip out on wearing sunscreen then the risk of getting burnt increases, which in turn incrementally increases skin cancer risk in later life.

We don't have statistics to hand on how often people misinterpret or misrepresent data – but it's almost certainly an everyday occurrence. Even the sources attributed to quips *about* statistics can be shaky. While it does seem to be writer Mark Twain who noted 'Facts are stubborn things but statistics are more pliable', it's not 100 per cent clear who first remarked, 'There are three kinds of lies: lies, damned lies, and statistics'. If it's any comfort, understanding statistical concepts such as the ones we've outlined here, and deploying a generous pinch of common sense, can help you navigate any hype.

'We don't have statistics to hand on how often people misinterpret or misrepresent data – but it's almost certainly an everyday occurrence.'

30

WHAT WILL POWER OUR HOMES IN THE FUTURE?

Hydrogen, wind, solar, perhaps
coal – what will we be plugging into in
2050? What will it take to make
them work? And is there any
role for nuclear power?

Nick O'Malley and Mike Foley

Three emerging technologies will help shape Australia's energy future, and one old one probably won't. There is a growing consensus that by 2050 the vast bulk of our electricity will be supplied by sources that are cleaner than old king coal.

Under the Paris Agreement, the federal government has committed to following scientific advice on how to meet Australia's contribution to keeping global warming under 2 degrees, while the states have set targets to source at least half of their electricity from renewable sources by 2050. Tasmania is aiming for 2022 and South Australia for 2030, while the ACT says it met its 100 per cent net renewable target in 2020.

So what are the new – or improved – technologies that will be powering the nation in the coming decades? And what else needs to be in place to make them work?

Why is there so much talk of hydrogen?

'I like to call it shipping sunshine,' said a chipper Australian chief scientist Dr Alan Finkel in late 2019 when he outlined a plan to develop a hydrogen energy industry that would not only one day help power Australia but also provide an export income in a post-coal world. Though the use of hydrogen as a clean energy might not yet be widely understood, it is already a proven technology. Germany started running the first hydrogen fuel-cell-powered train in 2016 while hydrogen-powered commuter buses were tested in Perth as far back as 2007. The only waste they emit is water.

The Hydrogen Council, an international body representing eighty-one leading energy, transport and industry companies, predicts that by 2050 there will be a global hydrogen market worth more than US$2 trillion per year. Finkel believes Australian exports could be worth AU$1.8 billion by 2030.

In the simplest terms, the process works by using an electrical current to split water into its component parts – oxygen and hydrogen. Hydrogen, which unlike other forms of renewable power has a similar energy density to fossil fuels, can then be used in vehicles equipped with hydrogen fuel cells or pumped into the mains gas network to be blended with natural gas for domestic consumption. It can be piped to power plants to sustain the grid or converted to synthetic natural gas for export.

Finkel believes Australia is ideally placed to produce enough hydrogen for it to become a key domestic power source, as well as an export industry – due to our size and clear, hot skies and our proximity to Asian markets that are expected to become major hydrogen importers, particularly Japan.

Even in the midst of political warfare in Australia over energy and resources, there is little disagreement over all this – but there is growing dispute over how best the industry should be scaled up. Commercial hydrogen, created by electricity drawn from renewable sources such as wind and solar farms, would be a totally emission-free energy, or green hydrogen; but that created by electricity generated by coal or gas would be brown hydrogen.

Finkel argues that to quickly grow the industry and secure a position for Australia in the export market we should employ fossil fuels in the short term and bank on cheaper renewables displacing them in the long run. 'We can use coal and natural gas to split the water, and capture and permanently bury the carbon dioxide emitted along the way,' he has said. Others, such as Richie Merzian, the director of climate and energy research at The Australia Institute, says that the infrastructure needed for brown hydrogen would be so expensive that we would lock in its use for years, further driving up Australian greenhouse gas emissions. The result of this debate might have an impact on exports, too. Some believe that customers of an Australian hydrogen industry might demand that the product be green.

Is the answer blowing in the wind?

Wind-generated power became almost as contentious as coal the moment utility-scale turbines began appearing on our horizons.

In 2014, then treasurer Joe Hockey lamented those that dotted the ridges above Lake George on the road between Sydney and Canberra as a 'blight on the landscape'. There are those who have suggested that coal mines and power plants are perhaps at least as offensive, but Hockey is not alone in his views. The energy and emissions reduction minister, Angus Taylor, has been an equally enthusiastic opponent of wind power over the years as well, once appearing at an anti-wind-power rally, but now accepts its role in Australia's future energy mix.

According to *National Geographic,* cumulative wind capacity around the world increased from 17,000 megawatts to more than 430,000 megawatts between 2000 and 2015 – by 2050, wind is expected to produce a third of the world's electricity. Wind overtook hydropower as Australia's leading source of clean energy in 2019, supplying 35.4 per cent of the country's clean energy and 9.5 per cent of Australia's overall electricity, according to the Clean Energy Council.

Australia is not the first country to see disputes arise from the impact of wind farms and the infrastructure needed to link them to the grid. In the United Kingdom, the cost of land and the imposing nature of turbines has prompted a huge expansion of offshore wind power. The first such farm in Australia is in early development stages off the coast of Victoria near Wilsons Promontory. If completed as planned, the so-called Star of the South project would see windmills generating 2000 megawatts – about as much as the vast Liddell Power Station in New South Wales – connected to the grid via existing infrastructure in the nearby Latrobe Valley, the traditional hub of Victoria's coal generation.

But Greg Bourne, who has served in such posts as energy adviser to Margaret Thatcher, Australasian chief of BP, chief executive of World Wildlife Fund Australia and chairman of the Australian Renewable Energy Agency, points out that wind energy in Australia faces different challenges and enjoys different benefits to the UK and Europe. Most of the waters close to our coastline are deeper than those of the North Sea, he says, making offshore wind farms more difficult to install. Land is more abundant here than in Europe, meaning there is more space to install them onshore without imposing on other land users, which would be a considerable cost saving.

Bourne, who is also chairman of Palisade, a company developing a wind farm at Granville Harbour on the west coast of Tasmania, says that advances in technology have made modern windmills ever more efficient and the power they generate commensurately cheaper. Turbines of the sort Palisade will install have masts that reach up to 70 metres and rotor diameters of more than 100 metres, each generating 4 megawatts of power. Due to the sheer size of these machines, fewer turbines can generate more energy, reducing the overall size of the farms. Rather than being installed on hilltops, where they may dominate skylines, in some cases they can be moved down slopes, reducing their visual impact. With such farms spread over Australia's land mass, the nation's wind resources can be better harnessed, with farms in the north providing power while those in the south might remain idle, and vice versa.

For all this energy to be put to best use at critical times, though, Australia must find a way to store it. Large-scale projects such as the Snowy 2.0 hydropower scheme will become critical, as will utility-scale batteries. But so will old-school rooftop solar systems, reinforced by a new wave of batteries and improved market regulation.

What's next for solar power?

Solar cells are as common to suburban Australian roofs as Hills hoists to our backyards, so it might seem odd to name them as one of the most exciting emerging energy technologies. But solar cell technology keeps improving – along with that of domestic batteries – and now a revolution is going on in the way they store and dispatch power. Together these changes are so significant that solar – along with batteries in homes, cars and other smart household appliances – is on the cusp of becoming so crucial to the national energy supply that it will displace the need to replace some of the ageing fleet of coal-fired power plants.

Also central to the growth of solar are long-awaited market reforms, with the Australian Energy Market Commission committing to reforming what is known as wholesale demand response. When the changes become effective in October 2021, big industrial power users such as smelters will be paid for reducing power consumption during periods of peak demand, such as in heatwaves when millions of air-conditioners are switched on at once. This will free up supply and bring down bills for households and industry alike – but the broader implications are far more significant. For the first time, the change will shift the balance between energy generators and customers and reward energy users for their contribution to the grid by way of reducing power demand. Until now it's been a one-way street with customers paying as they go.

What's a distributed energy grid?

The end goal of all of this power generation is what's known as a distributed energy grid, sometimes referred to as the two-sided grid. Energy customers of all sizes both pay for their consumption and get paid for their generation. A new form of energy player is already entering the market to make such a system even more efficient. Customers of these businesses pay to have equipment installed in their homes that monitors the price of power as it changes, minute by minute during the day, topping up batteries when it is cheapest and selling power when it is most valuable. This means that even more of the green energy produced by solar cells is used when it is most needed, easing total demand.

The Commonwealth Scientific and Industrial Research Organisation (CSIRO) has found that Australia could achieve net zero carbon emissions by 2050 with a large contribution to emissions reduction coming from solar power and the distributed energy grid – but targeted reforms to infrastructure and the market are needed to integrate widespread rooftop solar into the transmission network.

The two-sided energy market, where household customers are also paid for power generated on their premises and supplied back to the grid, could earn up to $2.5 billion a year, or an annual electricity saving of $414 to an average household.

State and Commonwealth governments, through the Council of Australian Governments, have worked on long-term market design that could apply from the middle of the decade, and a large part of which is the distributed energy grid. Agencies such as the Australian Energy Market Operation and the Australian Energy Market Commission are also developing reforms to help bring it on.

Voltage control will be a particular challenge for a distributed energy grid, and especially in Australia where more than 2 million of the nation's 13 million homes have been fitted with panels. That's because power supply into the grid has to be regulated to ensure it meets compatibility standards that make it as cheap and reliable as possible to accommodate a wide range of power sources.

Community batteries also hold exciting potential for the distributed energy grid. Servicing communities on a suburb or town basis, they would replace the batteries that some rooftop solar owners have in their home and enable customers to take a share in a more efficient and larger-scale resource.

The distributed energy grid reforms would need to ensure customers 'don't get double charged for transporting energy to and from the community battery,' says Australian National University Energy Change Institute director Dr Lachlan Blackhall. 'Under the current regulations, customers could be charged once for transporting energy to the community battery during the day as they generate energy from solar panels on their roof, and then get charged again later at night when they import and use that energy in their home,' Blackhall says.

> *'The industry body Energy Networks Australia forecasts that the electrification of transport could reduce annual household power bills as much as $162 by 2050.'*

In this system, electric vehicles, which currently draw on an already stressed grid, will start to help smooth its operation. Electric vehicle technology draws about the same amount of electricity as a small household for an average suburban commute, but advanced charging stations will ensure that when cars are plugged in to recharge overnight or at workplaces during the day they will contribute to the grid in the same manner as domestic batteries, effectively becoming a networked method of storing and supplying energy as needed. The industry body Energy Networks Australia forecasts that the electrification of transport could reduce annual household power bills as much as $162 by 2050.

Internet-connected smart devices will also play a role in the distributed energy grid by allowing retailers to tap into connected appliances such as air-conditioners and refrigerators and reduce power consumption when an appliance is not needed.

What role will nuclear power play?

One critic of the nuclear industry in Australia – such as it is – notes that it has always proved far more effective at generating reports about how much energy it might one day produce than it has been at producing any energy. Between 1952 and 2007, there have been at least five failed efforts to establish nuclear power plants in Australia, but the industry's indefatigable supporters ensure that debate over it never really ends.

The New South Wales, Victorian and federal parliaments have held inquiries into aspects of nuclear power, following a South Australian royal commission in 2016 – despite the fact that it remains illegal in Australia. Today, champions of nuclear power use the threat of climate change to bolster their case, arguing that only nuclear power can provide Australia with enough safe, cheap, reliable and clean energy to grow and decarbonise our economy. This argument is endorsed by a couple of heavyweights of the international climate action movement; the famed NASA climatologist James Hansen and the environmental speaker and writer Michael Shellenberger, who have become fixtures on an international pro-nuclear speaking circuit.

Nuclear advocates are now focused on an emerging technology, so-called Small Modular Reactors, or SMRs, that could one day be mass produced to bring down costs and trucked to distant sites to deliver power. Despite all this, the chance of an Australian nuclear industry being developed has been dismissed by environmental activists and avowed energy pragmatists.

Asked for his views on the issue, Dr Ziggy Switkowski, NBN chairman, RMIT chancellor and former chairman of the Australian Nuclear Science and Technology Organisation, simply provides his submissions to some of those former inquiries. They acknowledge the attractiveness of clean and reliable baseload power but say, 'with the additional levels of safety and security demanded post-Fukushima (and post 9/11), conventional nuclear reactors are now very expensive (more than US$1B per 100MW) with nearly half the costs associated with systems and technologies which one hopes are never activated in anger.' Reactors at the Fukushima nuclear plant on Japan's east coast went into meltdown after an earthquake and tsunami in 2011.

Switkowski notes that from a standing start it would take 'about fifteen years to reach normal operation (and generate revenues) through the stages of: changes to legislation, skill building, design, community consultation, site selection, environmental approvals, vendor selection, construction, accreditation and operation.' Such a project has no bipartisan political support and no widespread social licence, and in Australia no coherent business case for a nuclear energy sector has ever been presented, he says. Finally, he notes, the major reactor vendors that traditionally work in the civilian sector in the West – Westinghouse, GE and Toshiba – have all abandoned nuclear in recent years.

It is this final point that is perhaps most devastating to the case for nuclear in Australia, and it is underscored most effectively by the Paris-based energy analyst Mycle Schneider, lead author of the annual *World Nuclear Industry Status Report*. These reports paint a picture of an industry in serious decline: in May 2020 there were 413 reactors operating in the world, forty-nine under construction (most of them well behind schedule, two of them having started construction more than thirty-five years ago) and ninety-three whose construction had been abandoned. The average age of the reactors was over thirty years, and the share of nuclear power in the global energy mix had declined from 17.5 per cent in 1996 to 10.3 per cent in 2019. Meanwhile, the report shows that between 2009 and 2019 the levelised cost of electricity (the cost of energy generated by a plant over its lifetime, allowing for comparison between sources) from utility-scale solar fell by 89 per cent and wind by 70 per cent while new nuclear costs increased by 26 per cent.

Schneider argues that nuclear also fails as a technology to address climate challenges because meeting Paris Agreement carbon reductions demands not only that we embrace technologies that are cheap and emit little carbon but are also able to quickly displace carbon. As explained, a traditional reactor would take at least fifteen years to bring online in Australia, while small modular reactors do not yet exist outside testing facilities.

So what is the solution?

'We need to stop looking for a silver bullet,' says Schneider. 'Nuclear is not providing anything its low-carbon competitors cannot provide better, cheaper, faster. Wind and solar are complementary and they are part of the solution. You fill in the gaps with hydrogen and biomass [organic matter converted to fuel]. There are countless possibilities in energy storage and their costs are falling faster than solar's did.'

Rather than silver bullets, Schneider proposes a different metaphor for the energy solution of our future: 'We need an orchestra, a symphony.'

31

HOW DID THE ESKY BECOME A CULTURAL ICON?

It's been a staple of Australian life
for decades. How has the Esky
evolved – and what does it mean now?

Tom Cowie

Humans have long enjoyed a nice, cool bevvy. Centuries before chilled chardonnay, wealthy Romans would lower the temperature of their wine with snow that slaves had carted from nearby mountains. During the nineteenth century, the ice trade was big business, involving the mass harvesting, storage and export of ice from cool climates such as Norway and the east coast of the United States across the world.

Refrigeration using ice boxes allowed people to keep perishable food in their homes for the first time. Before then, most food was stored using preservation methods such as salting, pickling and drying. In Australia, the Coolgardie safe was an early answer to the need for cooling – a set-up involving hessian, a tray of water and the powers of evaporative cooling.

But keeping things fresh away from home was always a challenge. Nowadays, we use ice bricks or buy bags of cubed or block ice from service stations and supermarkets to fill up coolers for a day of fun at the beach or park. In Australia, these coolers are called Eskies. And, like few other products, the Esky has come to symbolise the Australian summer. It's an invention we take for granted as we reach into the plastic tub to pluck a cold drink from the sea of icy water on a sunny day.

So where did Eskies come from and how do they work? Are they a relic from another time or have they evolved?

Why are they called Eskies?

Esky is actually a brand name, short for Eskimo. It's a term for people who live in and around the Arctic that is now considered by many to be offensive, though it is still used in places such as Alaska. The name was registered by Australian whitegoods company Malleys in 1961 and was so popular that it became what's known as a generic trademark. That's when a brand name enters the local vernacular, such as Glad Wrap for cling film or Hills hoist for clothesline. It's a word specific to Australia; New Zealanders

> **The Esky has come to symbolise the Australian summer.**

say 'chilly bin' and Americans use 'cooler'. Early Esky slogans included 'Take the party with you' and 'Cool, man, cool'.

Where did they come from?

Before electric refrigerators were common in the home, people used chests that held blocks of ice to cool food. The inevitable evolution was a portable version, first sold in Australia in 1952.

Advertisements for the Esky Auto Ice Box trumpeted its 'lustrous green baked enamel and chrome'. Intended for use in cars, the galvanised iron boxes had cork insulation to keep things cool while travelling. By the end of the 1950s, it was claimed that '500,000 happy picnickers' were using Eskies.

'When you look at where Australia was in the 1930s and the rationing of the 1940s, the 1950s saw optimism and growth,' says Anni Turnbull, assistant curator at the Museum of Applied Arts and Sciences in Sydney, where an early Esky is part of the collection. 'Cars transformed the way of life, expanding leisure activities. The initial use of the Esky was about going to picnics and camping.'

What were Eskies used for?

It wasn't long before Australians were using Eskies to cart around tinnies and stubbies. 'It didn't start off associated with beer,' says Turnbull. 'It grew into that in the 1970s and 1980s.' Australia reached 'peak beer' in the mid-1970s, when annual consumption of alcohol was the equivalent of more than 500 stubbies per person per year. Drinking habits are now less than half that, as wine rivals the once dominant amber fluid as our favourite tipple and the health effects of booze come under increasing scrutiny.

Back in the 1970s, though, the lager-swilling Australian was a feature of pop culture, with characters such as Barry McKenzie revelling in downing (and regurgitating) Foster's on the big screen in *The Adventures of Barry McKenzie*. Super Dag, a character from the hit *The Paul Hogan Show,* carried an Esky that had special powers.

A heavy drinking culture led to the Esky becoming a popular twenty-first birthday gift, particularly with men. And, back in the days when BYO was permitted at sporting events, it was a common sight to see people lining up with beer-packed Eskies. These days, BYO alcohol is banned at venues such as the Sydney and Melbourne Cricket Grounds, and large items that won't fit under a chair are not allowed in.

Back in 1980, the unruly behaviour of cricket fans after consuming the contents of their Eskies prompted a Malleys sales rep to defend the brand. 'If you buy a shotgun and shoot yourself you don't blame the manufacturer ... the Esky was certainly not designed to disrupt the cricket,' he told *The Age*.

Meanwhile, a spokesperson for rival brand Willow was philosophical about the word Esky becoming part of the language. 'We can't lose sleep over it,' he said. 'It would take a massive marketing job to change that, which would cost us a fortune.'

In 2000, white polystyrene Eskies featured in the closing ceremony of the Sydney Olympics: they were part of an 'audience participation' souvenir kit, containing a fly swat in the shape of Australia, among other items.

What are Eskies made out of?

The Esky brand was sold in 1984 to manufacturer Nylex, which began constructing the coolers entirely out of plastic. Plastic was already being used for the lids and liners of Eskies, in addition to steel. US company Coleman had introduced the then wonder material in 1957, helping it to popularise the cooler in the United States after the first patent was filed in 1951. It would go on to buy the Esky name in 2009 and still sells it today.

Lighter, easier to clean and, most importantly, better at keeping things cool than metal, plastic was a game-changer for the portable cooler and is still what they are made out of. It took some time for the innovation to make it to Australia, with the all-steel variety rusting away in garages around the country until the 1970s. Eskies were soon made out of the likes of polyethylene and polypropylene, with styrofoam and later polyurethane used as insulation. Many people are now trying to cut down on using plastic, especially single-use; but rather than ending up at the tip, Eskies seem to be one of those items that linger in households for years.

Plastic has other benefits, such as buoyancy. Eskies have featured in several survival stories, where people have used them to stay afloat in the sea. In one example, two Burmese fishermen survived almost a month floating in a large Esky after their small wooden boat sank in the Torres Strait.

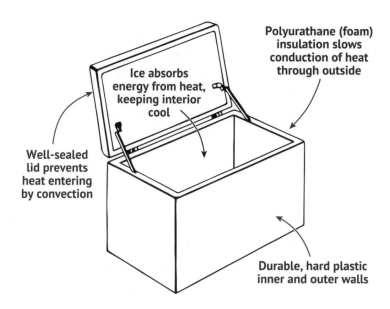

How do coolers work?

Heat is transferred in three ways: convection, conduction and radiation. When you touch something that feels cold, that's the energy of the heat leaving your fingers. With Eskies, it's about keeping the heat out rather than the cool in. Lucky, as science communicator Dr Karl Kruszelnicki says, 'you've got yourself a damned good insulator'.

The reason Eskies have insulation is mainly to prevent conduction, which is heat spreading between objects that are touching. The inner and outer shells, along with the foam on the inside, have low thermal conductivity, meaning the heat moves through slowly, a bit like double-glazed windows.

A more tightly packed Esky will perform better, as there is less room for air inside to warm things up.

Dr Karl uses the analogy of getting out of bed in winter and putting your feet on the floor. 'You step out of bed and onto the carpet, which is at a temperature of 4 degrees centigrade, but the carpet has very low thermal conductivity so your feet don't feel cold,' he says. 'And you take a few steps to the bathroom to have a wee and there are tiles. They're at the same temperature as the carpet but because they've got a high conductivity, the heat goes through quickly.' The thicker the material, the better with insulation because the heat will take longer to get through. The gas bubbles inside foam help lower conduction, too.

Convection involves heat transferring through air currents. Keeping an Esky lid shut obviously helps with that, as does a good rubber seal. This is also the reason why a more tightly packed Esky will perform better, as there is less room for air inside to warm things up.

Should you drain the water in an Esky?

This is a controversial debate and many people will swear black and blue that draining the water from an Esky is the way to go. But Dr Karl says you should always hold off on doing this for as long as you can. 'As long as it is cooler than the outside air temperature, you should keep the water with the beer or the holy water or whatever's inside,' he says. When ice cools things down, it is absorbing the thermal energy of the heat that would otherwise warm up the beer. As ice melts into water, it remains at the same temperature until it is all gone. Once that happens, the water heats up rapidly. The type of ice also has an impact. Cubed ice melts faster but chills things quicker. Block ice, due to having less surface area, lasts longer.

Are Eskies still a thing?

'Rotomoulding' is the latest innovation when it comes to coolers. It's a construction process that creates a cooler out of one continuous piece of plastic by heating it up and putting it into a mould before spinning it around. The companies that use rotomoulding say this improves performance as it ensures that the plastic is the same width and has fewer imperfections for heat to get in. It also makes things more expensive. Yeti, a cult brand in the United States that uses rotomoulding, sells its coolers for hundreds of dollars more than standard varieties. They say they hold ice for much longer, using stronger buckles to help lock out the heat.

It's all a long way from the first iron boxes produced in the 1950s. New sizes and shapes, even soft cooler bags, have come along. Extra features such as sets of wheels have made Eskies easier to use.

The basic idea still holds true, however: people want a place to keep things cool. It's what they put inside their Eskies that has probably changed the most. Mass-produced lager and Anglo food have given way to a variety of cuisines. It might still hold a slab of beer on a camping trip but an Esky is now just as likely to be used to cool an antipasto platter or a bottle of prosecco.

In some ways, the Esky has come full circle, back to the picnics it was taken to when first invented – just check out your local park on a warm evening or a sunny day.

'They're pretty remarkable, aren't they?' says Turnbull. 'They're still part of our icons of Australian leisure and summer.'

Author biographies

Max Allen has been writing about wine and drinks for almost thirty years and is currently booze columnist for *The Australian Financial Review*, honorary fellow in history at the University of Melbourne and author of *Intoxicating: Ten drinks that shaped Australia*. You'd think he'd know what he was talking about by now …

Ella Archibald-Binge, a Walkley Young Australian Journalist of the Year award winner in 2020, began her career in regional newspapers before working at SBS, NITV and *The Sydney Morning Herald* and *The Age* with the support of the Judith Neilson Institute. She is a proud descendant of the Kamilaroi people.

David Astle (alias DA on the puzzle page) has been making crosswords for *The Sydney Morning Herald* and *The Age* for over thirty-five years. A broadcaster with ABC Radio Melbourne, David is also the author of such wordy books as *Puzzled* and *Riddledom*, as well as Spectrum's weekly Wordplay column.

Sophie Aubrey is deputy lifestyle editor for *The Age* and *The Sydney Morning Herald* where she has written about everything from infertility, sexual violence and mental health to wellness, dating culture and TikTok. She started at News Corp where she covered breaking news, cultural trends and health.

Kate Aubusson is the health editor at *The Sydney Morning Herald* and an award-winning medical journalist. She has worked in breaking news at the *Herald* and as a senior journalist for several specialist medical news publications. Kate was also the presenter of the ABC documentary *Lest We Forget What.*

Michael Bachelard is the investigations editor of *The Age* and a former Indonesia correspondent for *The Age* and *The Sydney Morning Herald.* He has been a journalist since 1991, has won a number of awards including a Gold Walkley and has written two books.

Greg Baum is a journalist with forty years experience, mostly covering sport. For the past thirty years, he has worked for *The Age.* A Walkley Award winner, he was also editor of the short-lived *Australian Wisden* and has co-authored a number of books. He has not yet abandoned his dream of opening the batting for Australia while playing centre halfback for Collingwood. Sadly, his love for sport remains unrequited.

Craig Butt is *The Age*'s data journalist, charged with making statistics accessible and interesting to readers. He specialises in analysing data and producing data visualisations. He also teaches postgraduate subjects in data journalism and news writing at The University of Melbourne's Centre for Advancing Journalism.

Anthony Colangelo joined *The Age* in 2017, covering general news and sport. He now focuses on AFL, soccer and tennis. A Nick Kyrios fan, he has covered three Australian Open tournaments.

Tom Cowie is a reporter at *The Age* where he covers general news, often with a focus on colourful and quirky topics. He previously worked at *The Courier* in Ballarat and started out in journalism at online news website *Crikey.*

Melissa Cunningham started at *The Age* in 2017, reporting on breaking news and crime before moving to health in 2019. She won a Melbourne Press Club Quill Award in 2017 for her coverage of child sexual abuse in the Victorian regional city of Ballarat, where she worked at *The Courier*.

Mike Foley is climate and energy reporter for *The Sydney Morning Herald* and *The Age* in Canberra, a keen fisherman and voluntary craft beer inspector. He was previously a political reporter for *The Land* and other Australian Community Media mastheads.

Simone Fox Koob is a crime reporter for *The Age* where she began as a breaking news reporter after working on *The Australian* in Melbourne.

Dionne Gain is the creative director at *The Sydney Morning Herald* and has been a leading illustrator for the *Herald* and *The Age* for more than fifteen years, her work covering subjects from political commentary to lifestyle. She illustrated a number of the explainers in this book in their original format. She was highly commended in the Warringah Art Prize when she was twelve and has a penchant for jumpsuits.

Anthony Galloway is foreign affairs and national security correspondent for *The Sydney Morning Herald* and *The Age* based in the Press Gallery in Parliament House, Canberra. He previously covered federal politics for the *Herald Sun*. His hobbies include going for long hikes and watching too many James Bond films.

Sherryn Groch is the explainer reporter for *The Age* and *The Sydney Morning Herald*, digging into everything from COVID conspiracy theories to subsonic flight. She started her career at *The Canberra Times* in 2016, reporting on crime and social affairs, and picked up a Walkley Young Australian Journalist of Year Award in 2020 for her work in education reporting.

Peter Hannam has been the environment editor for *The Sydney Morning Herald* since 2014. Before that, he covered mostly business news, based in places such as Beijing, Tokyo, Singapore, Melbourne and Ulaanbaatar.

Felicity Lewis is the national explainer editor for *The Age* and *The Sydney Morning Herald*. She has worked in diverse roles on titles from *The Herald Sun* to *The Independent* to *theage(melbourne) magazine* and has won several awards, including a Walkley.

Liam Mannix started his career writing politics for *InDaily* in Adelaide before moving to *The Age* to cover breaking news. He is now the national science reporter for *The Age* and *The Sydney Morning Herald*.

James Massola is the South-East Asia correspondent for *The Sydney Morning Herald* and *The Age*. He was previously chief political correspondent in Canberra. Massola won the Kennedy award for 'outstanding foreign correspondent in 2019 and wrote *The Great Cave Rescue*, about the rescue of the Thai boys' soccer team from Tham Luang cave, in 2018. When he's not travelling off the beaten track, his pastimes are gardening, reading and building Lego with his three young kids.

Maher Mughrabi has worked for *The Age* since he emigrated to Australia from Britain in 2003. He is currently features editor and from 2014 to 2017 was foreign editor of *The Age* and *The Sydney Morning Herald*. The son of a Palestinian father and a Scottish mother, he has worked in newspapers for twenty-five years, including stints at the *Independent,* the *Scotsman,* the *Daily Mail* and the *Khaleej Times.*

Jake Niall is a Walkley Award–winning sports journalist and chief AFL writer for *The Age* where he has covered footy since 1995, except for two years in television at Fox Sports.

Nick O'Malley is the national environment and climate editor for *The Sydney Morning Herald* and *The Age*. As the Washington correspondent from 2012 to 2016, he covered the Obama White House and the Trump election. He is a Walkley finalist and twice won the United Nations Association Prize for news writing. His essay on the destruction of precious French botanical samples by Australian immigration officials was included in *The Best Australian Science Writing* 2018.

Miki Perkins is a senior journalist at *The Age* where she covers climate and environment stories. She spent five years as *The Age*'s social affairs editor, reporting on topics such as gender, sexuality, family violence, disability, mental health and Indigenous affairs.

Karl Quinn is senior culture writer at *The Age* and *The Sydney Morning Herald*. He has been writing about film and television since film was shot on film and TV shows were broadcast only by TV stations, on the television – yes, children, there really was a time before streaming, smartphones and screens in every room of the house – and he's still completely transfixed.

John Silvester is a Walkley Award–winning crime writer and writes the Naked City column for *The Age*. He has written and edited more than thirty crime books and is the co-author of the bestselling Underbelly series that was the basis of the hit Australian TV series *Underbelly*. Silvester is a regular guest on 3AW with his Sly of the Underworld segment.

Shane Wright has been the senior economics correspondent for *The Sydney Morning Herald* and *The Age* since 2018. He has been a member of the Canberra Press Gallery since 2000, writing about economics for Australian Associated Press and *The West Australian*. He started out at the *Cootamundra Herald* and worked for *The Daily Advertiser* in Wagga Wagga and the *Border Mail* in Albury-Wodonga. Throughout it all, he has been a devotee of the music of Kate Bush.

Tony Wright began his career on *The Portland Observer* in south-west Victoria in 1970. Since 1987 he has been variously political correspondent, foreign affairs correspondent and national affairs editor for *The Canberra Times, The Sydney Morning Herald, The Bulletin* and *The Age*. He is associate editor and special writer for *The Age* and *The Sydney Morning Herald*. He rides a Harley-Davidson and a Triumph Bonneville.

Emma Young is a reporter for *The Age* and *The Sydney Morning Herald*'s sister publication *WAtoday*. She has won seven WA Media Awards including the 2018 Matt Price Award for best columnist. Her debut novel *The Last Bookshop*, to be published in March 2021, was shortlisted for the inaugural Fogarty Literary Award in 2019.

Acknowledgements

Explainers at *The Age* and *The Sydney Morning Herald* exist in their current form because executive editor James Chessell and national editor Tory Maguire saw their potential, hired an explainer editor to make them happen, and have backed them all the way.

The brief? Give readers context to properly understand events as they unfold.

To this end, editors across our newsrooms have graciously allowed their reporters the time to bring clarity and perspective to knotty topics in explainer form – even when, as South-East Asia correspondent James Massola put it, this has involved 'HARD editing and questions big and small'. 'It's painful sometimes but it's great,' he added.

Among the writers featured is our first dedicated explainer reporter, Sherryn Groch, who started in the same week that reports surfaced of a mysterious virus in Wuhan. She has since unpacked a whirlwind of gnarly questions, about pandemics and much more besides, with great tenacity and flair.

There are many ways to shed light on a subject. Photographers and videographers, producers, graphic designers and artists have all contributed along the way, including *The Sydney Morning Herald*'s creative director, Dionne Gain, whose irreverent illustrations are featured in this book. We're delighted that Dylan Mooney let us include one of his striking artworks too, in the explainer about slavery.

Our newsrooms publish thousands of words every day – but not in books. Thanks to former *Age* editor Alex Lavelle for planting the seed for this anthology, to *Age* digital editor Mathew Dunckley for the nudge and to the *Herald*'s Spectrum editor, Shona Martyn, for so generously helping me develop my idea for Penguin Random House – where publisher Justin Ractliffe and editors Catherine Hill and Clive Hebard turned the tables on me with lots of 'questions big and small'. Michael Epis, Emma Woolley, Mex Cooper and Kate Doherty also offered insightful feedback at key moments while David provided good humour, a patient ear and schnitzel.

Most of all, I'd like to thank you, our readers, who inspire these explainers. 'What is a think tank?', for example, was a question emailed to the explainer desk by subscriber Peter Fleming. 'I had thought my suggestion had just disappeared into the ether,' Fleming wrote after reading Nick O'Malley's piece, 'but it's really good to know that someone, somewhere, took it seriously.'

You bet we do.

Discover a
new favourite

Visit **penguin.com.au/readmore**